Berthe Morisot

Masterpieces of Art

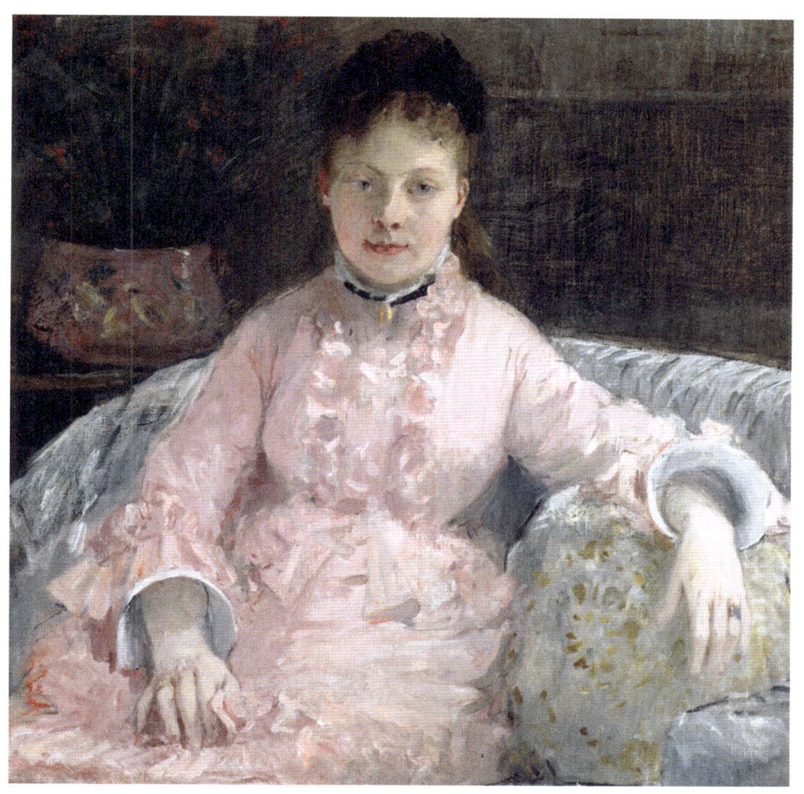

Publisher & Creative Director: Nick Wells
Editorial Director: Catherine Taylor
Copy Editor: Anna Groves
Art Director and Layout Design: Mike Spender
Digital Design & Production: Chris Herbert

Special thanks to Jen Veall, Dawn Laker, Helen Snaith and Frances Bodiam.

FLAME TREE PUBLISHING

6 Melbray Mews
Fulham, London SW6 3NS
United Kingdom

www.flametreepublishing.com

First published 2020

26 28 30 31 29 27
3 5 7 9 10 8 6 4 2

Image credits: Courtesy of The Metropolitan Museum of Art, New York: 1 & 85 The Walter H. and Leonore Annenberg Collection, Bequest of Walter H. Annenberg, 2002. Courtesy of akg-images: 3 & 114 The National Gallery, London; 4 & 75, 51, 125 Heritage Images/Fine Art Images; 13 & 30, 35, 67 Laurent Lecat; 15 & 34, 18 & 28 & 41, 21 & 92, 25 & 37, 36, 40, 71, 122; 46 Gift of Wallace and Wilhelmina Holladay; 53, 76 Album; 54, 74, 86, 91, 94, 95, 112 Heritage Images; 65 Erich Lessing; 116 Album/Oronoz. Courtesy of Bridgeman Images: 6 Private Collection/© Archives Charmet; 10, 56 Musee d'Orsay, Paris, France; 11 & 77, front cover & 14 & 31, 17 & 39, 19 & 73, 20 & 49, 52, 66, 72, 78 & 104, 89 Musee Marmottan Monet, Paris, France; 12 & 45, 38, 43, 44, 105, 108, 117, 123 Private Collection/Photo © Christie's Images; 23 & 103, 27 & 102 & 128, 69, 87, 97, 119 Private Collection; 57 Acquired 1925; 58 & 64 Santa Barbara, Museum Of Art/Photo © Photo Josse; 88 The Courtauld Gallery, London, UK; 90 National Museum of Western Art, Tokyo, Japan/Photo © Christie's Images; 93 gift of the Meadows Foundation, Incorporated; 124 Collezione Baron de Chollet, Fribourg, Switzerland/Photo © Luisa Ricciarini. Courtesy of Getty Images: 8 & 60 Picturenow/Universal Images Group; 120 Buyenlarge. Courtesy of National Gallery of Art, Washington DC: 9 & 80, 22 & 62, 81, 121 Ailsa Mellon Bruce Collection; 7 & 84, 48, 99 Chester Dale Collection; 26 & 68, 100 Collection of Mr. and Mrs. Paul Mellon; 82 Gift of Mrs. Charles S. Carstairs; Courtesy of Nationalmuseum Stockholm: 16 & 106 & 113 Photo: Erik Cornelius. Courtesy of Art Institute of Chicago: back cover & 24 & 32 Stickney Fund; 50 Berthold Loewenthal Fund; 101 Gift of Mrs. Frederic C. Bartlett; 118 A Millennium Gift of Sara Lee Corporation. Courtesy of Clark Art Institute/clarkart.edu: 33; 47 Acquired by Sterling and Francine Clark, 1949; 70 Acquired by Sterling and Francine Clark before 1955. Courtesy of Minneapolis Institute of Arts: 42 The John R. Van Derlip Fund. Courtesy of Yale University Art Gallery: 61 Bequest of Paul Mellon, B.A. 1929, L.H.D.H. 1967. Courtesy of The Cleveland Museum of Art: 96 Bequest of Leonard C. Hanna, Jr. 1958.41; 98 Gift of Mrs. Lewis B. Williams 1975.83; 110 Gift of the Hanna Fund 1950.89. Courtesy of Superstock: 109 Universal Images.

ISBN: 978-1-83562-794-5

Printed in China | Created, Developed & Produced in the United Kingdom

Represented in the EU for product safety and compliance by
Authorised Rep Compliance Ltd, Ground Floor, 71 Lower Baggot Street, Dublin, D02 P593, Ireland.
Contact at www.arccompliance.com

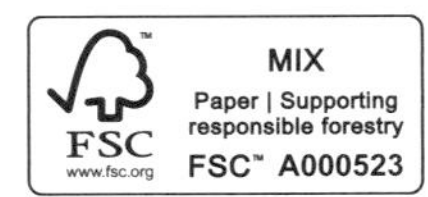

Berthe Morisot

Masterpieces of Art

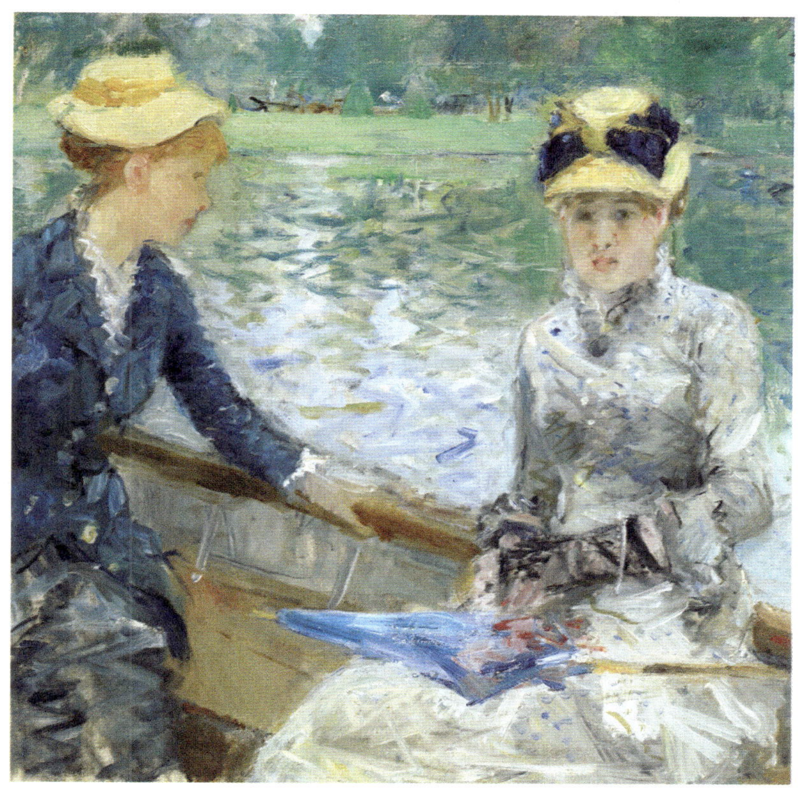

Ann Kay

FLAME TREE
PUBLISHING

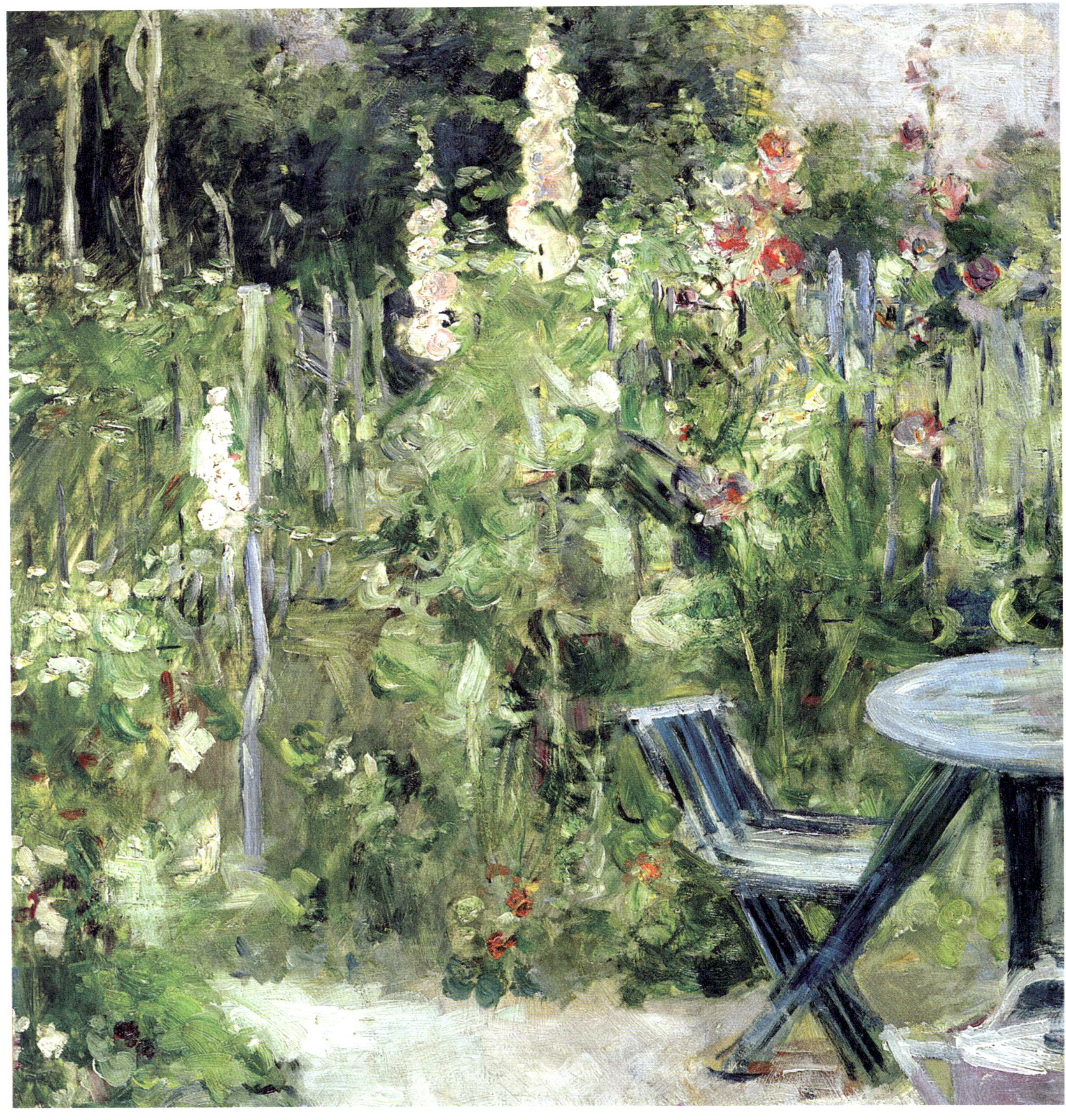

Contents

Berthe Morisot: Grande Dame of Impressionism

Much celebrated for her deft touch and beautiful use of colour, Berthe Morisot (1841–95) painted a beguiling portrait of what life meant for the nineteenth-century French woman. Hers was a middle-class perspective, but Berthe's work gave ordinary, fleeting domestic moments a special and timelessly universal quality. A pivotal member of the Impressionist movement, and close to key artists of the age, Berthe was highly proficient on canvas, paper and in print forms. She achieved some artistic success and recognition during her lifetime – no mean feat for a woman at that time – although her subject matter tended to obscure a considerable, and avant-garde, technical talent. However, from the later twentieth century her true stature as a major Impressionist artist began to be properly appreciated.

An Auspicious Start

Berthe's early life provided promising foundations for a future artist. She was born in Bourges, central France – a historic hilltop city of architectural gems, crowned by a Gothic cathedral – into a well-to-do family who went on to settle in Paris during her childhood. Her father, Edme-Tiburce Morisot (1806–74), was a senior government official who had once intended to become an architect. Her mother,

Marie-Joséphine-Cornélie Thomas (1819–76), was said to be descended from the leading French Rococo artist Jean-Honoré Fragonard (1732–1806). Berthe had two older sisters, Yves (1838–93) and Edma (1839–1921), and a younger brother, Tiburce (1845–1930?). At an early stage of her career Berthe would portray her mother and Edma in *The Mother and Sister of the Artist* (1869–70, *see* opposite and page 84).

Possessing artistic talents was considered a valued accomplishment for young bourgeois ladies, and many received some instruction, aimed at enabling them to produce delicate watercolours of flowers or attractive landscapes. So there was nothing especially unusual about the fact that in 1857, in her mid-teens, Berthe – and her sisters – came under the tutelage of the painter Geoffroy-Alphonse Chocarne (1797–1857?). However, it seems that the Morisot girls had greater artistic ambitions than simply fostering a delightful hobby, and Berthe was already keen to become a painter. Their brother Tiburce described how his sisters came home from lessons despondent and 'reduced to a stupor' of boredom by Chocarne's teaching. Berthe and Edma were found another teacher in the form of artist Joseph Guichard (1806–80), a former pupil of Jean-Auguste-Dominique Ingres (1780–1867) and an admirer of Eugène Delacroix (1798–

1863) – two artists who were regarded as being sharply opposed in the artistic battles of the day, Ingres as the classical traditionalist and Delacroix the Romantic modernist.

Flouting Convention and Making Connections

Guichard quickly realized that his two new charges had considerable talent – enough to become true painters. According to brother Tiburce, Guichard was 'almost frightened by his discovery', and he warned their mother that becoming artists would be 'revolutionary, I might almost say catastrophic' for young ladies from their upper-middle-class milieu. To many people, dabbling in art was one thing, but being a professional painter was thought rather bohemian and unseemly. However, it appears that Berthe and Edma's parents were far from being shocked, which suggests that they were unusually broadminded, and so Berthe and Edma began sessions with Guichard in the Louvre in spring 1858, copying from masterworks there.

Guichard's presence was required because at this time women were not allowed to undergo such sessions unchaperoned; they were also barred from formal state art training and usually not allowed to draw from nude models, even when attending private art lessons. Berthe's career undoubtedly gained a massive boost from her parents' enduring support, though of course also from their wealth, which made acquiring good tuition possible.

At the Louvre, the sisters met other artists such as Félix Bracquemond (1833–1914) and Henri Fantin-Latour (1836–1904). Berthe destroyed many of her earliest works, one survivor being a painting of a Normandy farm from 1859–60. This shows her growing determination and exacting standards – traits that would soon take her away from Guichard to follow a new direction under a different artistic master.

Lessons with 'Papa' Corot

This new master was Camille Corot (1796–1875), by the 1850s a hugely influential figure admired by those in the know for his poetically natural and luminous landscapes. The Impressionists, and painters like Corot and the French Barbizon School who paved the way for them, brought a new emphasis to painting out of doors – *en plein air* – and producing painterly truths to nature. Berthe and Edma were determined to get outside too, and were fervent admirers of Corot. So in 1860, they left Guichard to take up instruction with Corot.

The girls studied with Corot in his studio in Paris and in 1861, persuaded their parents to summer at Ville d'Avray – a town on the edge of the capital marked by lovely landscapes where Corot owned a property – in order to be close to him. Corot became a firm family friend, dining with the Morisots every Tuesday evening. Stimulated by his advice on naturalism, in 1862, the girls summered in the

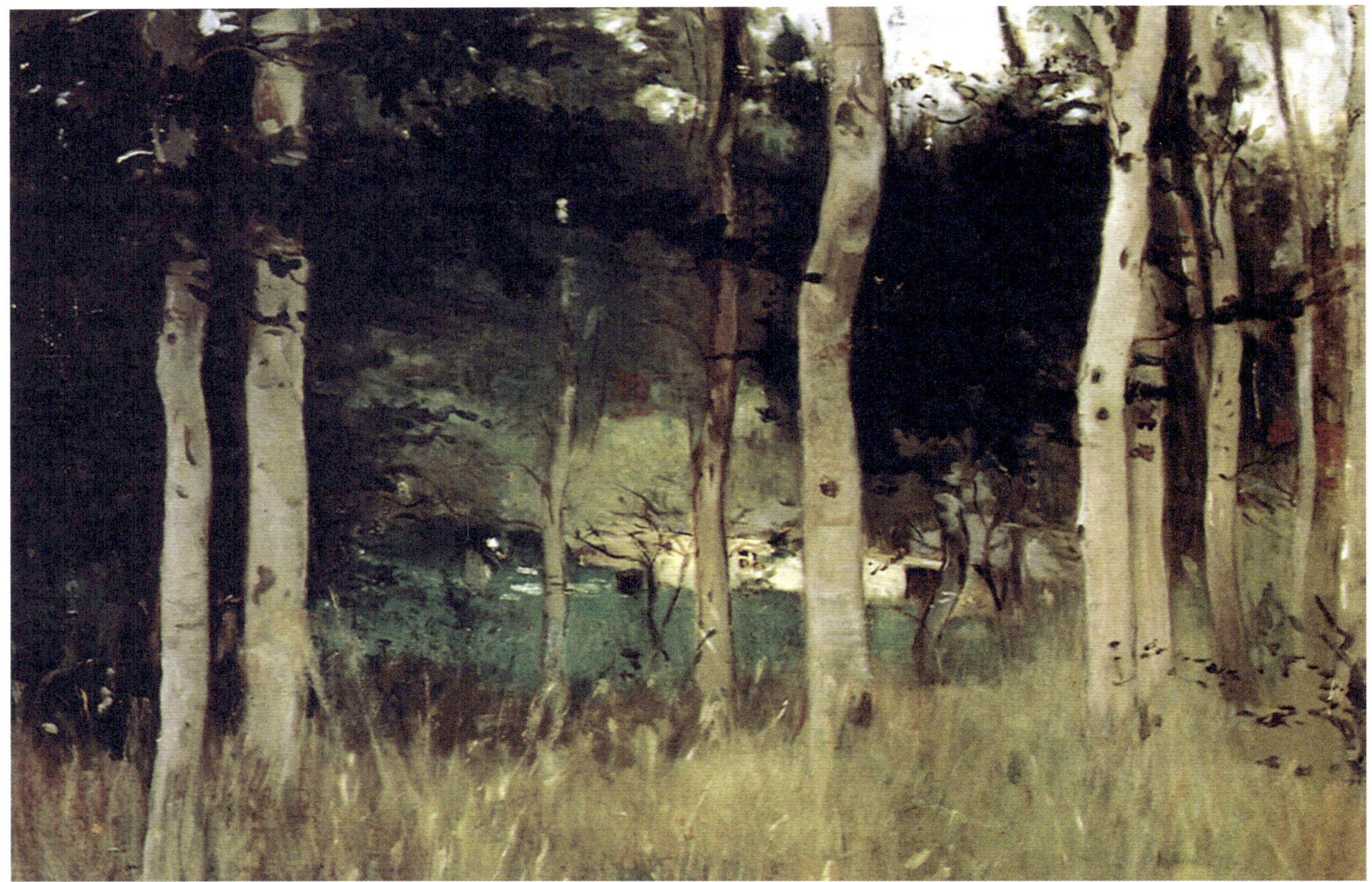

Pyrenees, riding mules and horses and painting the landscape. Among other things Berthe would take from Corot, whom she (like many others) called 'papa', was a love of blues and greens used together and of the play of light across a scene. This high regard was shared by Impressionist Claude Monet (1840–1926), who supposedly said: 'There is only one master here – Corot. We are nothing compared to him, nothing.'

Working Outdoors

During 1863 and 1864, Berthe and Edma enjoyed further outdoor painting trips with the family near Auvers, just outside Paris, and in Beuzeval, Normandy, and received some instruction from Corot's pupil

Achille-François Oudinot (1820–91). At Beuzeval, Berthe, already a determined professional, would head off into the country for the day, complete with backpack and painting gear, eager to catch light effects at different times of day. There were meetings with other notable artists on these trips, such as Honoré Daumier (1808–79).

Berthe's painting of her artistic companion from this time – *The Artist's Sister Edma Seated in a Park* (1864, *see* opposite and page 80) – shows that she was learning quickly from such trips. It is clear from the painting that she was already adept at depicting both landscapes and people, and able to work in the tricky medium of watercolour, which she practised a great deal in the earlier part of her career and which was easy to carry outdoors.

Gaining facility with watercolours fed into the fresh, spontaneous-looking strokes and colours that would also characterize her pastels and oils. She struggled with mastering oil painting; watercolour was certainly better suited to capturing luminous light effects. Returning to Beuzeval in 1865, Berthe produced the promising oil painting *Thatched Cottage in Normandy* (1865, *see* opposite and page 60). Exhibited at the 1866 Salon, this shows a debt to Corot, for example in its poetic aura and harmonious palette. However, it also reveals Berthe developing an individual Impressionist sensibility with her convincing play of light on the softly delicate grass.

Salons and Early Successes

Berthe – and Edma – exhibited at the Paris Salon for the first time in 1864 and were favourably reviewed by prominent novelist-journalist Edmond About. Berthe showed two landscapes, one of which featured a lane in Auvers. This was quite a coup, as these Salon exhibitions were hugely influential in the nineteenth-century Western art world. Acceptance into them was all-important and the public flocked to see the exhibits.

The history of these Salons was one of royal and state backing, with a background of being dominated by the prescriptive, generally conservative, taste of members of the Académie Royale de Peinture et de Sculpture. These tastes had traditionally decreed painting of historical and mythological subjects in the grand manner to be of much more value than landscapes, still-lifes or genre scenes of everyday or modern life.

By the 1860s, tastes were shifting slightly in the Salons, but the somewhat stuffy and traditional guard was still very influential. Meanwhile, the art world was now alive with artists who wanted to counter this guard. They sought to experiment with new approaches and explore areas such as modern life and the reality of nature, in all its startling light and colour effects.

Just the year before Berthe's Salon debut, artists who had been refused by the Salon selection process had their protests answered when Emperor Napoleon III decreed that a Salon des Refusés

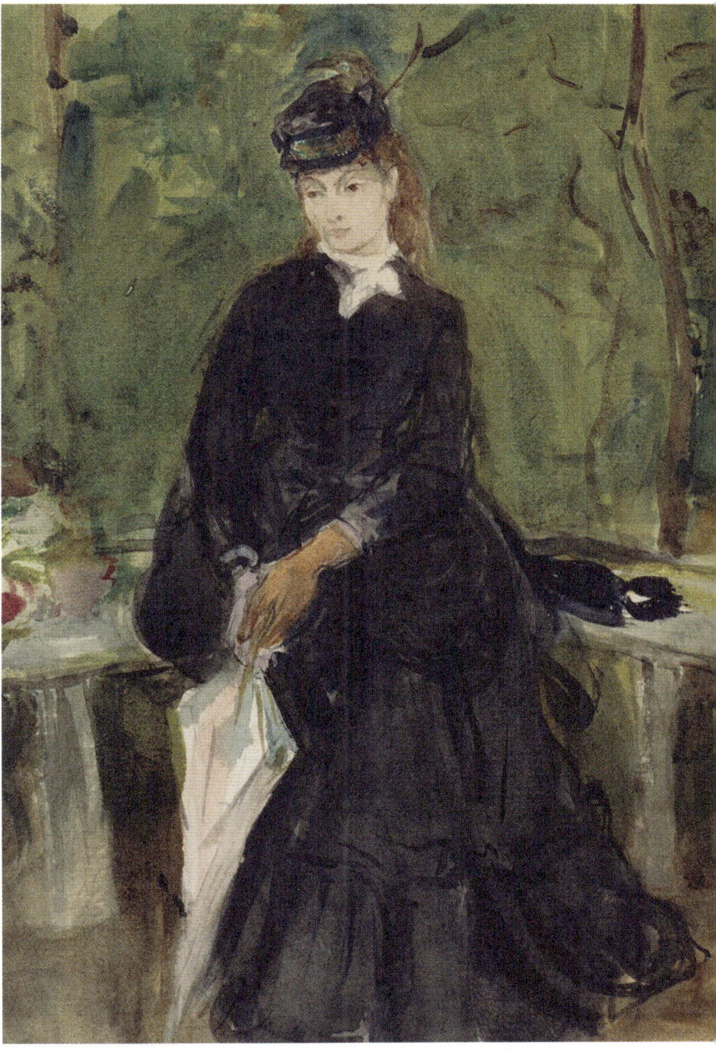

should be mounted to show their work and let the public decide its merit. Sadly that public laughed derisively at much of the work, which included that of Paul Cézanne (1839–1906), Fantin-Latour, Camille Pissarro (1830–1903), James McNeill Whistler (1834–1903) and Edouard Manet (1832–83) – notably the latter's then-shocking *Déjeuner sur l'Herbe* (1863). However, a precedent had been set and this gathering of refuseniks laid foundations for later non-official shows such as the Impressionist exhibitions – which would prove so important to Berthe – and those of the Salon des Indépendants (1884 onwards).

Marriages and Meeting Manet

Between the late 1860s and early 1870s, Berthe's work, and sometimes that of Edma, was shown in various places, including most years at the Salon exhibition. But changes were afoot for the Morisot sisters. In 1866, Yves married tax inspector Théodore Gobillard, and in 1869, Edma wed naval lieutenant Adolphe Pontillon and ended any plans to continue as a professional artist. Berthe and Edma, the steadfast painting companions, both felt their separation keenly. As for Berthe, she continued to follow an artistic path and make useful connections, with her mother worrying that she might never marry.

In 1868, Berthe was formally introduced to Edouard Manet via Fantin-Latour and this was to have various important repercussions,

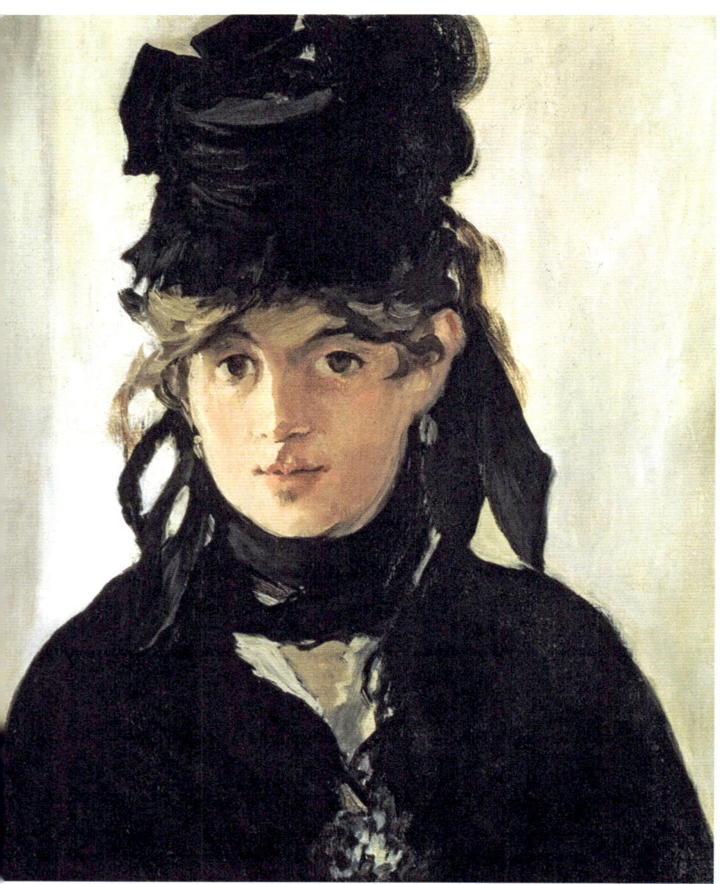

both professional and personal. Manet and Berthe soon became good friends and colleagues – a vital friendship that would endure – and the Morisots and Manets also socialized with each other, helping to bring together Berthe and her future husband Eugène Manet (1833–92), Edouard's brother. The Morisots already had a well-connected artistic circle, now expanded even further through the Manets, so Berthe was mixing with figures at the heart of nineteenth-century culture, such as Edgar Degas (1834–1917) and Emile Zola (1840–1902).

The friendship with Edouard Manet also ushered Berthe further into the world of Impressionism, although this was a complex matter as Manet in some ways distanced himself from the artists who became known as the Impressionists while simultaneously coming to be seen as one of their major players. At any rate, the two enjoyed painting together and learned much from their mutual artistic admiration: she from his boldly brushed contrasts of light and shade and he from her love of working *en plein air*, which probably loosened and lightened his art. Manet had shocked the public and critics with the perceived sexuality of *Déjeuner sur l'Herbe*, and again with *Olympia* (1863), and so Berthe found herself consorting with, and being advised by, a figure identified at this time as a leader of the avant-garde who felt he found little real success with his work.

Appropriately, quite a few images of Berthe were done by Manet, notably modelling for the seated figure in his masterful *The Balcony* (1868–69), which attracted some critical derision at the 1869 Salon, and *Berthe Morisot with a Bouquet of Violets* (1872, *see* left). Such works show her strong but pleasant gaze and the 'Spanish' good looks that many remarked upon.

Shaken by War

In 1870, French life took on a very different edge with the outbreak of the Franco-Prussian War (1870–71) and its repercussions, in which France suffered humiliating defeat, Paris was besieged and the Third Republic (1870–1940) was established. For a brief spell in 1871, revolutionary forces in the French capital – backed by radical thinkers, including some artists – formed the Paris Commune and refused to accept the authority of the French government. The Commune governed Paris for two months, until it was violently suppressed by the regular French Army, most infamously during *La Semaine Sanglante* (The Bloody Week)**,** with the death of many thousands.

These were testing times, and very hard ones for people in Paris, even those well-padded by privilege. Berthe initially stayed in the capital with her family during the troubles. Her painting studio at the Morisots' home on Rue Franklin was requisitioned as soldiers' quarters and she produced mostly watercolours during the seige (*see* right and page 77 her later *Tulips* of 1890). Manet and brother Eugène did their bit in the National Guard and Berthe's brother Tiburce joined the French forces and was imprisoned by the Germans before escaping.

The fall-out of this period was that Europe's map and balances of power changed, including the creation of a united German empire. Many French people suffered something of a crisis of identity, especially as the war had highlighted divisions and problems. Berthe herself is often said to have undergone her own personal crisis around this time, perhaps deepened by fighting for life as an artist in a world that expected her to be a homemaker, and by suffering under the hardships and shortages that befell Paris. Her health was affected in ways that would permanently weaken her, though her resolve to be an artist seems, if anything, to have strengthened.

Family Life Versus Painting

By 1872, sister Yves had produced a little girl and a boy, Paule Marie and Marcel, and Edma two daughters, Jeanne and Blanche. Berthe's *The Mother and Sister of the Artist* (1869–70, *see* pages 7 and 84) shows Edma pregnant with Jeanne, undetectable thanks to her discreetly loose dress. Berthe loved her sisters' children but felt torn at this stage between a desire for marriage and motherhood and the pull of art and independence. She spoke of 'asserting my determination to emancipate myself' and wrote to Edma: 'however fond one is of one's husband, one does not relinquish a life of work without some difficulty' and 'I both lament and envy your fate … life gets more complicated by the day here now I am gripped by the desire to have children; that's all I need!'

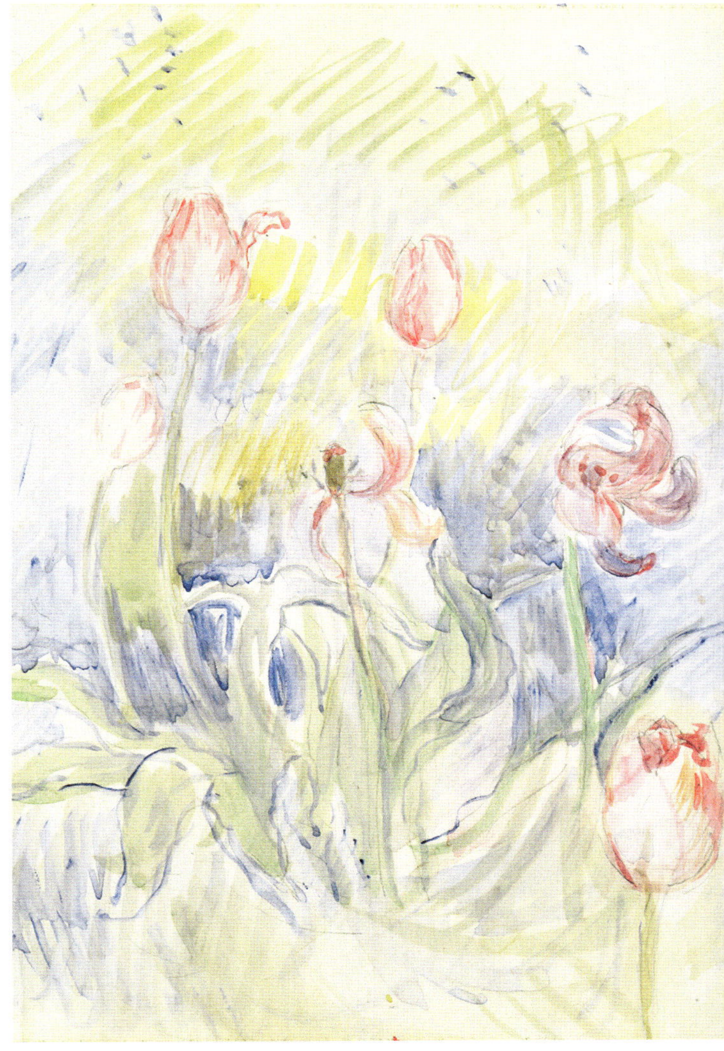

The year 1874 did, however, bring marriage for Berthe, but marriage with a difference by the usual standards of the day. On 22 December, Berthe wed Manet's brother, Eugène, and she appears as 'without profession' on the licence. Eugène was a painter himself but one who would effectively give up his own artistic pursuits in favour of supporting Berthe's, which she continued under her maiden name (although Eugène did have other non-artistic employment and ample money behind him). A few years after marriage, Berthe would also experience motherhood for herself.

One of the couple's wedding presents came from another member of the Morisot-Manet circle: Degas. He gifted them a portrait he had painted of Eugène; just a few years earlier he had also produced two portraits of Berthe's sister Yves. Degas was certainly an influence on Berthe's work, especially in her use of pastels and mixed media, in using white to show brilliant light effects, and in a fondness for fleeting images of women unselfconsciously occupied with their toilette, such as her later pastel study *Young Girl with Naked Shoulders* (1885, *see* below and page 45).

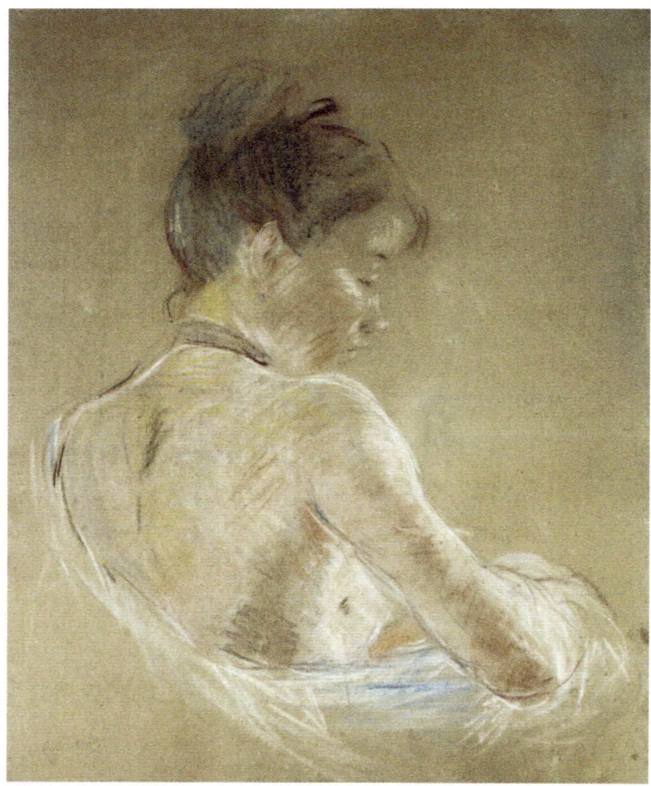

The Official Birth of Impressionism

Apart from her engagement and marriage in 1874, the year proved a momentous one for Berthe in other ways. It began with her father's death in January. Then, on 15 April, the very first Impressionist exhibition opened, at 35 Boulevard des Capucines, Paris – the

former studio of leading French photographer 'Nadar' (Gaspard-Félix Tournachon, 1820–1910) – and ran for a month. Berthe was the only female exhibitor and a key organizer. She contributed ten works – in oils, watercolour and pastels – including *Hide and Seek* (1873, *see* page 109), an engaging work that tackled a topic close to her experimental contemporaries' hearts – how to paint figures in an outdoor setting.

Edouard Manet tried to dissuade Berthe from getting involved in this show, but she was determined. This was also the year when she had no Salon submissions accepted; she would never submit works there again. Other artists involved in the first Impressionist show included Cézanne, Degas, Monet, Pissarro, Pierre-Auguste Renoir (1841–1919) and Alfred Sisley (1839–99).

These artists' work received some exposure at this show, as well over 3,000 people visited. Much of the critical reception, however, was pretty brutal, the works considered crude and unfinished compared to typical Salon exhibits. The participants had not as yet called themselves or their movement Impressionist/-ism, but for this show had chosen the term 'Société Anonyme Coopérative d'Artistes Peintres, Sculpteurs, Graveurs, etc'. However, one of Monet's exhibits at the 1874 show was titled *Impression, Sunrise* (1872–73) and one damning review, titled 'Exhibition of the Impressionists', was bitingly sarcastic about such 'impressions', loosely painted in a way that seemed unfinished to traditional tastes. A term was born and generally embraced.

Many of the artists themselves used the term as they were in any case accustomed to the word being used to talk about direct, unmediated sensations and perceptions striking individuals, and how this might be captured in art. Although participants in the 1874 show were highly divergent artists, they were united in their desire to break away from 'academic' accepted norms and express these kinds of individualized sensations. As one of the 1874 reviews said: 'They are *Impressionists* in the sense that they render not the landscape but the sensation produced by the landscape.' A large part of this was painting *en plein air*, trying to capture the effects of precise weather, light and atmosphere at specific times of day with a new painterly realism.

Berthe as an Impressionist

So it was that this and following Impressionist shows effectively cemented and officially launched the namesake movement. There were eight Impressionist exhibitions, held between 1874 and 1886, and Berthe took part in all but one of them (1879, the year after her daughter was born), playing an involved role that included giving financial support.

The first show also included one of Berthe's most enduringly popular images, *The Cradle* (1872, *see* below and page 30). Here there is a clear debt to Manet in the strong, dark figure juxtaposed with whites. The subtly tinted whites echo Degas as well as 'symphonies in white' by Whistler – whose painting she admired – such as *Symphony in White, No. 1: The White Girl* (1862), a portrait of a white-dressed girl standing against white drapes. This had been turned down for the 1863 Paris Salon and appeared in the Salon des Refusés show,

where it was berated but also found some critical praise. Whistler's images play with spatial arrangements and tones to produce almost semi-abstract works, and often pose people sideways or at angles unconventional for the time. All of these elements can be seen in *The Cradle*, painted before Berthe's marriage and probably expressive of her especially conflicted feelings about motherhood versus career around this time.

Berthe's credentials as part of the Impressionist movement were impeccable. She was involved from the first Impressionist exhibition and knew the key players. She had learned some of her craft from Corot himself, a 'papa' to the movement, and shared many objectives with other artists who would be labelled as Impressionist, notably a brave and increasingly experimental aim at realism and portraying everyday life that used radically loose brushwork and a love of direct encounters with nature. Also, by the time the Impressionist shows were

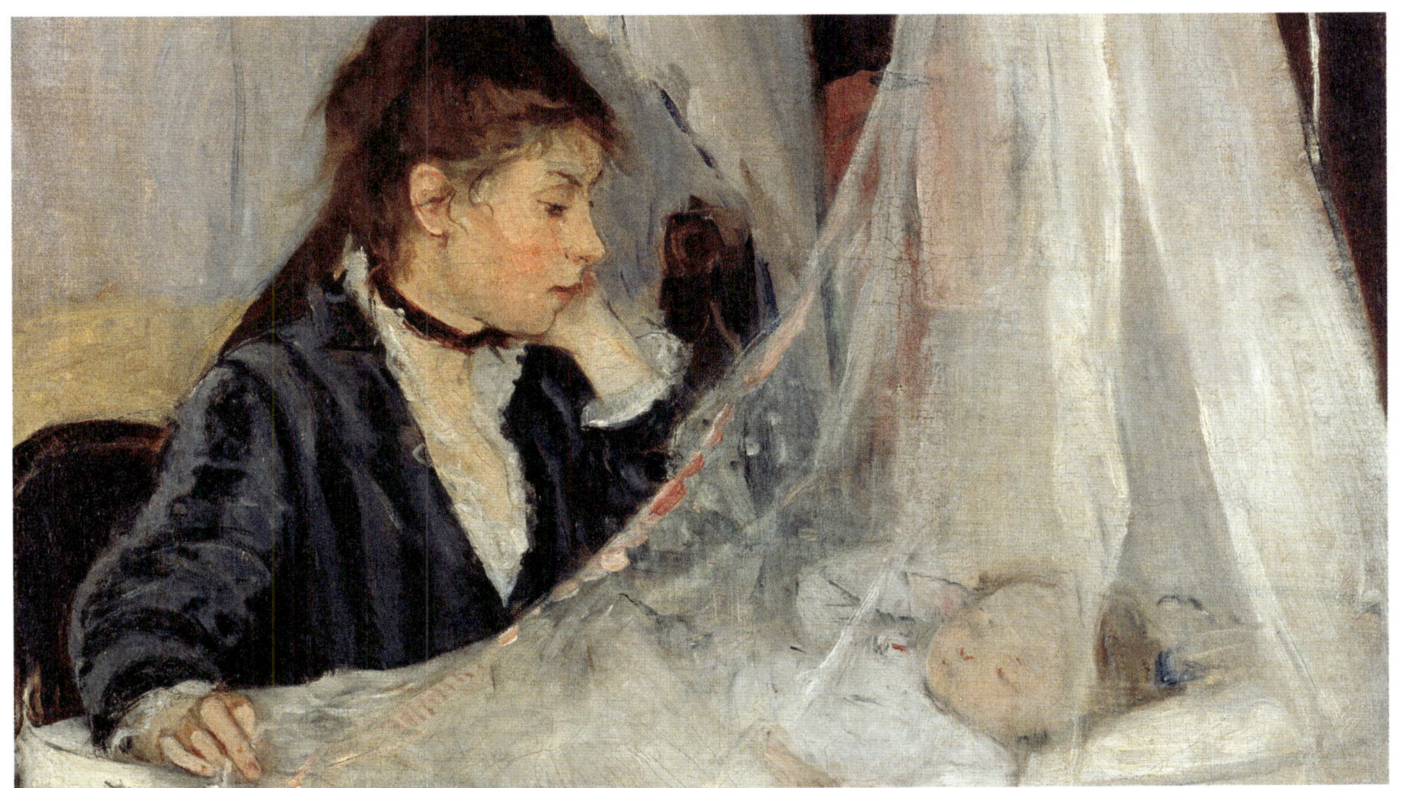

launched, she had started to sell work via an art dealer whose name would become synonymous with Impressionism – Paul Durand-Ruel (1831–1922) – and getting some respectable prices. For example, in 1873, her *View of Paris from the Trocadéro* (1871–73, *see* page 64) was bought swiftly for 750 francs by leading Impressionist collector Ernest Hoschedé (1837–91).

Life with Eugène

Berthe seems to have felt positive about her marriage, writing to brother Tiburce: 'I have found an honest and excellent man, who I think loves me sincerely. I am facing the realities of life after living for quite a long time in chimeras that did not give me much happiness.' It seems that Berthe probably did, at times, suffer from depression.

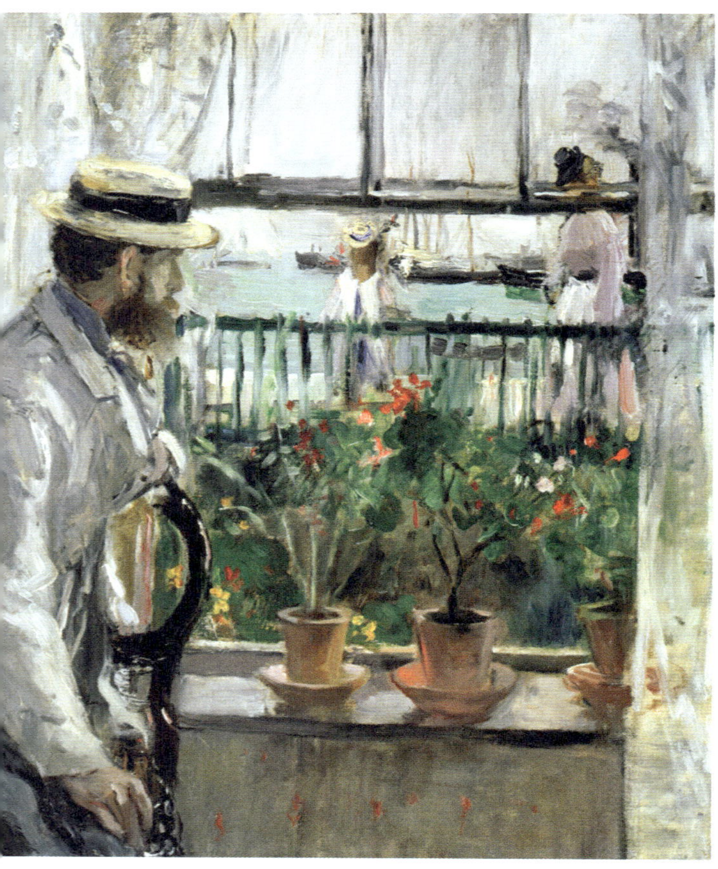

In 1875, the year after getting married, Berthe and Eugène honeymooned in England. However, a honeymoon did not involve stopping work for the determined Berthe, and during this trip she painted one of her best-regarded pictures, *Eugène Manet on the Isle of Wight* (1875, *see* below-left and page 31). She enjoyed painting out of doors and in boats on the trip, admired works in London's National Gallery and met successful French artist James Tissot (1836–1902). Like Berthe, Tissot chronicled modern life, albeit a privileged 'Society' slice of it.

The couple settled at 7 Rue Guichard, moving the following year, 1876, to Avenue de Saint-Cloud (known today as Avenue Victor Hugo). That year also brought the death of Berthe's mother. Berthe continued to sell work here and there and to produce and show various paintings, although critical reception of Impressionism in general remained very mixed and often unfavourable. She showed 20 works at the second Impressionist exhibition in 1876, varying from *At the Ball* (1875, *see* page 89), a beautifully coloured portrayal of stylish Parisian life, to *Before a Yacht* (1875, *see* page 70), a work in a very different type of palette that shows her technical talents with watercolour.

There were still the critics to deal with. The 1876 show was famously referred to in a scathing *Le Figaro* review of the time as follows: 'Five or six lunatics, one of them a woman, a group of unfortunate creatures … have met to exhibit their works…. A frightful spectacle of human vanity working itself up to the point of dementia.' That woman was Berthe. Her now-husband Eugène was so enraged over this comment that he considered challenging its perpetrator, art critic Albert Wolff, to a duel.

Some Critical Acclaim

Wolff aside, however, other, more radical publications than *Le Figaro* were finding some good things to say about Impressionism, and it seems from comments she made at the time that, overall, Berthe was simply pleased that the show's work was getting attention. In fact, Wolff's infamously rude article had included hints of a positive attitude towards Berthe and she was garnering some encouraging comments from other critics by the late 1870s, even if some were slightly doubtful about the free, sketchy style she would make her own. Reviews of the third Impressionist exhibition, in 1877, were mostly very positive for Berthe and included this glowing response from Paul Mantz: 'if there is a single Impressionist in the group, … it is Berthe Morisot…. Here is where we really find the impression perceived by a sincere eye, faithfully rendered by a hand that does not lie.'

Berthe's *The Psyche Mirror* (1876, *see* right and page 34) received the most praise of all of her exhibits at the 1877 show. An accomplished harmonizing of shades of white, it stands as one of her most acclaimed pictures. Mirrors are a common feature in her art as they allowed her to play with light and with reflections, which fascinated her. Critical reception of such toilette pictures by Berthe was often good, leading critic Philippe Burty to label her 'a truly gifted artist', with potential appeal to both the public and the press. The year after the 1877 show, she would earn a chapter in the first edition of Théodore Duret's *Histoire des Peintres Impressionnistes,* solidifying her place as a founder member of the movement (she would also gain a place in further written surveys in the early 1890s).

The Birth of a Daughter

In 1878, on 14 November, a baby girl – to be named Julie (1878–1966) – was born to Berthe and Eugène and would be their only child. Berthe's health was poor after the birth, no doubt adding to underlying weaknesses resulting from the days of the Seige of Paris.

Julie was one of the principal models for Berthe's art, from being a baby and then a little girl engrossed in play, as in *On the Veranda* (1884, *see* page 43), to the sophisticated-looking teenager of *Julie Manet and Her Greyhound Laërte* (1893, *see* page 104). She also modelled for other artists in her mother's circle, including Renoir and her uncle Edouard Manet.

It is clear from the wide variety of pictures of Julie that mother and daughter developed an especially close bond and that Berthe saw her daughter, even as a little girl, as a strong and independent entity in her own right. Julie herself would later say of her mother: 'Until her death, when I was 16, we were always together. I was very spoiled. It

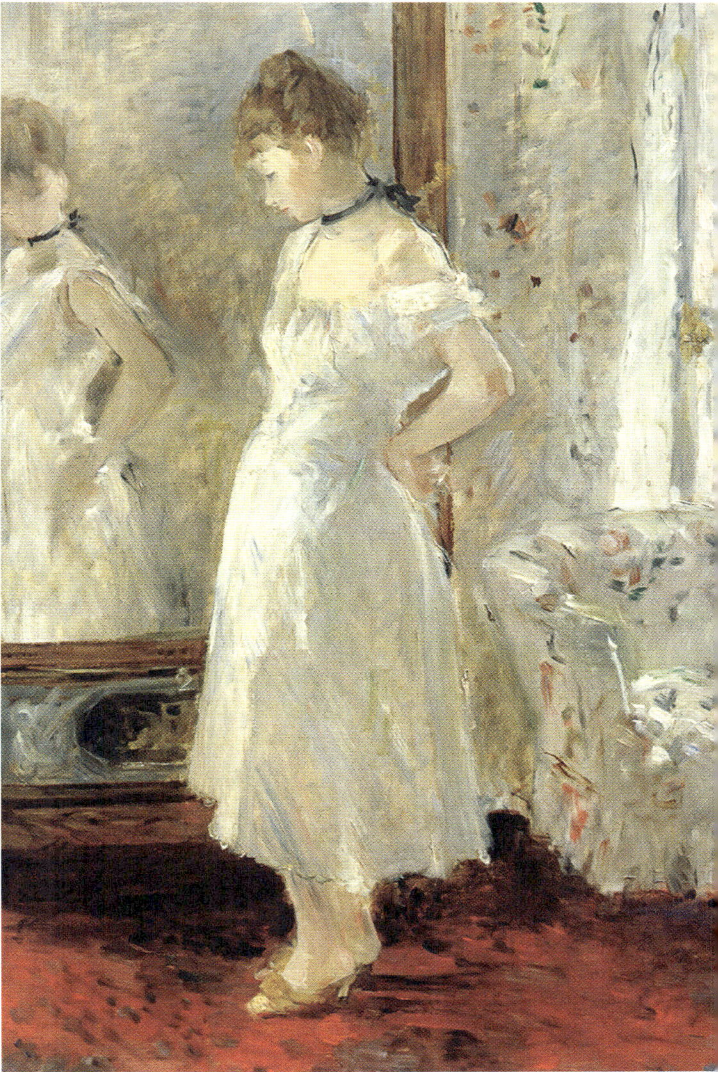

was almost as if my mother knew she wouldn't live for very long; she looked after me, painted me and drew me, with all her strength and tenderness.'

Having a constant but changing model and a powerful emotional model-artist connection appears to have released a rewarding stream of creativity. Berthe's many images of Julie stand as a richly moving and fascinating chronicle in paint of the nature and changing stages of a mother-daughter relationship.

The Early 1880s

It was probably because she was unwell after the birth and busy with
a new baby that Berthe did not exhibit at the fourth Impressionist
exhibition in 1879. However, she was back with a wide variety of work
for the fifth, sixth and seventh shows in 1880, 1881 and 1882.

Around 1880, she was especially preoccupied with painting in
watercolour and also started her first explorations of painting on
unprimed canvas – an approach also pursued by French artist Eva
Gonzalès (1849–83) and her mentor, Edouard Manet. Applying paint
to the heavy textural material made Berthe's strokes looser and
sketchier, affecting her style. Colours became brighter in the 1880s,

too, compared to her muted palettes of the 1870s. She made many
images during her career where areas of pale painting surface were left
bare and she often effectively drew with colour, applying it
to the final surface without any preliminary drawing.

Berthe's exhibits in 1880's Impressionist show were especially
impressive. They brought her much praise from reviewers – even
from the notorious Albert Wolff. Works that she showed included
the shimmering dressing scene, *Woman at Her Toilette* (1875–80,
see pages 24 and 32).

Family life was very busy in the early 1880s. In 1881, using a financial
loan, she and Eugène bought a lot on Rue de Villejust (now Rue Paul
Valéry) in order to build a new family home for themselves and their
daughter, with potential also to create apartments that they might rent

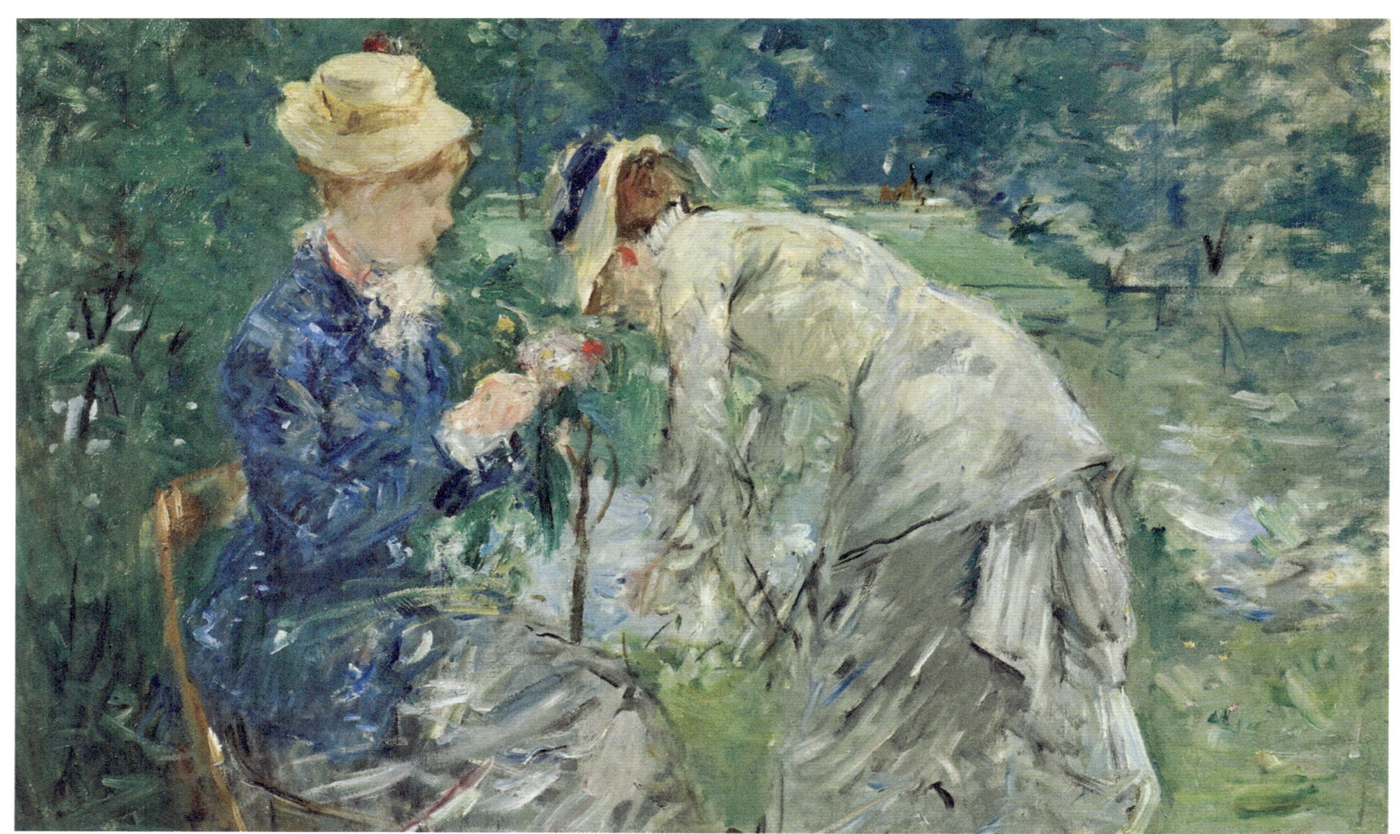

out. They quickly started to organize planning and building work on the property, and doing this took up a great deal of their time.

The new house was located in a convenient spot close to the Arc de Triomphe and present-day Avenue Foch and poised between one stretch of the Seine and the Bois de Boulogne. The latter, with its lakes and lush greenery, provided excellent subject matter for many notable paintings by Berthe that played to her skills in portraying the leisured classes in outdoor settings. These works included *In the Bois de Boulogne* (*c.* 1875–79, *see* opposite and page 113) and *Bois de Boulogne* (1893, *see* page 125).

Discovering Bougival

Around this time there were also various spells away from their Paris home. These included visits to Nice and to Italy, where Julie fell ill with bronchitis while staying in Florence. More notably, there were summers spent at Beuzeval-Houlgate, a fashionable resort area in Normandy that included an impressive sandy beach, plush villas and the imposing Grand Hotel, reminiscent of a French chateau.

Through the early 1880s they also spent sizeable chunks of time in Bougival, another fashionable spot, but this time closer to home in a suburb on the western edge of Paris. In 1881, they found a small house to rent at Bougival which they became very fond of and held on to for a few years, returning on various occasions. This became a convenient bolthole in 1882, when they passed both the summer and winter there while building work on their new house was completed.

Bougival and the area around it – places such as Louveciennes, further to the west – became extremely popular with various Impressionists and other artists as a place to stay and to paint. Pissarro, Sisley, Renoir and Monet all immortalized the area in paint, just as J.M.W. Turner (1775–1851) had before them, and the colourful Post-Impressionist and Fauvist Maurice de Vlaminck (1876–1958) would also paint there. Artists were drawn to attractive pockets of greenery and especially to life along the River Seine in this area – painting its locks, barges, bridges and the sky and water at different times of year and in different lights. Berthe, for example,

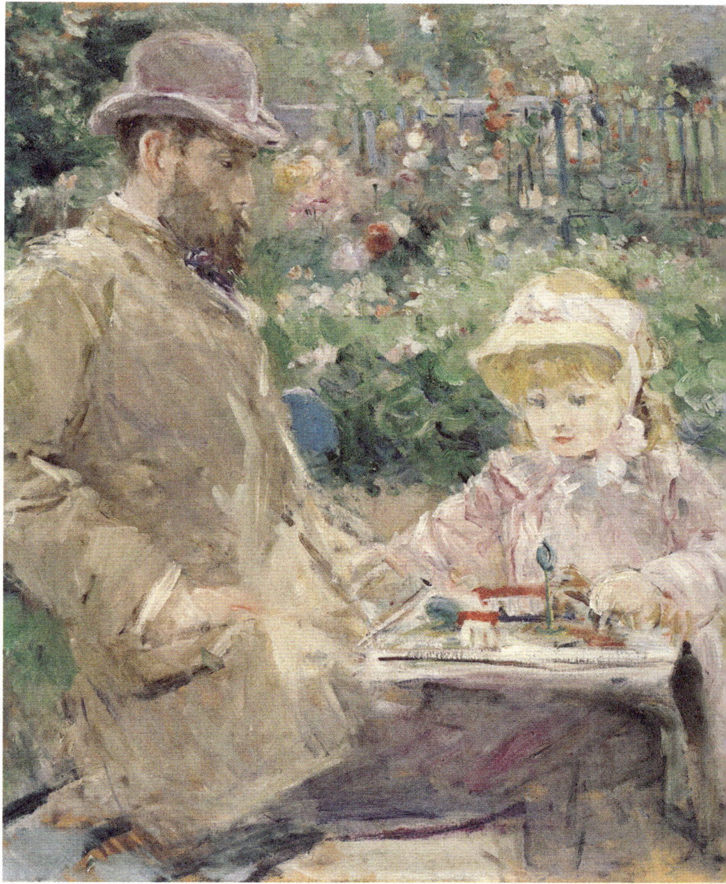

painted Bougival's quay, setting herself up in a small boat there in order to get the best viewpoint.

Berthe also painted her little girl Julie in the garden at the rented house at Bougival – spending time with her father, playing happily on her own or with maid Pasie, for example. Such works include *Mud Pies* (1882, *see* page 40), *Eugène Manet and His Daughter in the Garden at Bougival* (1881, *see* above and page 39) and *The Fable* (1883, *see* overleaf and page 41).

Bougival's Contribution

Some commentators have noted that the pictures from this period at Bougival show a new looseness in Berthe's style and approach, as well

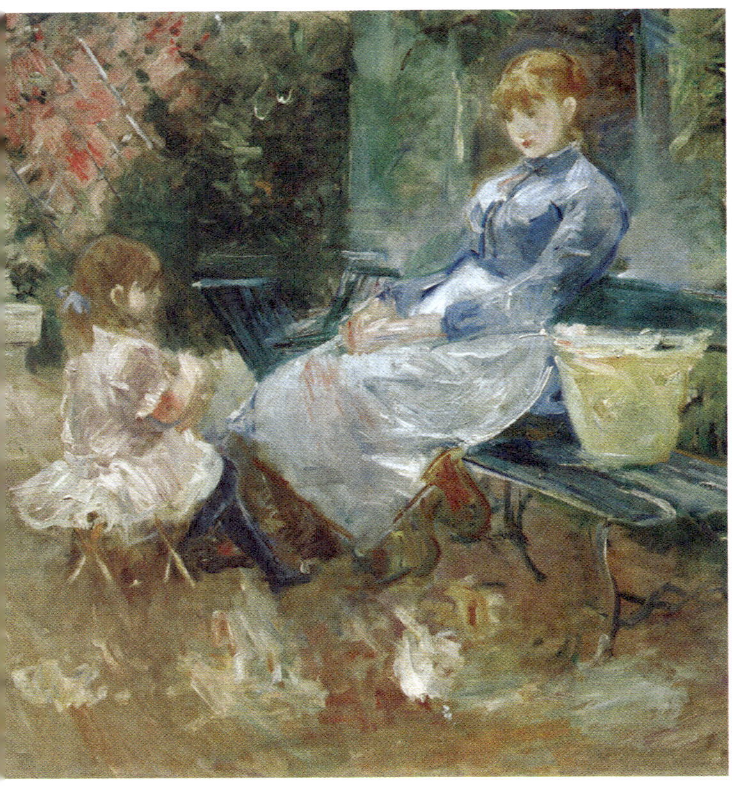

as a particular way of blending figure and surroundings. The rented
house, at 4 Rue de la Princesse, provided a wonderful context for a
painter such as Berthe. There was a glazed veranda that offered a
good painting space and looked out on to lush greenery and attractive
houses. The garden, complete with roses tumbling over trellises, was
a delight, and celebrated in works including *The Garden at Bougival*
(1884, *see* page 74), which was typical of her direction in the first
part of the 1880s, with its loose blending of forms. Such a setting
was a gift for someone so in love with the play of light and colour.

The Bougival pictures certainly seem to offer a poetic glimpse
into an atmospheric and specially charmed world. But was it that
simple? The puzzling content of *The Fable*, where the mood and
activities are enigmatic, perhaps hints at something more reflective,
even melancholic.

Whatever the truth about *The Fable*, it seems that good and special
times were had at Bougival, and times that were extremely fertile from
a creative point of view – a large proportion of Berthe's total output was
produced there. Berthe said of her sojourns at Bougival that they
were 'the happiest time of my life' and wrote of Julie to a friend: 'she
makes advances to all the children in Bougival, and is very popular
there. From every door one hears "Good day, Mademoiselle Julie".'

Artistic Alliances and Rifts

Another artist to be found summering in the environs of Bougival at
this creatively happy time in the early 1880s was American-born Mary
Cassatt (1844–1926). In the summer of 1880, for example, Berthe
made frequent visits to the Cassatt family's holiday villa, at Marly-le-
Roi. Cassatt greatly admired Berthe's work, writing to her about the
1880 Impressionist exhibit – in which they both participated – that she
felt Berthe had a great body of work to show and that she was 'very
envious' of Berthe's talent, signing off as 'Affectionate friend'.

Cassatt became another highly important member of the
Impressionist circle, well respected by her peers. She had first
exhibited in the Impressionist exhibition of 1879, invited to take
part by Degas, who was a driving organizational force in that
enterprise. Berthe and Cassatt had much in common. Both brought
a new stature and modern subtlety to explorations of everyday life
for women, working in oil, pastel and print. Both, too, seemed to
emerge particularly well compared to their fellow artists from the
sixth Impressionist exhibition of 1881. In general, the 1881 outing
became something of a shambles, a sad decline from the great
promise of the first show back in 1874.

The problems of 1881 would hardly have come as a shock to those
involved. Tensions had been brewing throughout the life of these
exhibitions. Degas took a prominent role that other participants found
overly domineering and some felt that he imposed the participation
of artists who did not share the core principles of the movement.
Premises chosen often did few favours to the works shown and some
critical derision continued, while visitor numbers were, in general, not

overly impressive. Gustave Caillebotte (1848–94), Monet, Renoir and Sisley actually abstained from taking part in the 1881 show.

The chasms opening up among those exhibiting in these shows were also caused by disagreement over participation in the Salons versus exclusively independent exhibitions. In other words, trying to reform things from inside or setting up against it, although Salon involvement brought with it a seal of approval that might lead to greater financial stability and general recognition. Monet, Renoir and Sisley were key figures who continued to show at the Salon, while Caillebotte, Cassatt, Degas, Morisot and Pissarro opted to never show at the Salon and chose total independence. Degas believed that only those turning their back on the Salon should be permitted to show with the Impressionists. According to Degas, Morisot had agreed in 1879 to send no more submissions to the Salon, and in fact showed nothing there after 1873.

Endings …

The year 1883 (the date of *Haystacks at Bougival, see* below and page 73) was a momentous one – in good and bad ways. In the spring, on 30 April, Berthe's brother-in-law and longstanding mentor, Edouard Manet, died at the age of just 51 after a tortured ending, throughout which Eugène and Berthe visited him regularly. Manet's health had been poor for some years and his death was brought on by gangrene following the amputation of a leg, which in turn had been precipitated partly by severe syphilis.

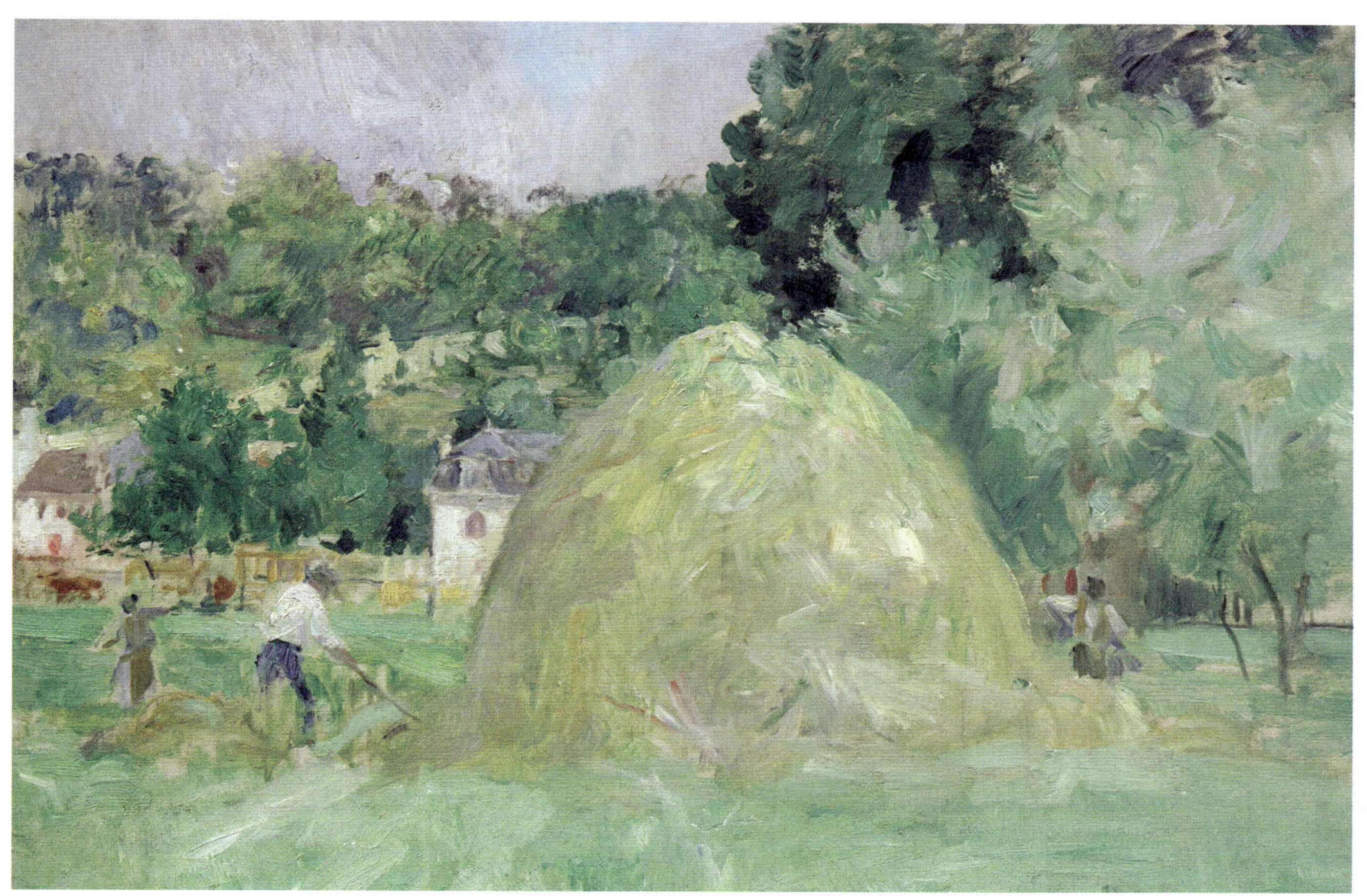

Berthe wrote feelingly to sister Edma and to a friend about her grief and profound sense of loss. Speaking of the 'almost physical emotions' of watching him suffer in agony and of their 'old bonds of friendship', she described herself as 'crushed'. She summarized: 'Edouard and I were friends for many, many years, and he is associated with all the memories of my youth; moreover, he was such an attractive personality, his mind was so young and alert, that it seemed that more than others he was beyond the power of death.'

Apart from the personal loss, Manet's passing was also something of a symbolic ending to the era of early excitements and scandals associated with Impressionism and its related circle, the rebellion of the Salon des Refusés, and of a time before the experiment of the Impressionist exhibitions had begun to seem increasingly like a failing one. In many ways Manet had distanced himself from Impressionism

throughout his career, while simultaneously helping to pave its way. During 1883, Berthe helped out with the planning of a retrospective exhibition of Manet's work, which took place the following year. In August of 1883, another blow came when Manet's mother had a stroke that caused paralysis. She moved in with Berthe and Eugène and was in their home when she died 18 months later, shortly after the death of her son Gustave, brother to Edouard and Eugène, who died at the young age of 49.

... and Beginnings

Late in 1883, Berthe, Eugène and Julie finally moved into their substantial new home on Rue de Villejust (where *Children at the Basin*, *see* left and page 49, was to be painted a few years later). This had been a large, demanding and draining project, causing a rather nomadic home life and closely involving Berthe and Eugène in the planning and execution each step of the way. Fortunately, they seemed in accord during the process and to respect each other's opinion. In general, they appear to have got along in a thoughtful and caring, if not over-effusive, way. By January 1885, Berthe's parents were gone, as were all of Eugène's immediate family, and so the couple must have felt rather lost. With the house completed, living there offered a kind of positive new start for them. Monet – who admired Berthe's work and had paintings by her in his own house – offered to paint a work specially to hang in their new home.

The couple and their little girl took the ground floor and mezzanine as their own living quarters and rented out the rest – a common strategy in Paris at the time. Eugène had planted up a flower-filled garden for the family to use. All the rooms in the apartment were modestly sized save for the salon, or living room. This was the heart of the home and a handsome space that Berthe also chose to use as her painting studio, although she sometimes painted in the dining room.

A Cultural Hub

Berthe's new salon would become highly important to her life and her art, which were inextricably intertwined. As a studio, it offered good credentials. Very large, with a high ceiling and high windows, it was

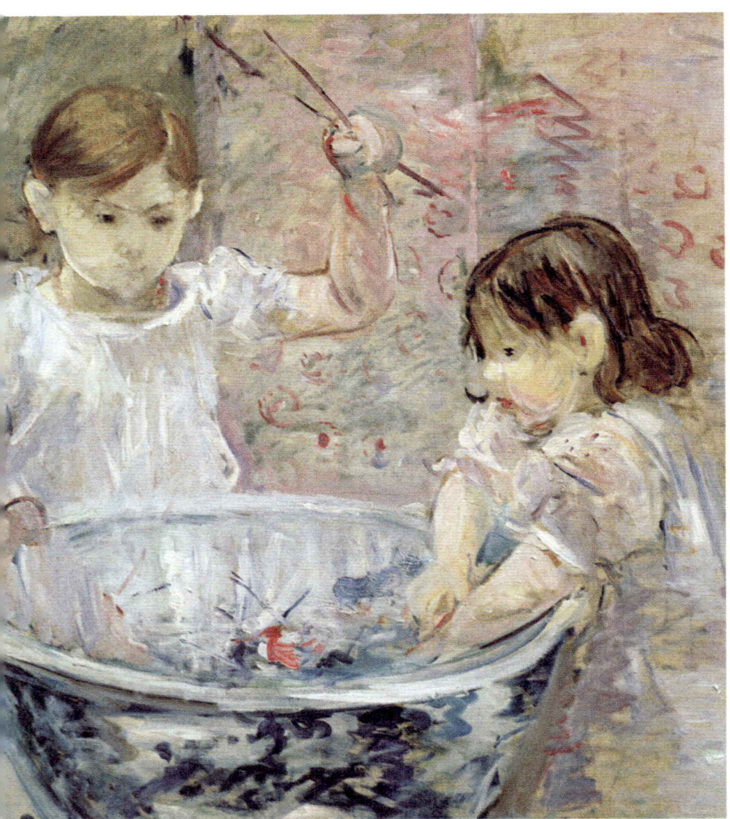

painted white and floored with well-polished parquet. Copious amounts of light bounced between the outside world and the shiny floor, controlled by pale-coloured blinds on the windows.

The room was furnished with elegance and lovely colour. Furniture in the French neo-classical empire style of the early 1800s jostled with the Japanese prints and decorative screens that were so fashionable at the time. Representing Berthe's experience as a copyist at the Louvre, the room also featured her copy of one part of *Vulcan Presenting Venus with Arms for Aeneas* (1757) by François Boucher (1703–70), a quintessential piece of French Rococo artistry.

A partly concealed cupboard in the salon meant that all of Berthe's painting equipment could easily be tucked away when the room was used for family or social life. This was important as this was also the room where Berthe and her husband hosted cultural 'salons' – a meeting place for many of the most artistic and interesting minds of the day, ranging from Monet and Whistler to the poet Mallarmé. These often took the form of regular Thursday-night dinners. The apartment's garden also made an important contribution as it became a favourite place for Berthe to indulge her love of painting *en plein air*. The year 1885 was a particularly intense one for painting in this garden and in the nearby Bois de Boulogne.

Japonisme

The decorative elements in the salon at Rue de Villejust reflected a contemporary fashion in nineteenth-century Europe for all things Japanese. *Japonisme* was a term coined in 1872 by the prominent French critic Philippe Burty to describe this general interest in Japanese art and design and its influence.

Scholars argue about exactly when this artistic trend began in Europe, but it was certainly especially marked from the mid-1800s. It received great encouragement from 1854, the year in which trading between Japan and the West was opened up considerably by the Kanagawa Treaty. In France, Fantin-Latour, an important early connection for Berthe and the agent of her introduction to Edouard Manet, was a founder member in the 1860s of a secret society based around

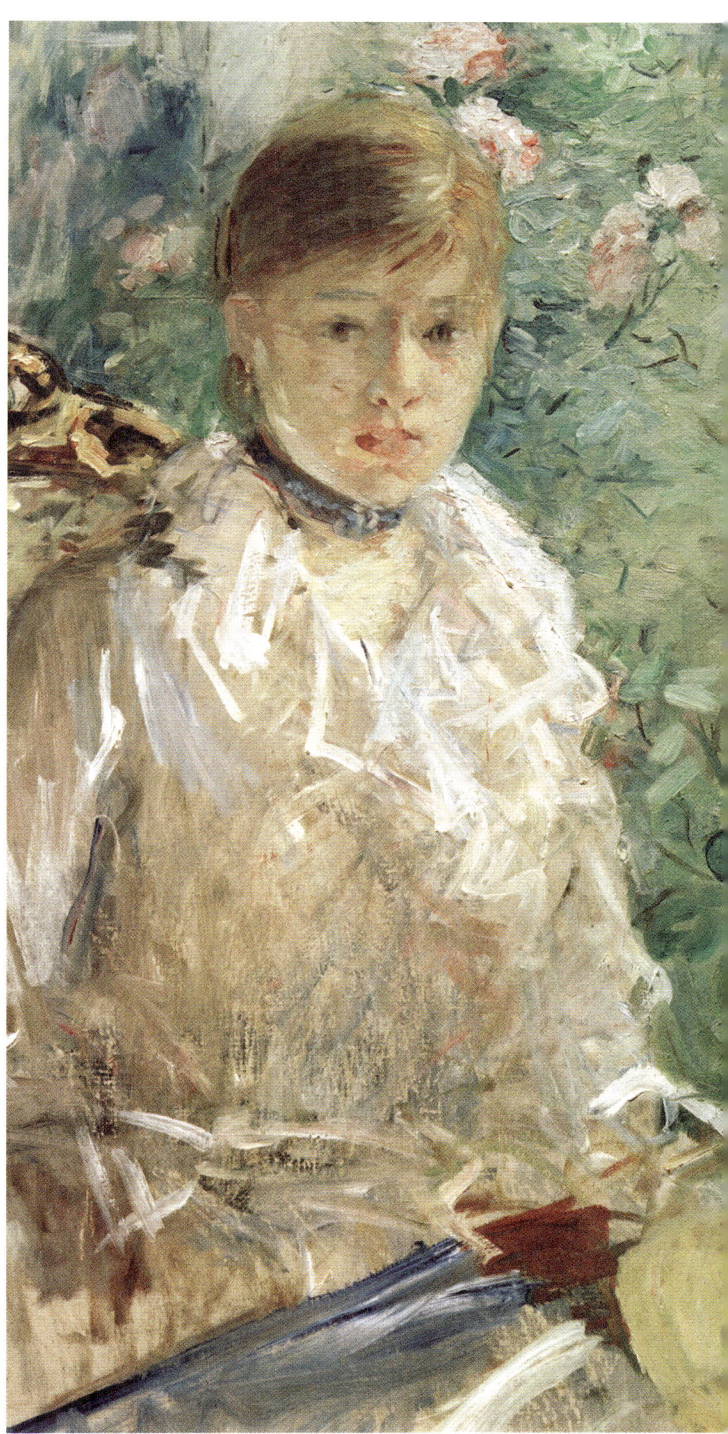

studying Japanese culture. Numerous influential French writers and artists of the day from Berthe's circle, including Charles Baudelaire (1821–67), Zola, Degas, Edouard Manet and Monet, started to collect Japanese art and artefacts just as she herself did. The American-born painter Whistler, whose influence is clear in some of Berthe's work, was a leading convert to the cause.

Japonisme had a profound effect on modern French painting in general and Impressionism in particular. Japanese woodblock prints contained many important influences which fed into the development of a more 'modern' vision: off-centre compositions, broad swathes of patterning and often-flat colour, lack of modelling, bright colours and depictions of everyday life. Artefacts such as Japanese screens showed a love of beautifully coloured decorative pattern and detailing. As just one example, Degas is famed for his visually powerful asymmetrical picture crops.

Berthe's varied work shows experiments with all of these aspects to a greater or lesser degree. These range from the large, schematized areas of colour and flattened perspective of *Two Girls* (*c.* 1894, *see* page 57) to the delicate, decorative background of *Summer* (1879,

see pages 21 and 92). In fact, in the latter work, the way that figure and surroundings are made to form part of an overall pattern must have been to some extent the result of Japanese influence, an effect that became a part of her famed style of blending figures with their background.

The Rise of Photography

Another central influence on the nineteenth-century artist was the inexorable rise of photography. Key people from the very early history of the photograph around the 1820s and 1830s were, in fact, French: Nicéphore Niépce (1765–1833) and Louis Daguerre (1787–1851).

The field of photography gathered pace during the nineteenth century. There was a massive rise in commercial photography in the West and practitioners were often influenced by the kinds of standards, such as symmetrical composition, that they were used to seeing in traditional paintings. Once techniques had been refined, some photographers moved from simply capturing what was before them to producing creatively 'arty' photographs, also often inspired by paintings. Because

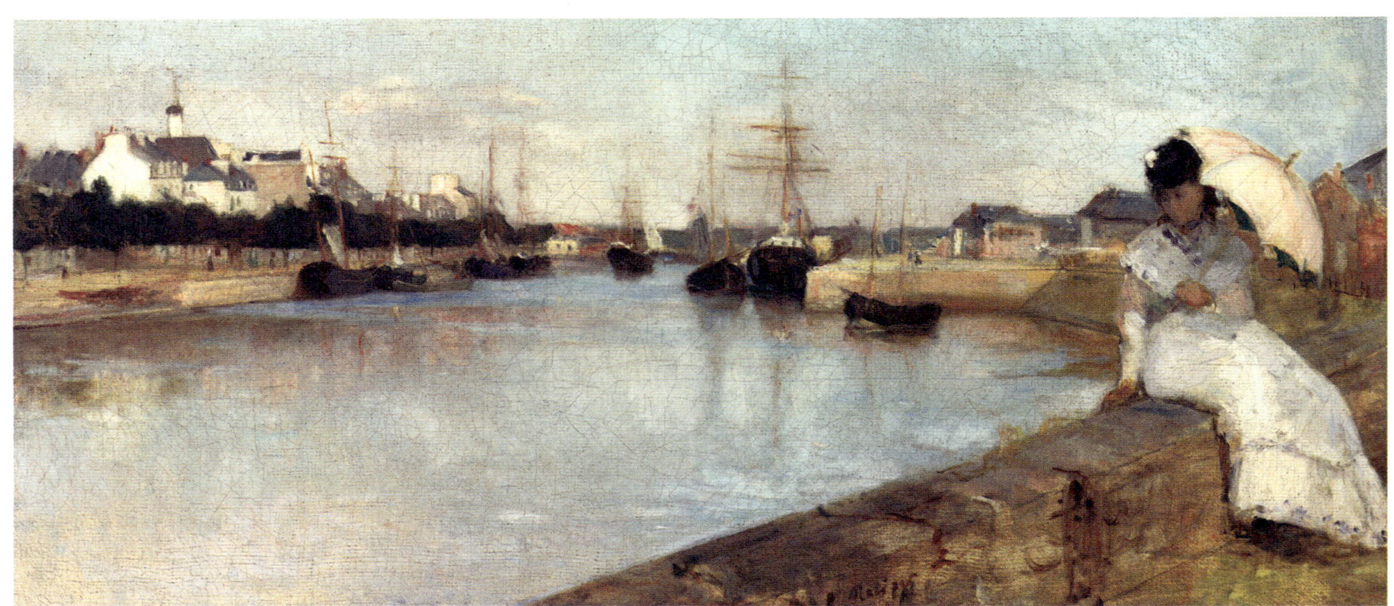

the photograph, as a momentous revolution in ways of seeing, also changed how painters viewed the world and their art, an interesting two-way art-photography relationship came into being.

This two-way traffic of influence was a complex affair with a web of different effects. As far as painters were concerned, many were fascinated by how photography could seemingly freeze a moment in time (even if it was hardly a fleeting snapshot in reality, as taking a photograph could be a lengthy process involving long exposure times). This was especially pertinent to Impressionism, which often sought to depict transient states of weather, light, time of day and season.

Photographs made artists look more closely at how they 'cropped' their own images and experiment with different crops, especially if they wanted to convey a feeling of having caught a fleeting moment. Artists were inspired by photographic 'mistakes' such as blurred moving figures and people or objects chopped off by the photo's edge. Berthe's *The Harbour at Lorient* (1869, *see* below-left and page 62) pushes a large figure right to one edge of the frame, as did many of her pictures.

Because photography was essentially painting with light, artists started thinking in creative ways about how they captured light with paint or pastel – central to Impressionist thought. There was also perhaps less need for artists to concentrate on portraying a traditionally objective, apparently 'realistic' portrait of the world as photographs had a form of that covered, freeing artists to turn their attention to making other, different, truths of their own – some attempting scientific precision related to how the eye receives light, and others undertaking more emotional responses.

Friendship with Renoir

Meanwhile, back in Berthe's personal artistic and family life, one of the important features of her last decade, from the mid-1880s, was her growing friendship with Renoir. Berthe had great admiration for his drawing skills and for the preparatory drawings he produced for his work. No doubt influenced by this, she started to focus more on drawing and to make a greater number of preparatory sketches,

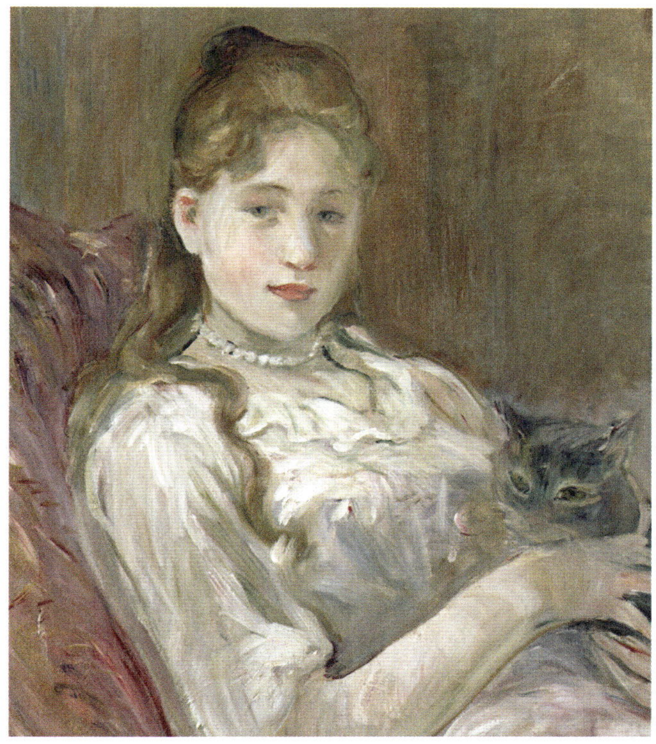

using coloured pencils as one of her media. Her pastel study of a little boy (for a painting that has been lost), *Little Saint John* (1890, *see* page 98), shows how much she was able to convey through well-judged line.

Berthe's style took some new directions in its final stages in the later 1880s and 1890s and Renoir's influence was certainly an important factor here. Her figures now often emerged from their backgrounds with a greater solidity of the kind seen in Renoir's work, aided by some outlining, as in *Young Girl with Cat* (1892, *see* above and page 103). The two artists shared an admiration for Boucher, a master of the solid figure set within a Baroque interior, enlivened by beautiful colours and light effects, and all these aspects can be glimpsed in their work. They also appreciated Peter Paul Rubens (1577–1640), whose well-lit figures also showed a certain strong realism; Berthe had praised Rubens after seeing a work by him in Amsterdam on a family trip to Belgium and Holland in 1885.

The friendship and mutual appreciation were further cemented by Berthe and Eugène asking Renoir to paint a portrait of Julie. He duly obliged and produced a charming picture that shows her wearing a prettily embroidered dress and hugging a cat: *Julie Manet* (1887). This was not Renoir's only portrait of Julie and he produced a striking and unusual double portrait of Julie with her mother right at the end of Berthe's life, in 1894.

Another area where Berthe would have learned from Renoir was in his wonderful use of pastels, a medium that she too used to such good effect. Like hers, his pastels sing out with vivid colours and are illuminated by a seemingly inner light. For artists such as Berthe, with a fascination for light effects encouraged by working outdoors, pastels offered the perfect medium, seen for example in *In a Park* (*c.* 1874, *see* page 65). Pastels deposit tiny particles that reflect the light and spread it across an image, producing a softly brilliant surface.

Attention Abroad, Problems at Home

By the late 1880s, Berthe's work was gaining some attention further afield thanks to a period of being included in a good range of international exhibitions. Between 1886 and 1890, she took part in both Les XX and Exposition Internationale shows in Brussels as well as various exhibitions in New York.

American collectors and critics were taking an active interest in Impressionism and the dealer Durand-Ruel was a key player in the New York outings – one of them was at a gallery he had opened there. The New York Impressionist show in which Berthe participated in 1886, with nine pictures, including the incandescent *Woman at Her Toilette* (1875–80, *see* left and page 32), was called *Works in Oil and Pastel by the Impressionists of Paris*. It took place at the American Art Galleries and was mounted in association with the American Art Association of New York. It did well enough to travel on for a further showing at New York's National Academy of Design.

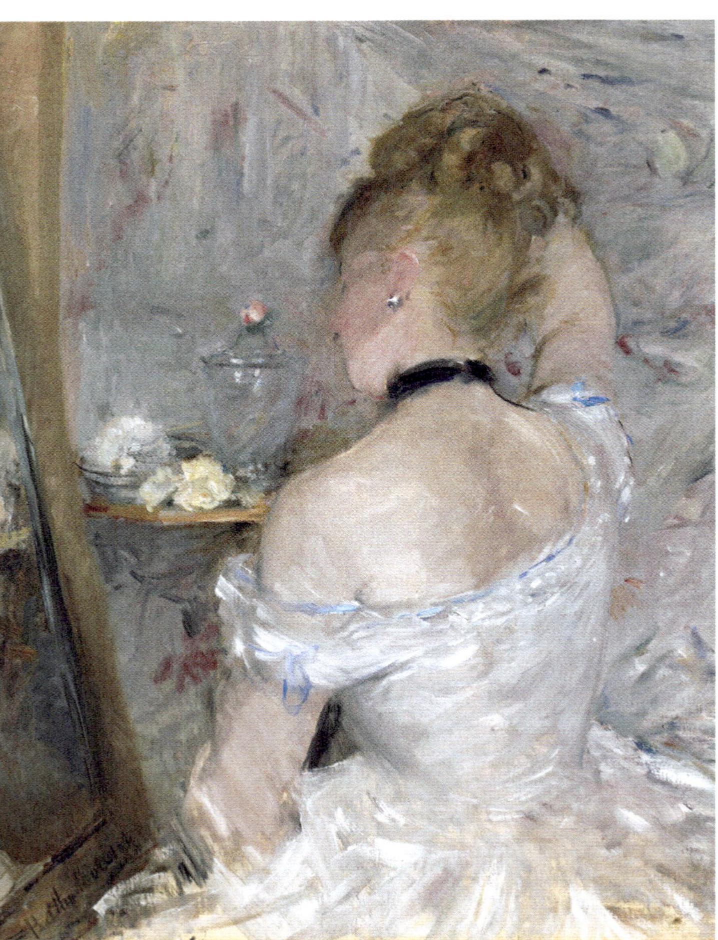

This era was also when Morisot took part in the eighth and last Impressionist show, in the summer of 1886, a venture now deeply riven by disagreements between participants. Berthe and Eugène helped to back it financially and she exhibited a good number of works. A significant proportion were in watercolour or pastel and she also included oils from her final happy summer at Bougival in 1884 – *Hollyhocks* (1884, *see* page 76), with its characteristically bold crop, is a lovely representation of the flower-filled garden there.

At home, there were health problems to contend with. Winter 1885 saw Julie catching a very dangerous disease, scarlet fever, through which Berthe successfully nursed her, throwing a children's fancy-dress ball for her daughter after her recovery by way of celebration.

Julie was dressed as a Greek girl. This illness came closely after
the death of Eugène's immediate family and caring for his mother.
Berthe also worked intensely on her painting during 1885 and was
contending with trying to organize another Impressionist exhibition
(which would eventually become the last one the following year)
amid all the personality clashes. Little wonder that in 1885, she
wrote to her sister Edma: 'I am not myself these days … the burden
of life seems hard to bear.'

To make matters worse, after a family trip to Gorey, Jersey, in the Channel
Islands, Eugène fell ill. Sadly this was the starting point for a period of poor
health that ended with his premature death in the early 1890s.

Living Her Painting, Painting Her Life

By the 1880s, Berthe had worked hard all of her adult life to produce
an impressive body of work, in a range of media. Her subject matter
was the everyday life of a nineteenth-century Parisian woman of some
means: the domestic life of women and children, including maids
and nannies; portraits of friends and relatives; women at their toilette,
bathing or getting dressed; scenes of leisure in gardens and parks;
attending the theatre or a ball; small children at play or with parents
or carers; landscape, garden, town and harbour views; some still-lifes;
and moments of rest, reading, dreaming or *ennui*. In other words,
a small, privileged and intimate world.

So Berthe painted what she herself knew best – often a good strategy.
In the words of French poet Paul Valéry (1871–1945), who in 1899
married Yves' younger daughter Jeannie, her special talent was 'to live
her painting and to paint her life, as if this was a natural and necessary
process essential to her well-being. He added that it was rather like
keeping a journal in visual form.

It might be said that, as a woman, Berthe had little choice but to
paint such subjects. Society at the time certainly did not in general
encourage women to become professional artists and they did not have
the ready access, as men did, to official training and aspects of it such
as painting nudes. It was not seemly for a woman to frequent the cafés

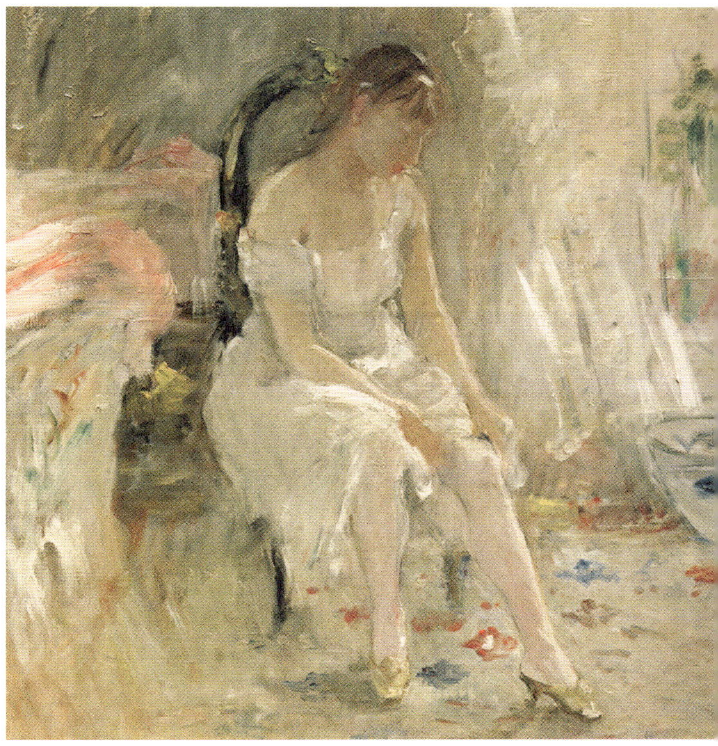

and bars featured in many of her artistic male peers' takes on modern
life, and so Berthe's domain became the domestic sphere.

Her domestic subject matter can also be seen in a different and more
subversive light, true to the aims of many Impressionists, and that is
in portraying modern life as opposed to the traditionally appreciated
grander, often historical, topics – and the life of a modern woman at that.
There are other aspects to her vision too. Berthe had money behind
her but she was always extremely serious about her painting (indicated,
for example, by a willingness to pay to use professional artists' models
as well as friends and relatives) and was eager to sell her work. It may
be that her toilette pictures, often slightly seductive in tone, were partly
aimed at male buyers, even including more experimentally executed
examples such as *Young Woman Putting on Stockings* (1880, *see* above
and page 37). Perhaps she also saw this strategy as a mode of paving
the road to acceptance for her many highly abstract scenes in the vein of
Hanging the Laundry out to Dry (1875, *see* overleaf and page 68).

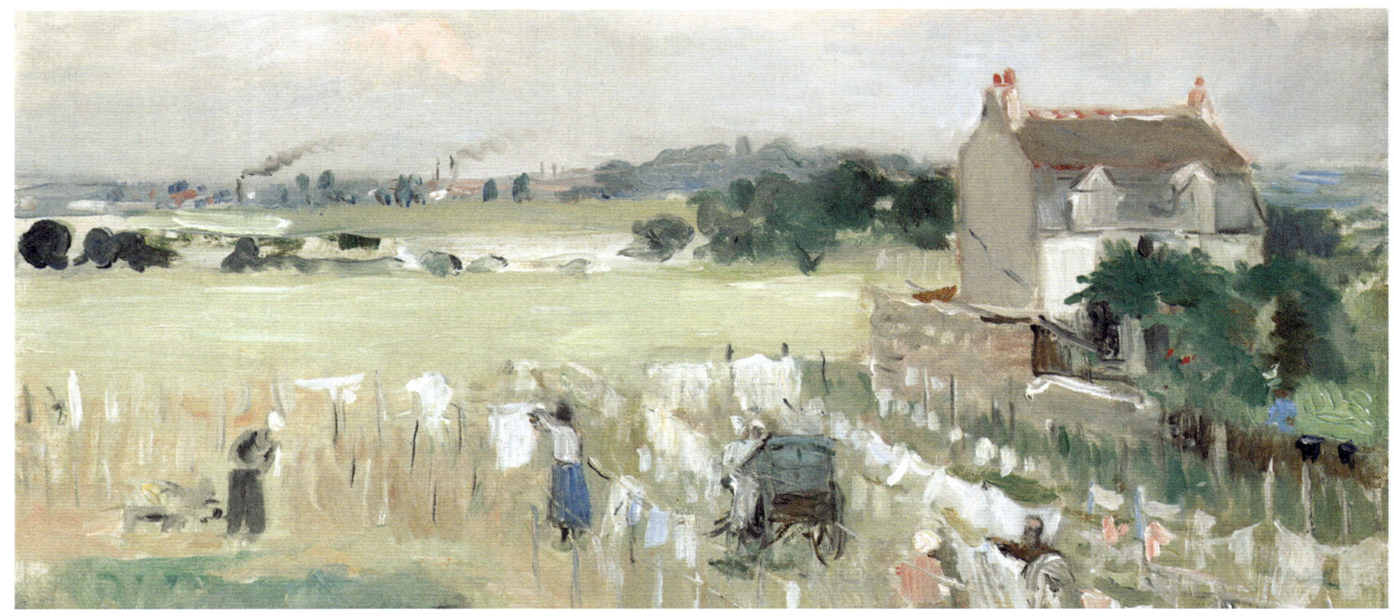

Something Old, Something New

Although Berthe forged a way to picture the modern woman, inevitably she in fact drew on past traditions to create a clever amalgamation of approaches. It is telling that she commented towards the end of her life: 'modern painters bore me – I like either extreme novelty or things of the past'. Many commentators have mentioned that she drew significantly from eighteenth-century Rococo artists held dear in France such as Boucher (greatly admired by her), her possible ancestor Fragonard and Jean-Antoine Watteau (1684–1721). Borrowed Rococo aspects included lovely colours, a light delicacy and intimate interior settings.

Such aspects are especially clear in her much-loved toilette images. The irresistibly lovely *Woman at Her Toilette* (1875–80, *see* pages 24 and 32) dazzles in a froth of dancing light and delicately coloured strokes. This is luxurious-looking Rococo-like frivolity, yet the sitter is very much a contemporary woman. As scholars have noted, such pictures can be seen as a modern take on the eighteenth-century Rococo tradition of the *fête champêtre* and *fête galante*, a genre of paintings that included well-to-do folk enjoying themselves in parkland

settings and semi-dressed women at their toilette. These were very popular in the nineteenth century, circulated widely as prints. As for the enigmatic facial expressions for which Berthe is well-known, Watteau's work also has a kind of poetically wistful melancholy that may have been influential.

Another notable area of Berthe's work that was indebted to eighteenth-century French art involved still-life elements in her paintings. Jean-Siméon Chardin (1699–1779) was a leading expert at clever still-life composition and the play of light across objects – often rendered with loose strokes. The water flask and lemons arranged artfully on the left of *In the Country (After Lunch)* (1881, *see* page 38) seem to echo his work.

The Late Years

The early 1890s brought a range of personal and professional changes. At the close of 1890, Berthe became ill with rheumatic fever, a seriously undermining condition. At the same time, Eugène's health was also failing and there were trips to Mézy-sur-Seine just outside Paris in the hope of bolstering it. At Mézy, Berthe painted outdoor images such as *The Cherry Tree* (1891, *see* page 52).

While travelling around the Mézy area in 1891, the couple discovered a seventeenth-century chateau along the Seine, west of Mézy at Juziers, and bought it that autumn. However, they were never able to enjoy it together as, tragically, Eugène died just six months later, in the spring of 1892. Stoical as ever, Berthe continued working, preparing for her first-ever solo exhibition, *L'Exposition de Tableaux, Pastels et Dessins par Berthe Morisot*, which opened the month after her husband's death.

Berthe's style took a new direction in the 1890s. Pictures such as *The Artist's Daughter with a Parakeet* (1890, *see* page 99) and *Julie Manet with a Straw Hat* (1892, *see* below-right and page 102) deploy more relaxed, less choppy – almost flowing – strokes than earlier work. There is more definition, and even outlining, of figures. The strange feel of some pieces, as with *Bois de Boulogne* (1893, *see* page 125), begins to seem akin to the Symbolism of Edvard Munch (1863–1944), whose famed *The Scream* was also painted in 1893, or of Berthe's friend Mallarmé.

Berthe continued to paint, exhibit and hold her Thursday-night soirées. In 1894, her 1879 picture *Young Woman in a Ball Gown* (*see* page 91) became the first Berthe Morisot to enter a museum when it was bought by the Musée du Luxembourg. This important milestone of recognition came just in time. Berthe became ill with flu the following year and died, at the age of 54, on 2 March 1895, leaving Julie an orphan at the age of 16. Berthe was laid to rest in the Manet family vault at Passy cemetery.

An Impressive Legacy

In 1876, Berthe's good friend Mallarmé praised the 'fresh charm' of her 'feminine vision'. He noted her 'marked economy of means' and stated that she 'succeeds marvellously in capturing the intimate presence of a woman or child'. He went on to talk about states of anxiety or sorrow that subtly underlie some of her enigmatic images. There is much that is complimentary here, and he certainly seemed to be tuned in to many of her aims. However, the word 'charm' or 'charming' was often used by other critics who sought to praise Berthe but in fact failed to fully understand her. Seemingly favourable reviews stressed her bright, fresh

colours and delicacy – often rightly praising her talents as a colourist and in orchestrating shades of white and light – but did not see just how groundbreaking her formal experiments were.

Berthe Morisot, a founder member of the French Impressionists and one of few women to show regularly with them, was highly admired by her circle but received little real recognition until the later twentieth and twenty-first centuries. However, her work made a mark along the way via its very probable influence on Manet and on other artists such as Frenchmen Edouard Vuillard (1868–1940), a firm admirer, and Pierre Bonnard (1867–1947).

Among her greatest achievements was to persevere as a professional painter at a time when the odds were stacked against women doing so. In her work, she succeeded in raising up, and documenting, the everyday life of the modern woman as a subject of interest and worth and with a degree of realism; even her toilette pictures show women without saccharine sentimentality. The final words are best left to Berthe herself: 'I do not think any man would ever treat a woman as his equal, and it is all I ask because I know my worth.'

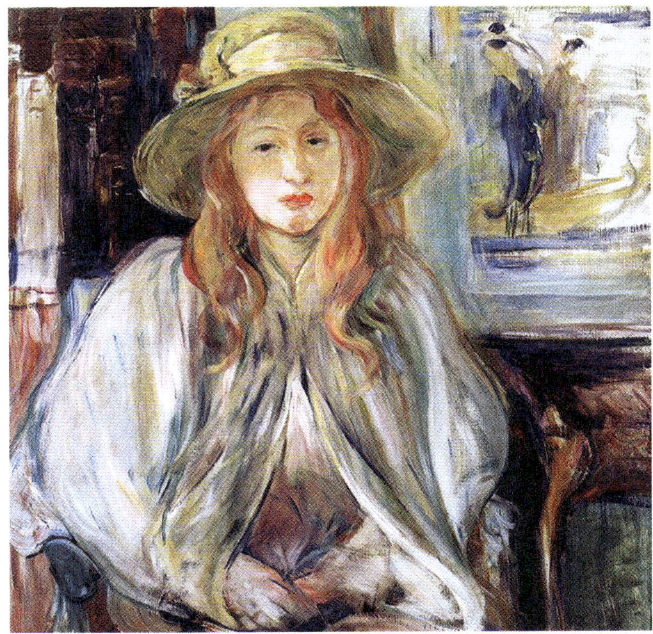

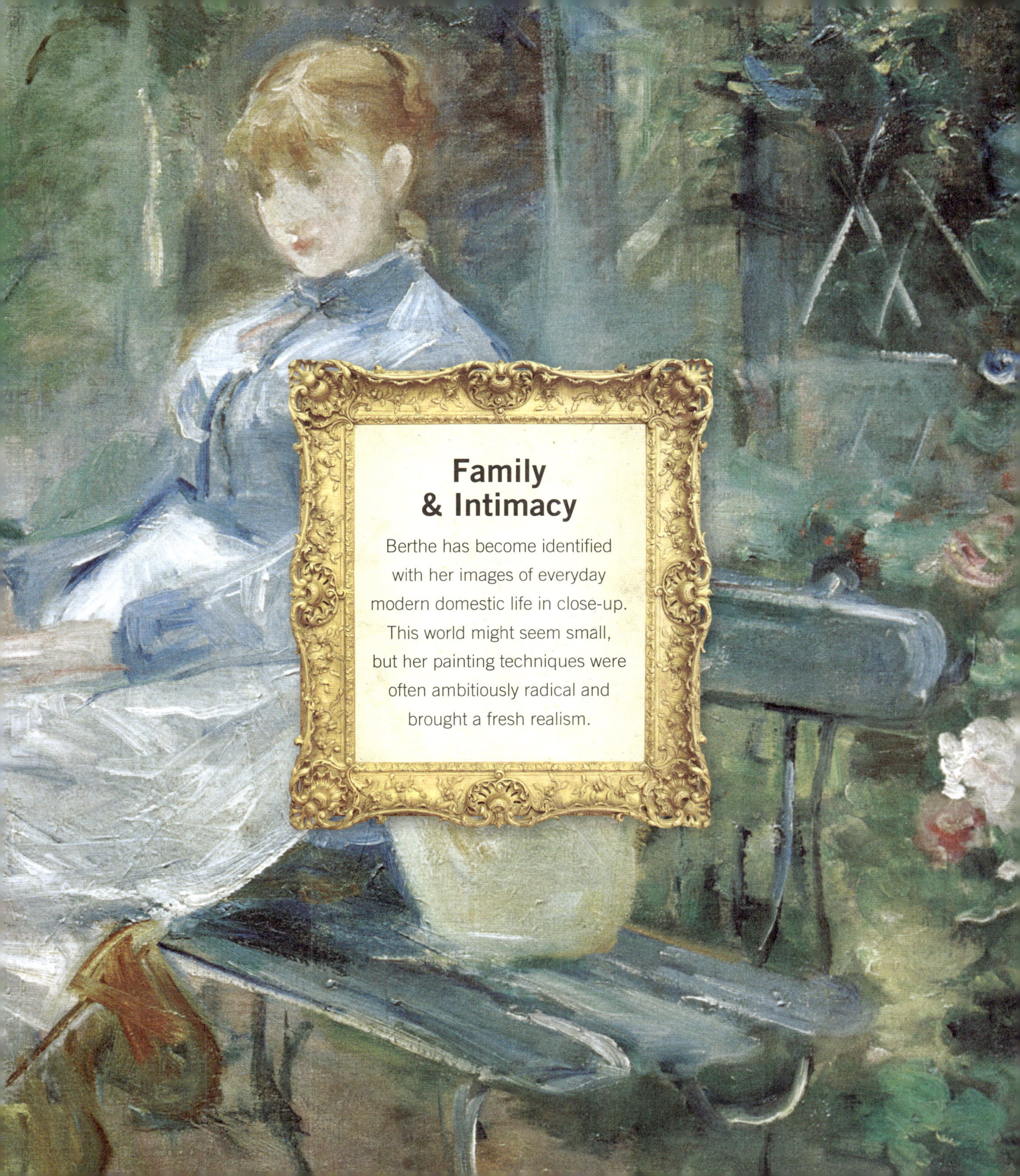

Family
& Intimacy

Berthe has become identified
with her images of everyday
modern domestic life in close-up.
This world might seem small,
but her painting techniques were
often ambitiously radical and
brought a fresh realism.

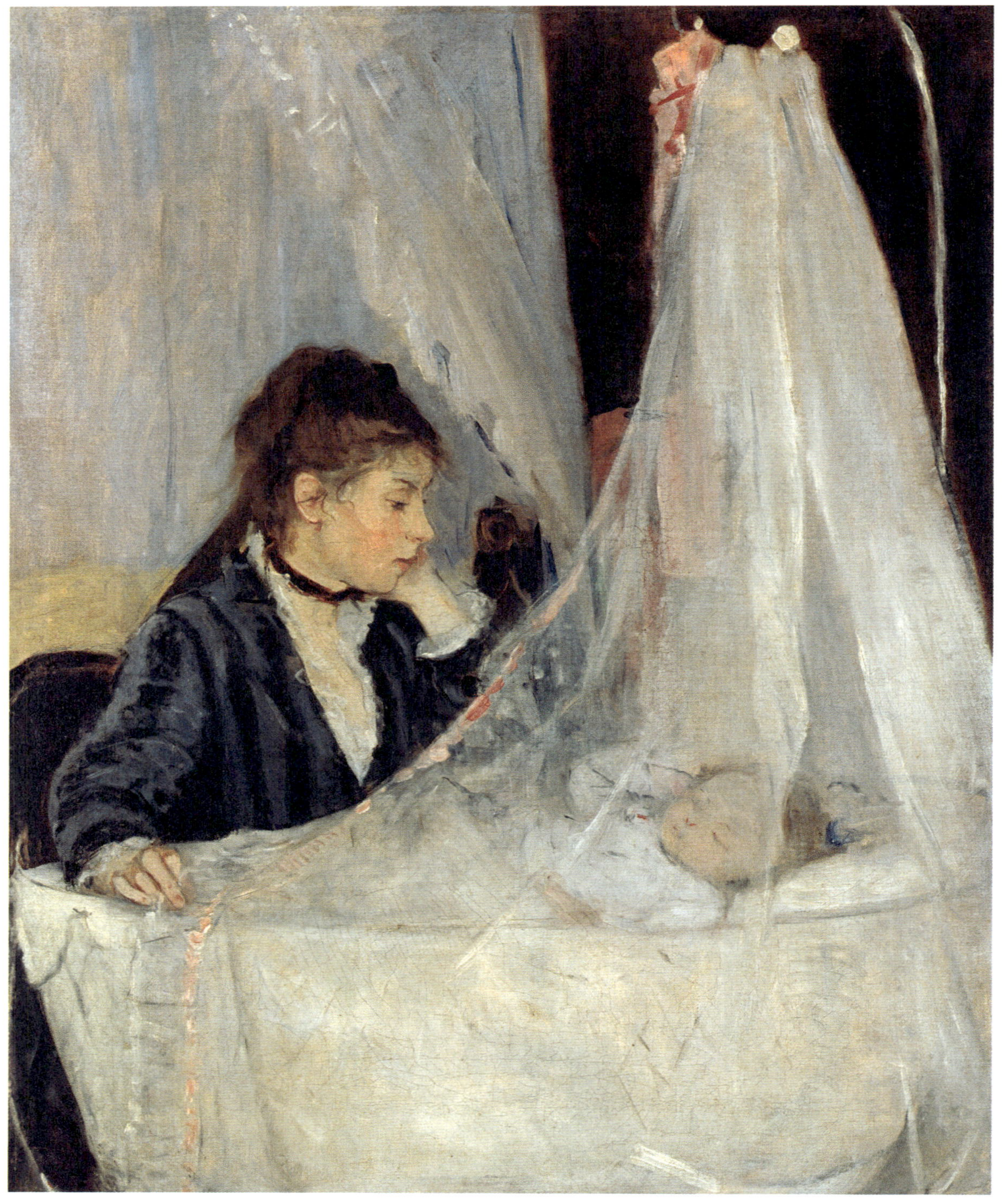

The Cradle, 1872
Oil on canvas, 56 x 46 cm (22¹⁄₁₆ x 18⅛ in)
• Musée d'Orsay, Paris

Sister Edma gazes at her baby daughter Blanche, in a famous picture whose prominent drapes add to its intimacy. It was painted at a time when Berthe was struggling with the conflict of wanting children and keeping her independence.

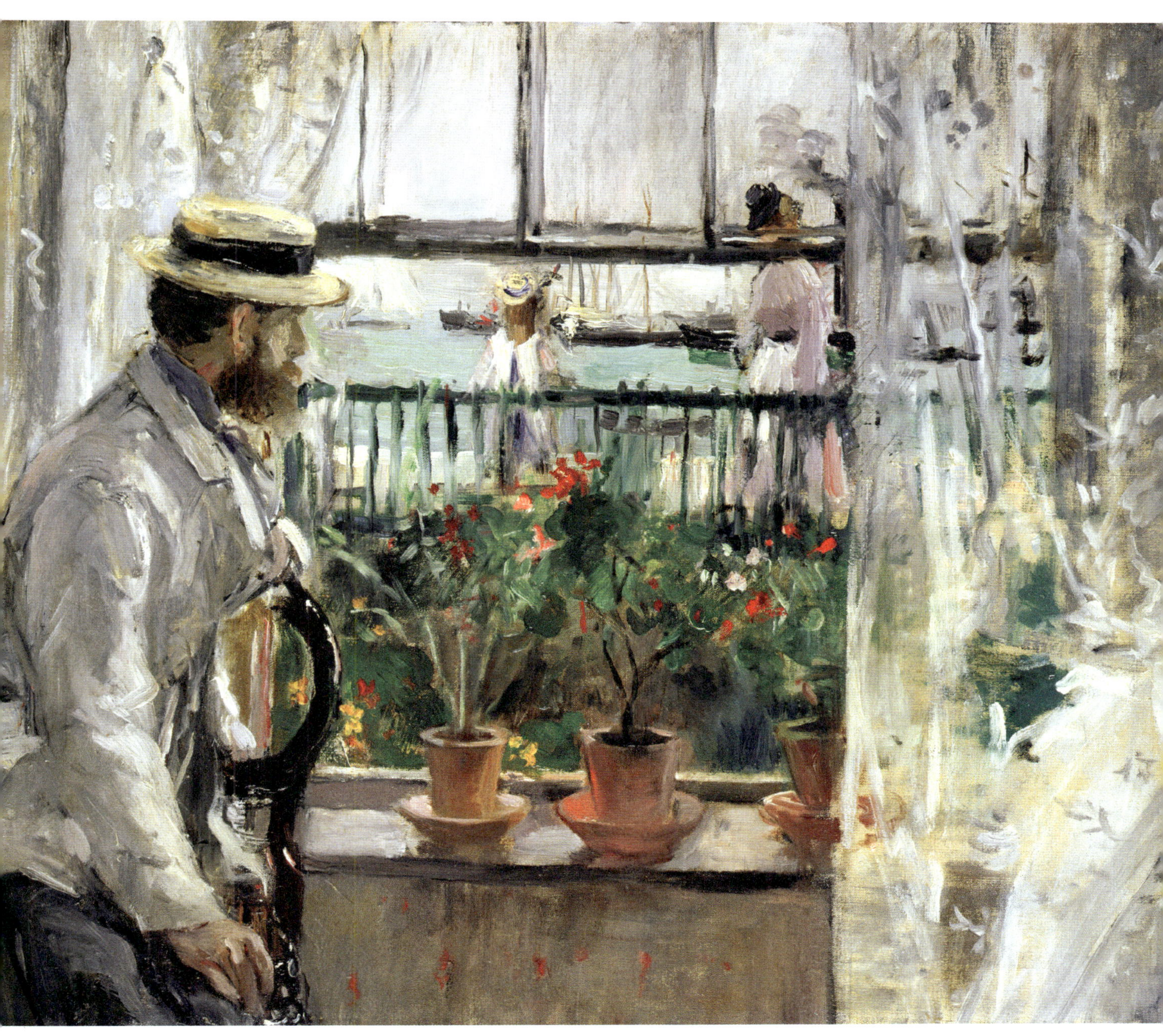

Eugène Manet on the Isle of Wight, 1875
Oil on canvas, 38 x 46 cm (15 x 18 in)
• Musée Marmottan Monet, Paris

Honeymooning in England in 1875, Berthe captures her new husband looking out from Globe Cottage, Cowes. Despite finding him an impatient model, her tonal balances and lively lighting cleverly unite an interior, a green mid-ground and distant boats on water.

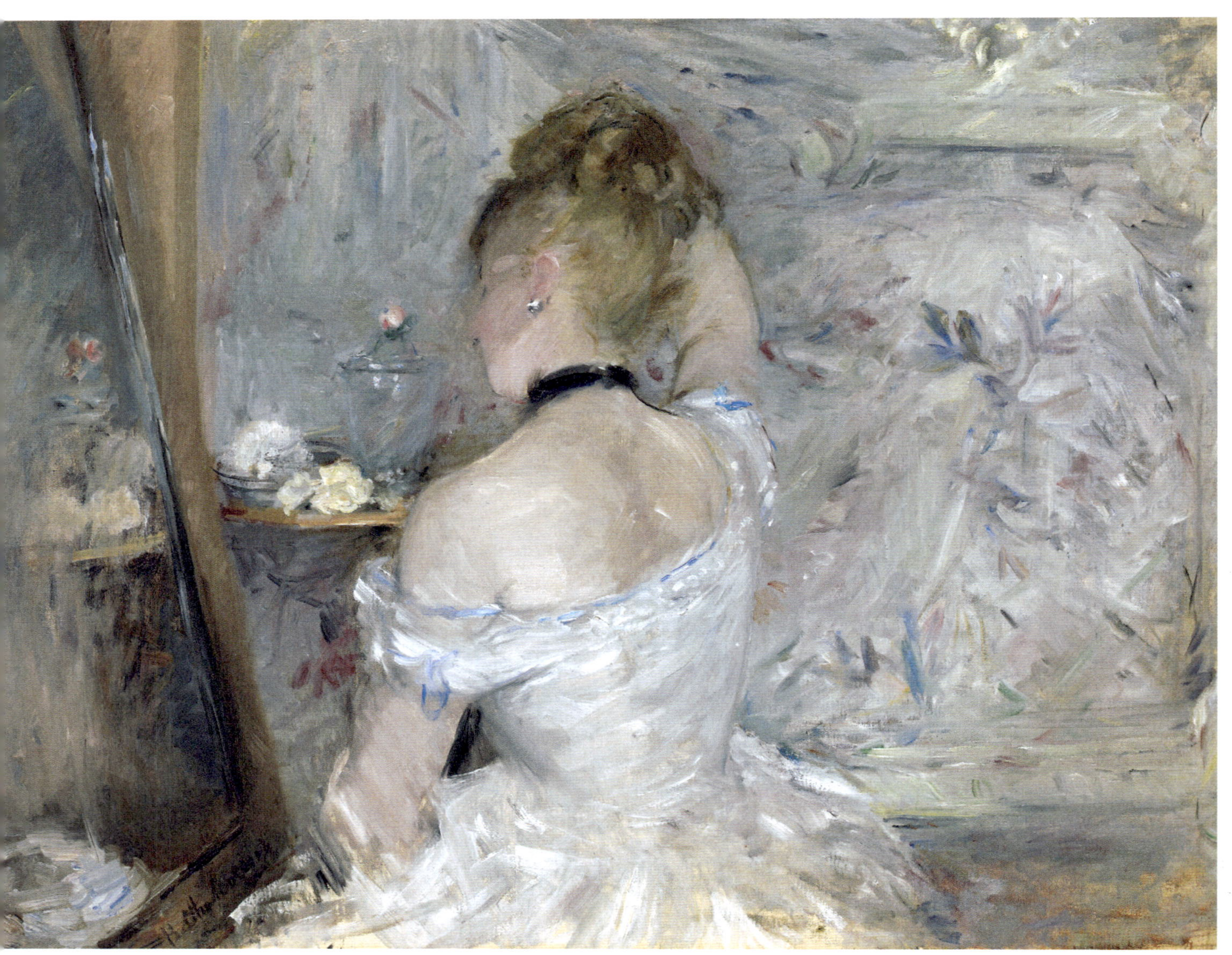

Woman at Her Toilette, 1875–80
Oil on canvas, 60.3 × 80.4 cm (23¾ × 31½ in)
• The Art Institute of Chicago

Fabric, glass, jewellery and hair sparkle irresistibly amid a flurry of breathlessly rapid feathery strokes in a picture that bears parallels with work by her friend Renoir. Berthe has signed it along the bottom of the mirror's frame.

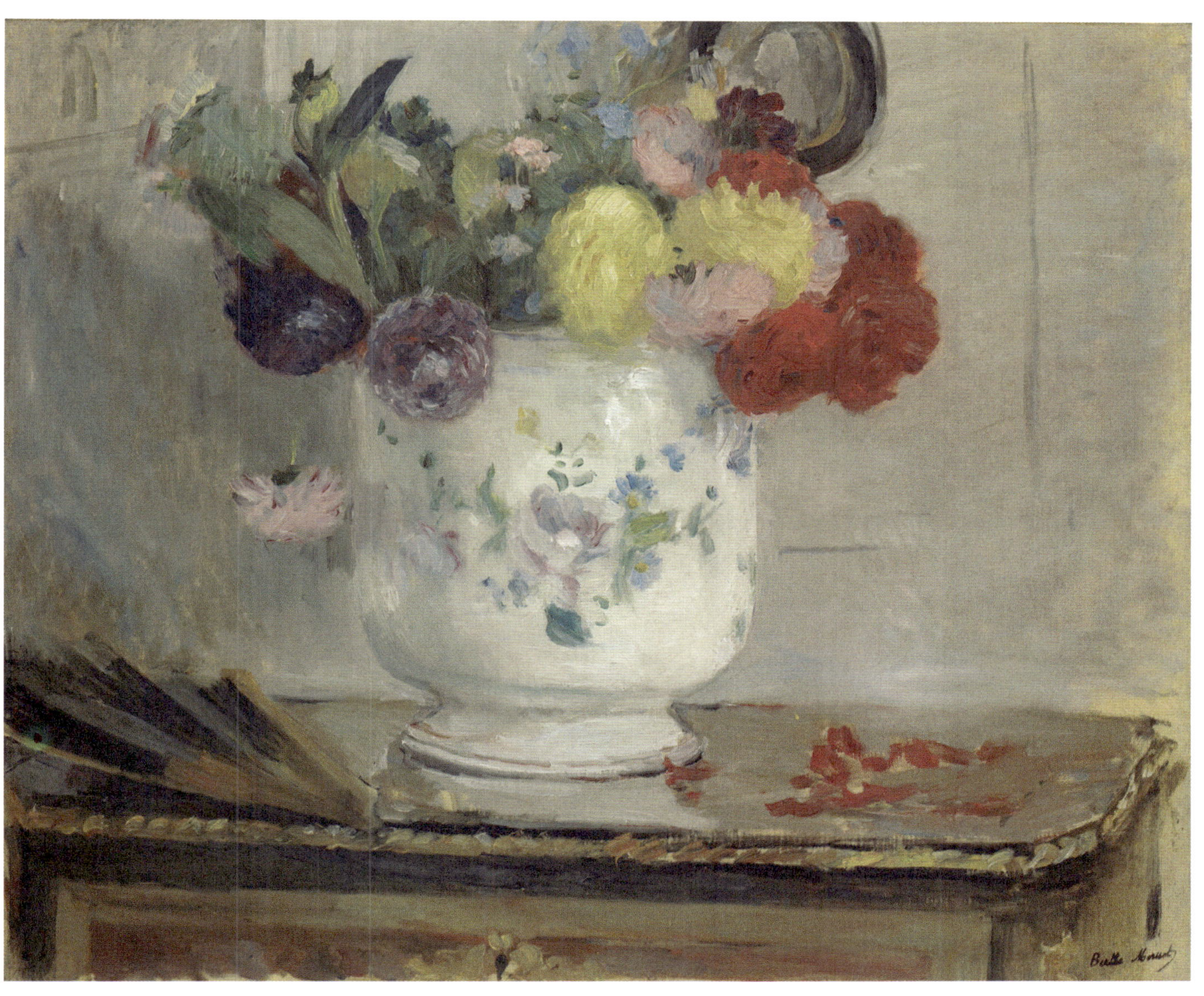

Dahlias, 1876
Oil on canvas, 45.7 x 56 cm (18 x 22 in)
• The Clark Art Institute, Williamstown, Massachusetts

Berthe produced few still-lifes. Here she creates a beautifully colourful study with aspects of the avant-garde: the flower vase is pushed much too close to the top of the image to meet traditional standards of symmetry and balance.

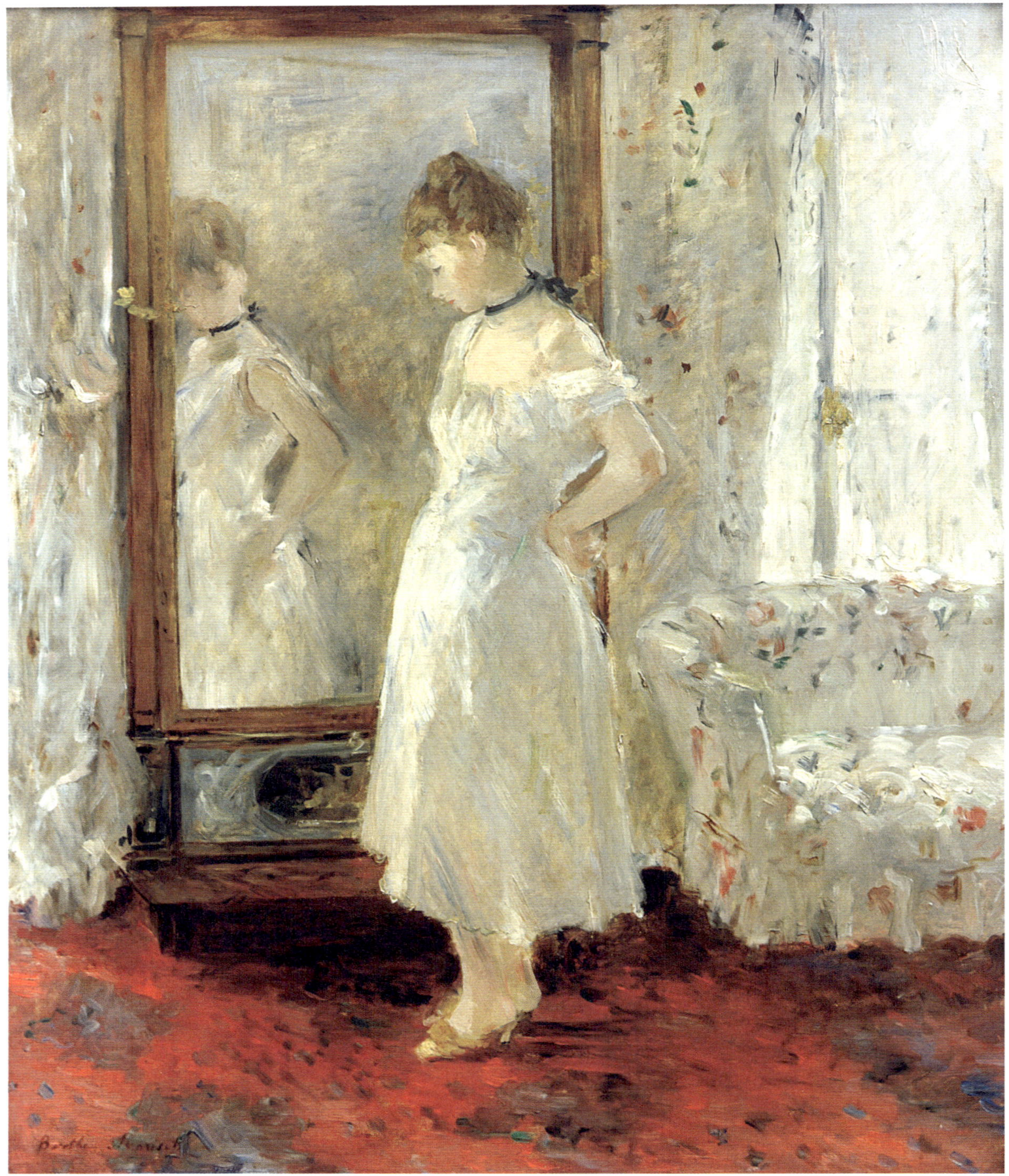

The Psyche Mirror, 1876
Oil on canvas, 65 x 54 cm (25⅔ x 21¼ in)
• Museo Nacional Thyssen-Bornemisza, Madrid

This flirtatious essay in light and whites was originally called *La Psyché*. Psyche is a beautiful princess from classical myth who was loved by Cupid but was also the name for a long dressing mirror – perhaps intentional wordplay?

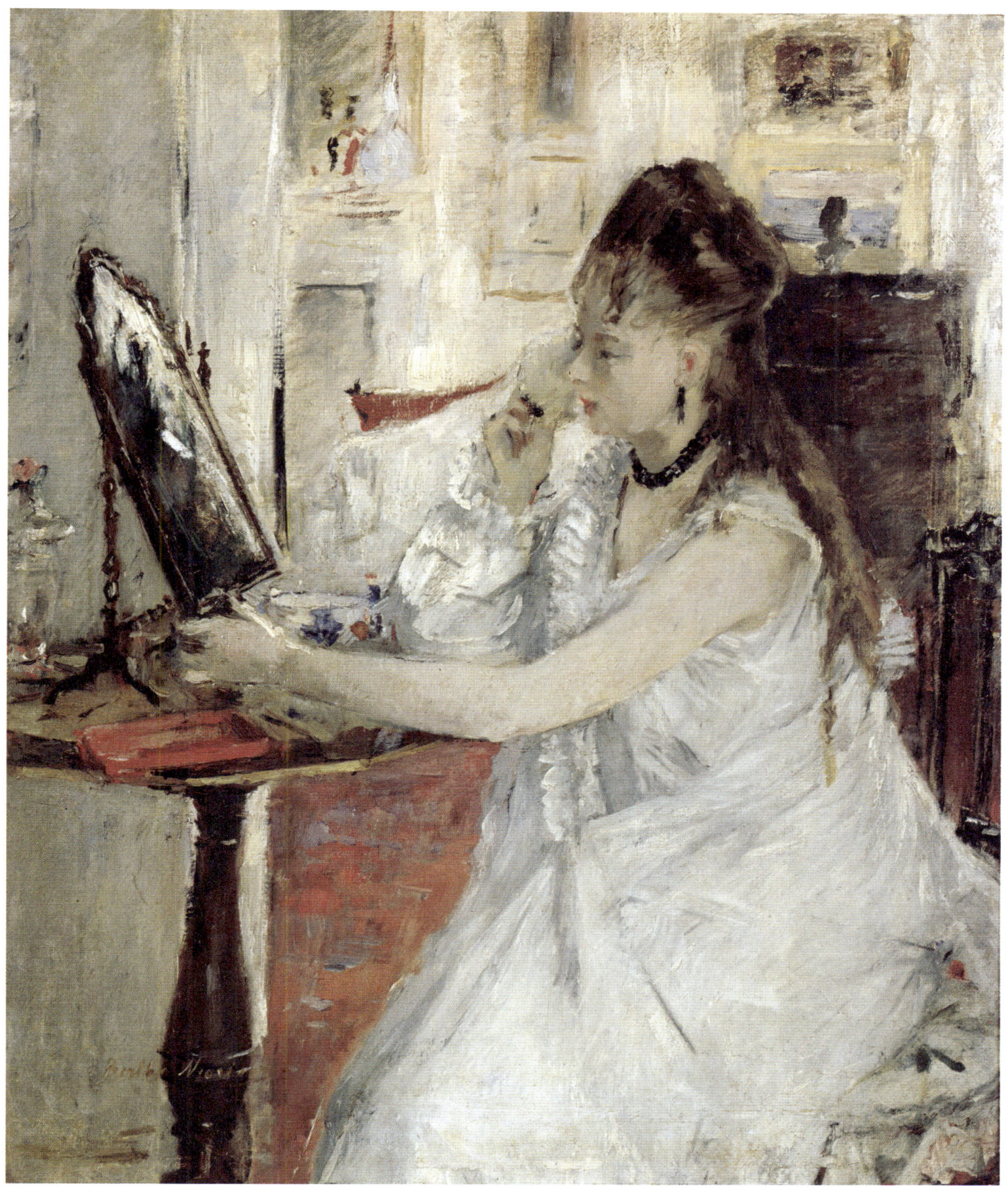

Young Woman Powdering Her Face, 1877
Oil on canvas, 46 x 39 cm (18 x 15⅓ in)
• Musée d'Orsay, Paris

This toilette picture feels more down to earth than some others by Berthe. Dashes of pink and red, from the subject's lips to a flower low down on her dress, send the eye exploring round the canvas.

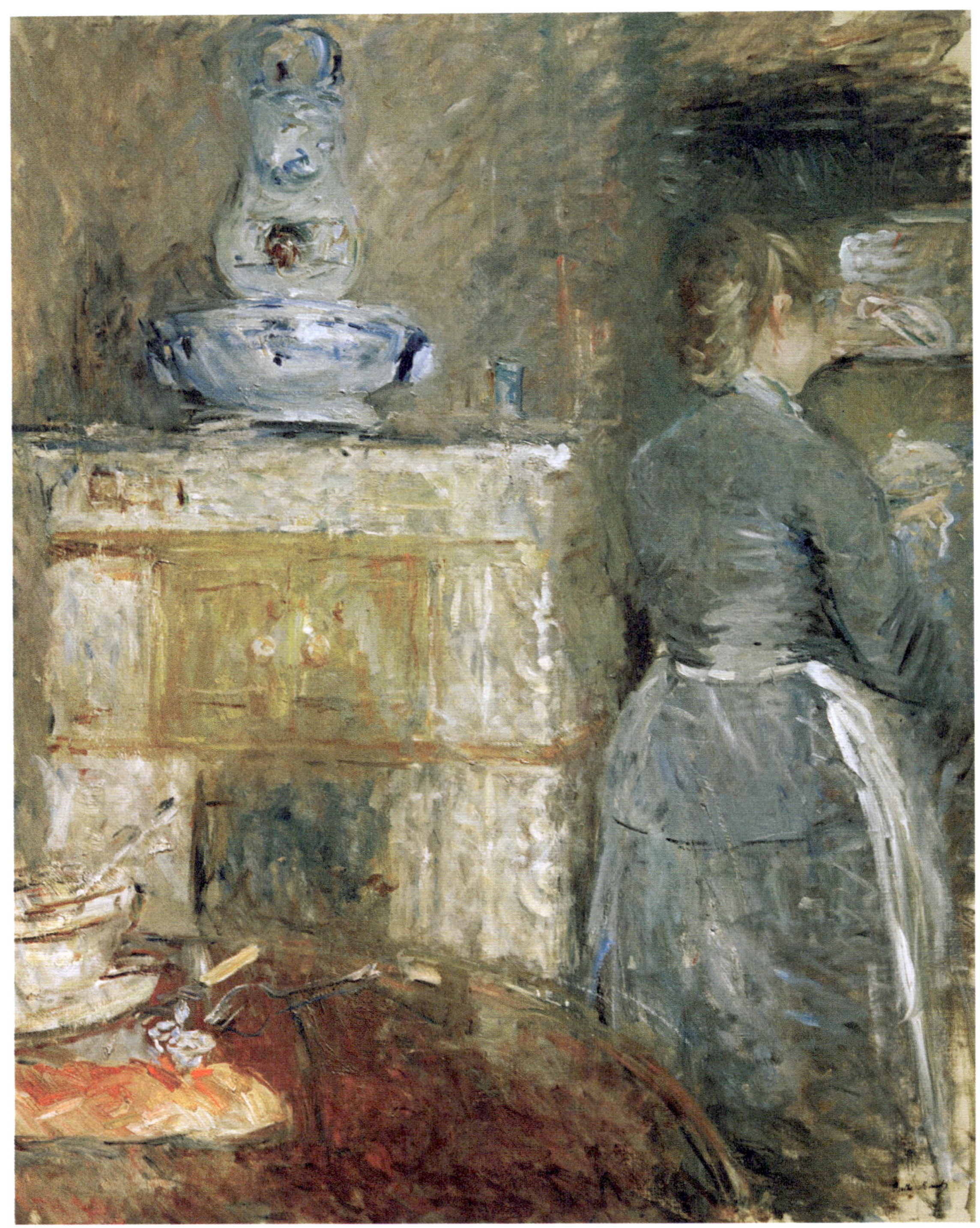

In the Dining Room, 1880
Oil on canvas, 91.8 x 73 cm (36 x 28¾ in) • Private Collection

The composition here is non-traditional: chopped off and off-centre with its principal player, the housemaid, facing away from us – creating a snapshot of everyday life. Broad blocks of colour echo the Japanese prints that influenced much Impressionism.

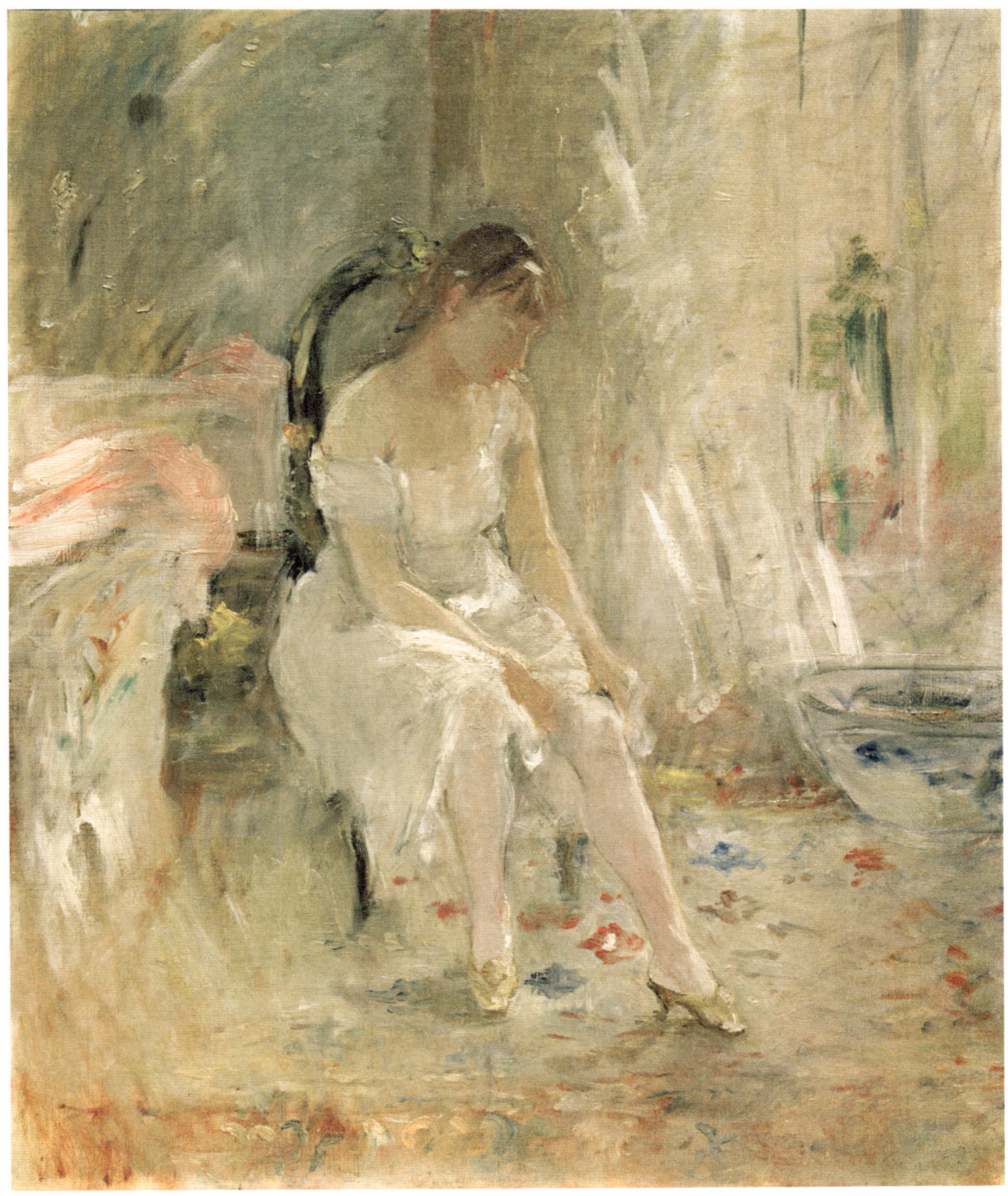

Young Woman Putting on Stockings, 1880
Oil on canvas, 55 x 46 cm (21⅔ x 18 in) • Private Collection

Here the central figure is clearly painted, but much of the rest of the picture seems to be dissolving into a sea of light and sparkling colour brushed with thick, loose and almost frenzied strokes.

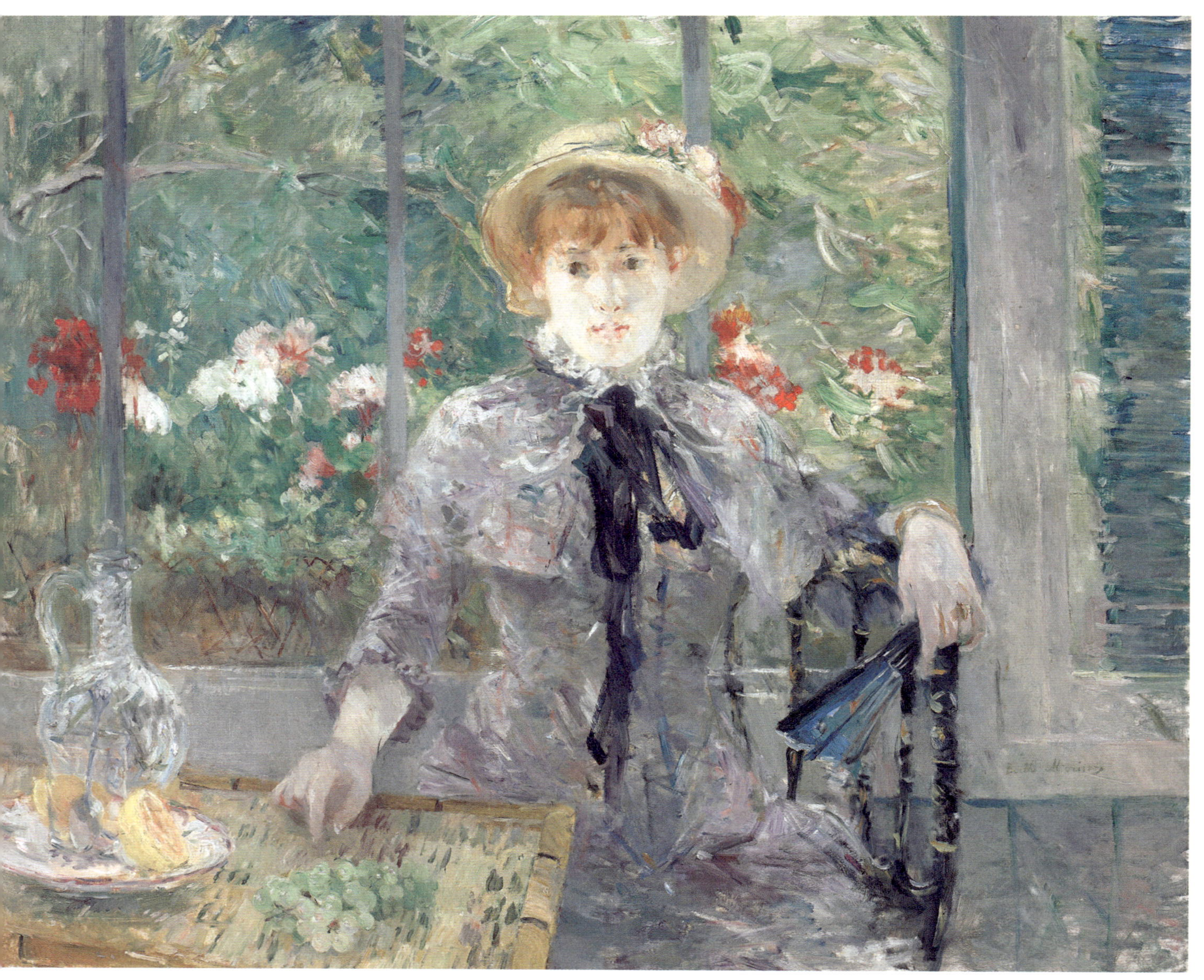

In the Country (After Lunch), 1881
Oil on canvas, 80.7 x 100 cm (31¼ x 39⅓ in) • Private Collection

Fan in hand and seated in a conservatory-like space, this young woman looks out of the picture with an intriguingly enigmatic expression – a common feature of Berthe's women. Is she relaxed, bored, preoccupied or melancholic?

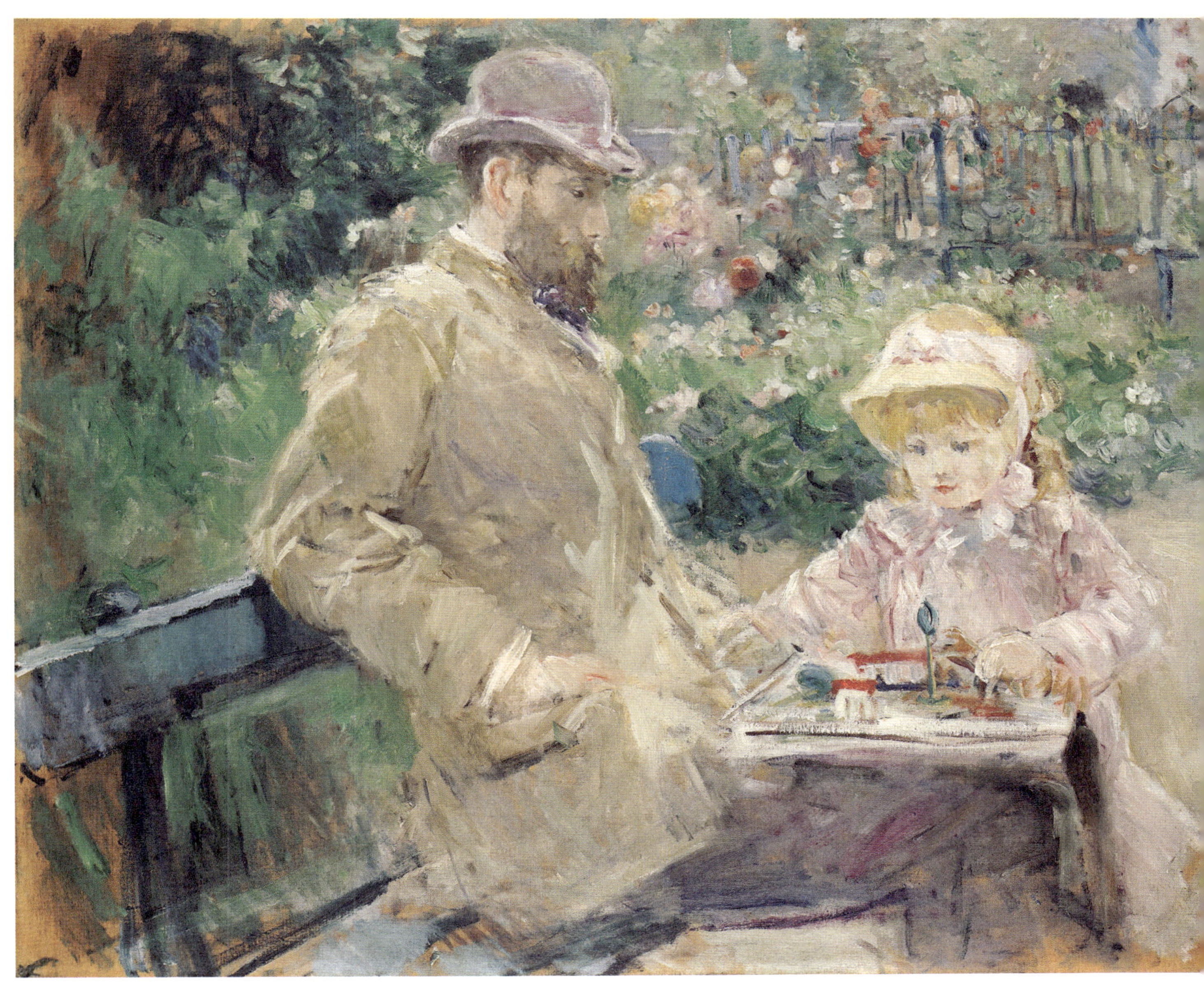

**Eugène Manet and His Daughter in the
Garden at Bougival, 1881**
Oil on canvas, 73 x 92 cm (28¾ x 36¼ in)
• Musée Marmottan Monet, Paris

In summer 1881, Berthe and Eugène rented a house in Bougival, a fashionable suburb of Paris, where Berthe enjoyed painting her daughter in the garden. The area in and around Bougival was much painted by several Impressionists.

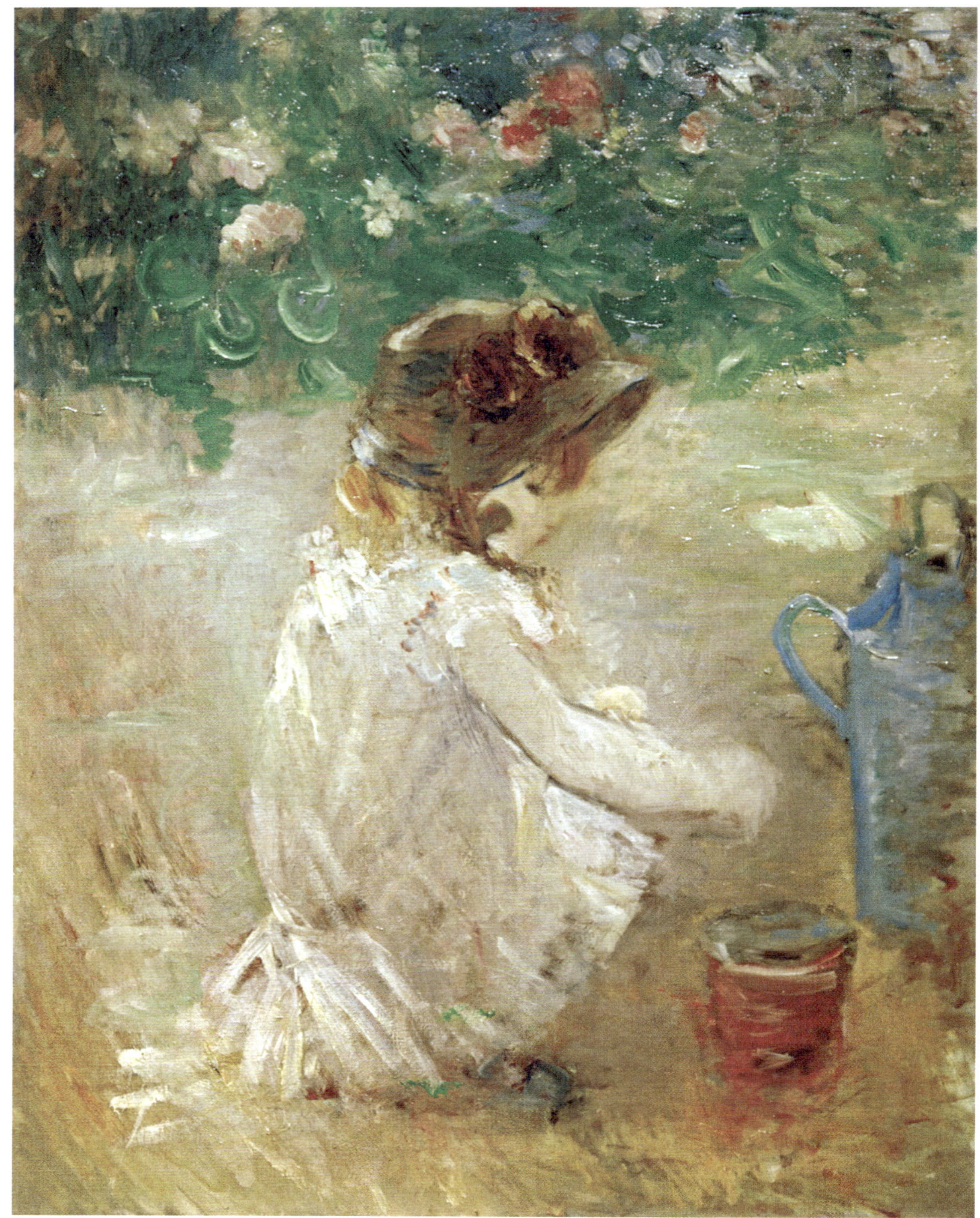

Mud Pies, 1882
Oil on canvas, 92 x 73 cm (36¼ x 28¾ in) • Private Collection

Producing real, unsentimentalized images of children was one of Berthe's strong points. In this beautifully coloured painting, Berthe captures her daughter Julie at Bougival, conveying the focus of a small child intent on her task.

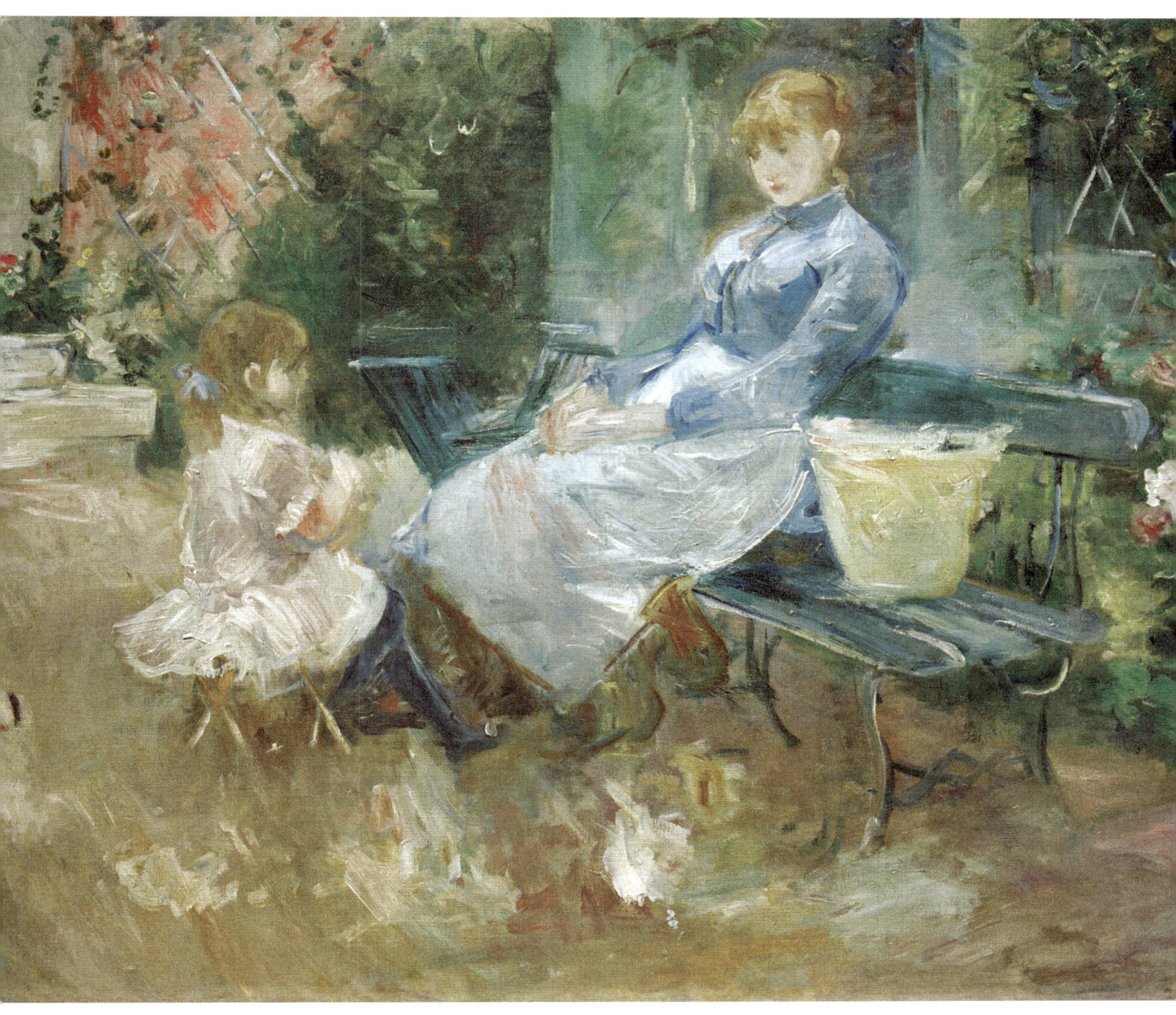

The Fable, 1883
Oil on canvas, 65 x 81 cm (25⅔ x 32 in) • Private Collection

The picture title – an idea from Berthe's poet friend, Stéphane Mallarmé (1842–98) – of Julie and maid Pasie at Bougival is enigmatic. Is a fairy tale being read aloud? Is Pasie subject to the ennui of many of Berthe's pictures?

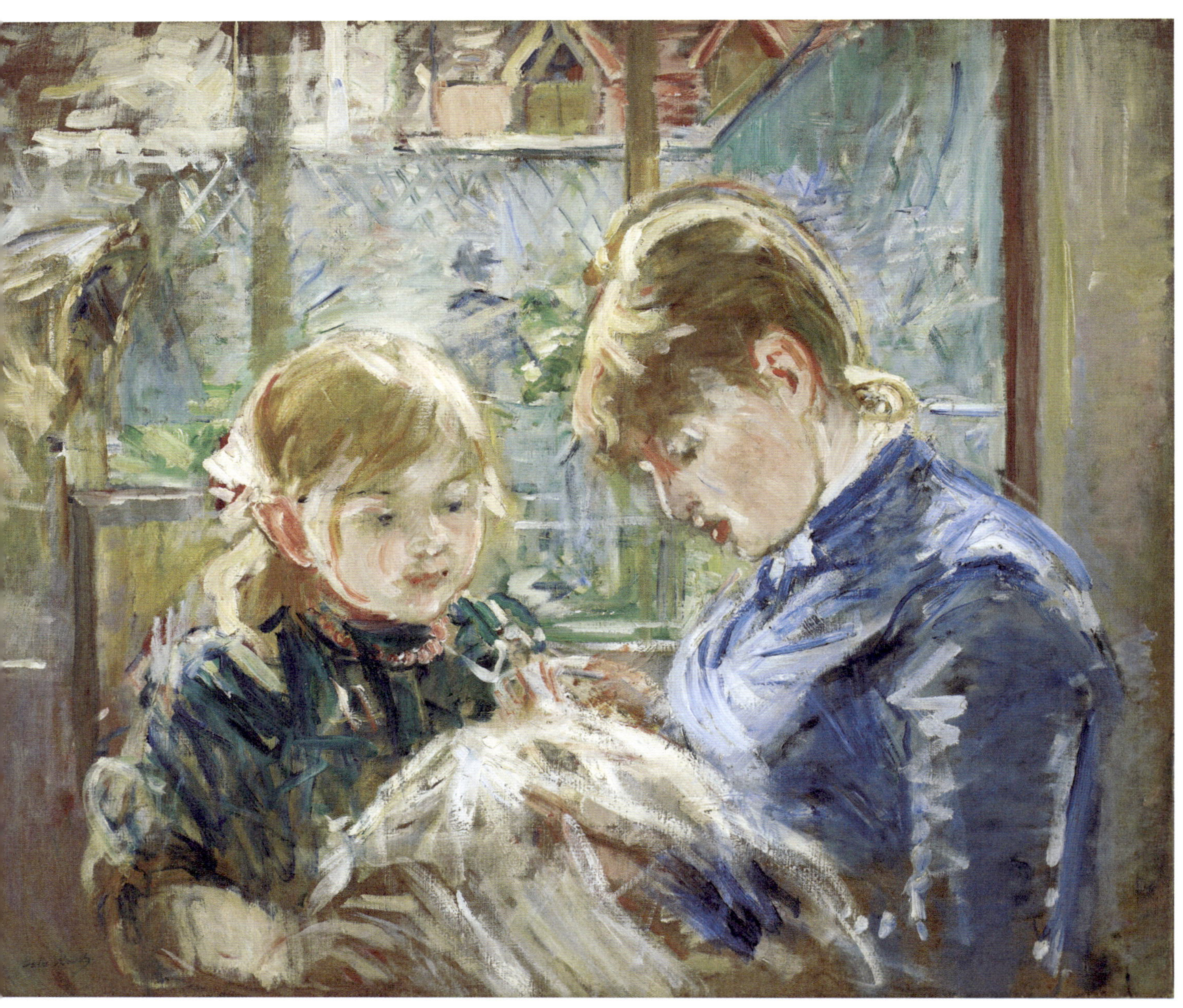

The Artist's Daughter, Julie, with Her Nanny, _c._ 1884
Oil on canvas, 57.2 x 71 cm (22½ x 28 in) • Minneapolis Institute of Art

Also known as _The Sewing Lesson_, this work uses rapid, sketchy brushstrokes. These blend a wide range of colours and tones and bring the whole to life by bathing it in a lovely bright light.

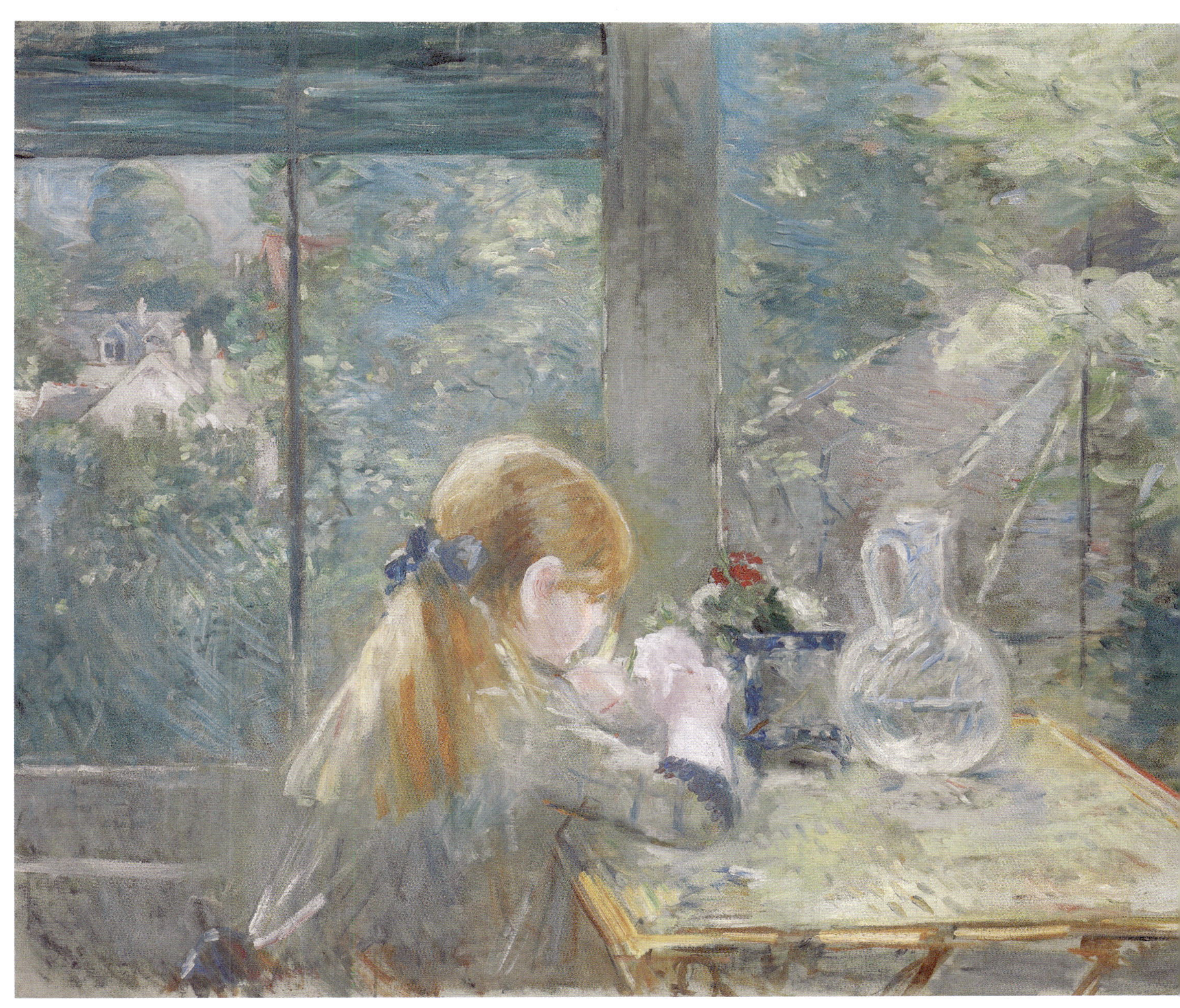

On the Veranda, 1884
Oil on canvas, 81.2 x 100.2 cm (32 x 39½ in) • Private Collection

Plants on the veranda, plus the flowers that Julie is studying while seated at a table and the greenery outside the window seem to blend into one in this image, dissolving distinctions between outside and inside worlds.

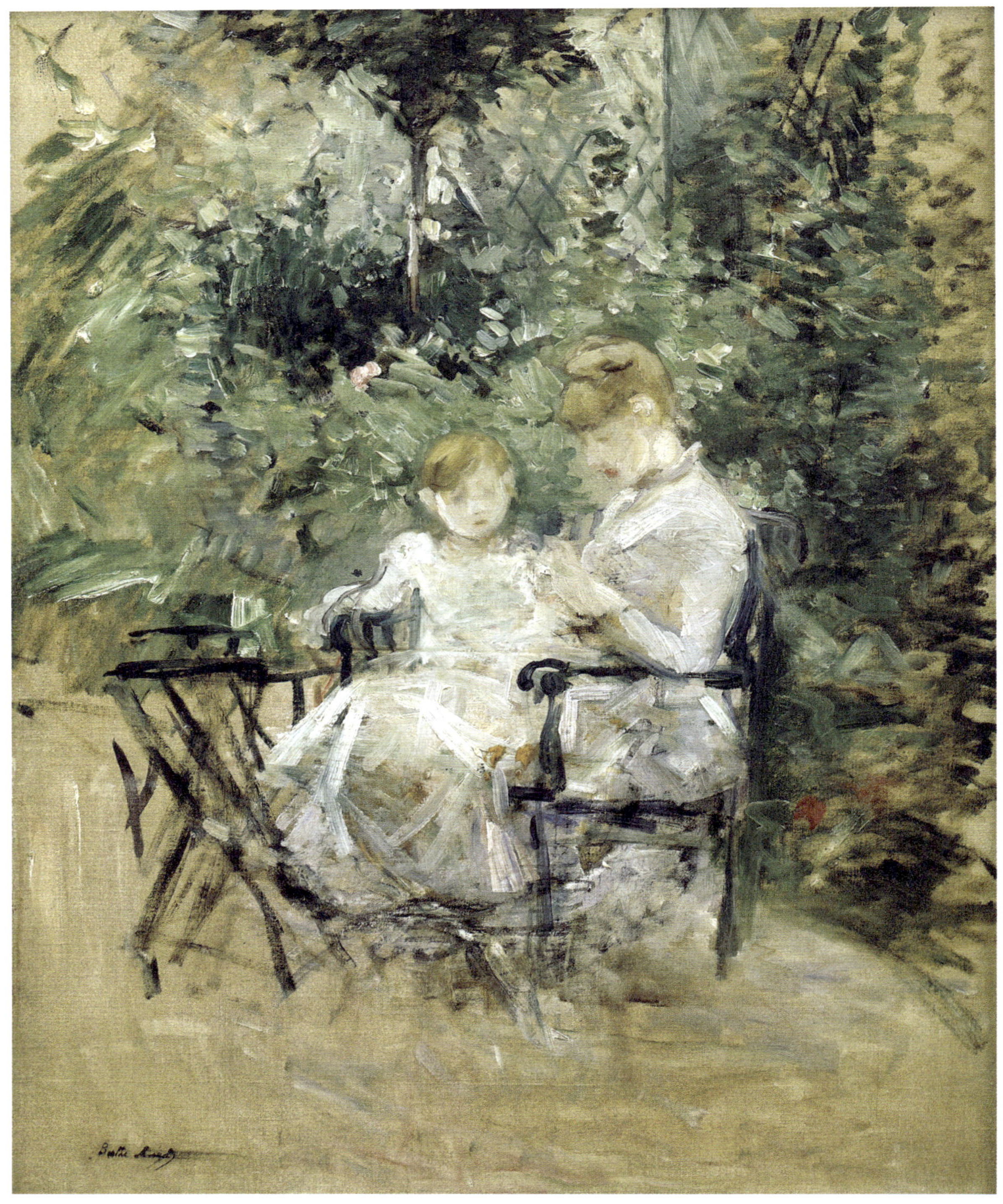

In the Garden, *c.* 1885   Berthe often left work less 'finished' around the edges, evoking a slightly strange spatial context.
Oil on canvas, 65 x 54 cm (25⅔ x 21¼ in) • Private Collection   The furniture is created convincingly from the most minimal of strokes – a great skill of hers.

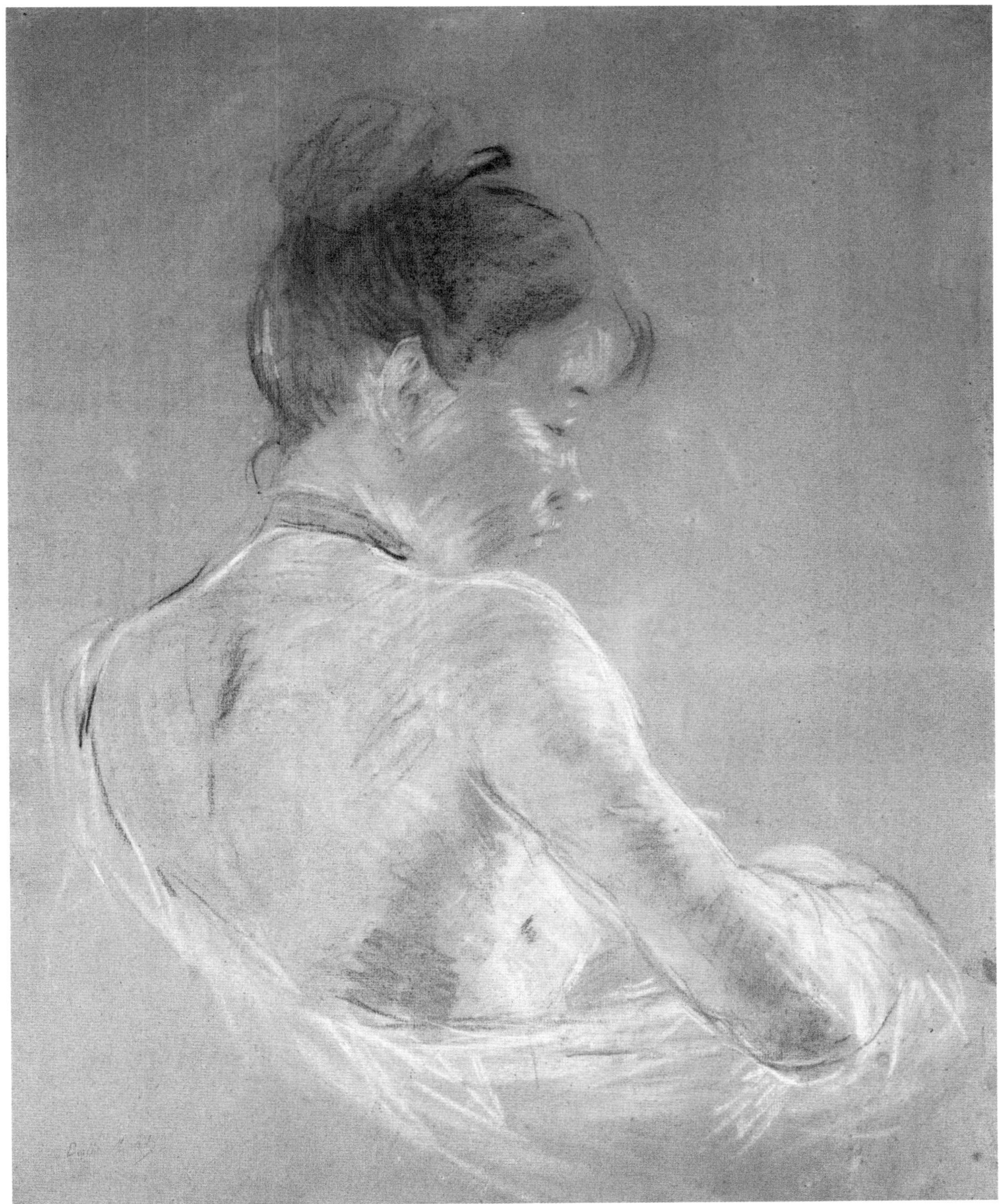

Young Girl with Naked Shoulders, 1885
Pastel on paper, 56 x 45.8 cm (22 x 18 in) • Private Collection

This graceful and understated master study in the quality of light on skin and fabric shows how well Berthe's drawing skills responded to pastels. Just enough lines are used – any fewer or more would have ruined the effect.

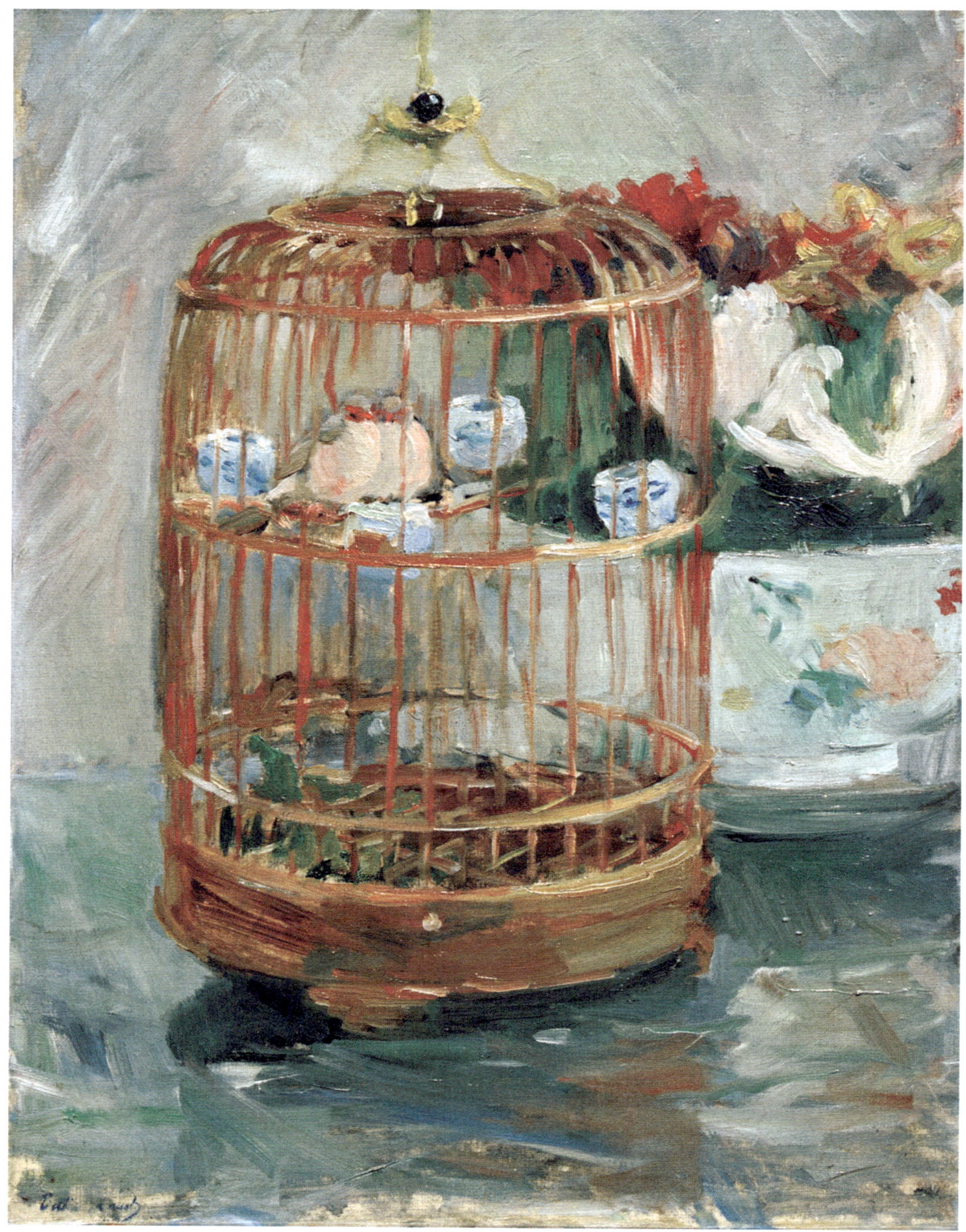

The Cage, 1885
Oil on canvas, 50.5 × 37.7 cm (20 x 14¾ in)
• National Museum of Women in the Arts, Washington DC

As Berthe's style matured in the 1880s it generally became freer, so that objects like this birdcage and flower bowl seem to float in a sea of strokes, although they 'read' as being on a stable surface.

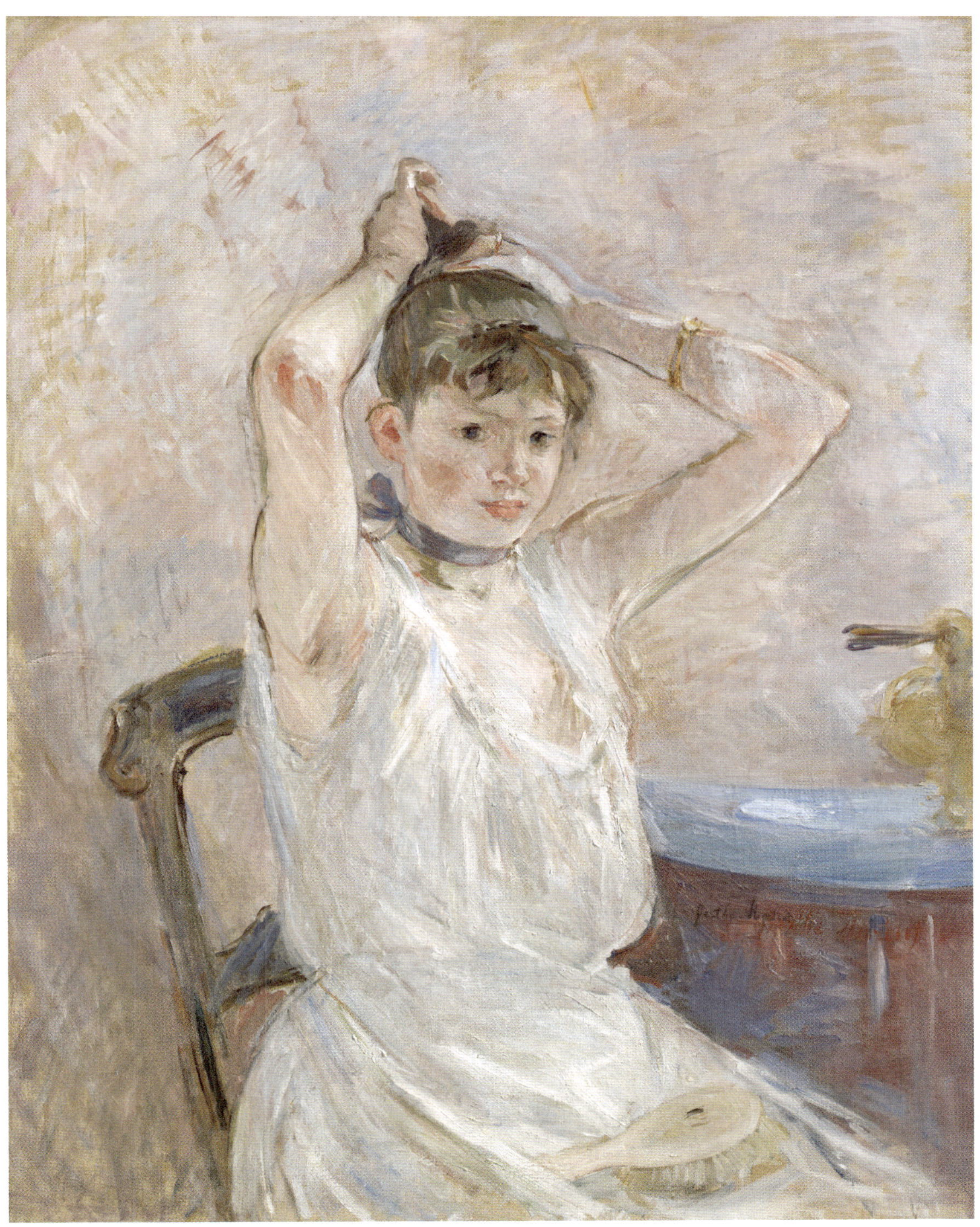

The Bath, 1885–86
Oil on canvas, 92 x 73.3 cm (36¼ x 28¾ in)
• The Clark Art Institute, Williamstown, Massachusetts

Figure and background partly blend into each other in this study of an everyday intimate domestic moment, differentiated by clear delineation of the girl's arms and face, demonstrating Berthe's drawing skills.

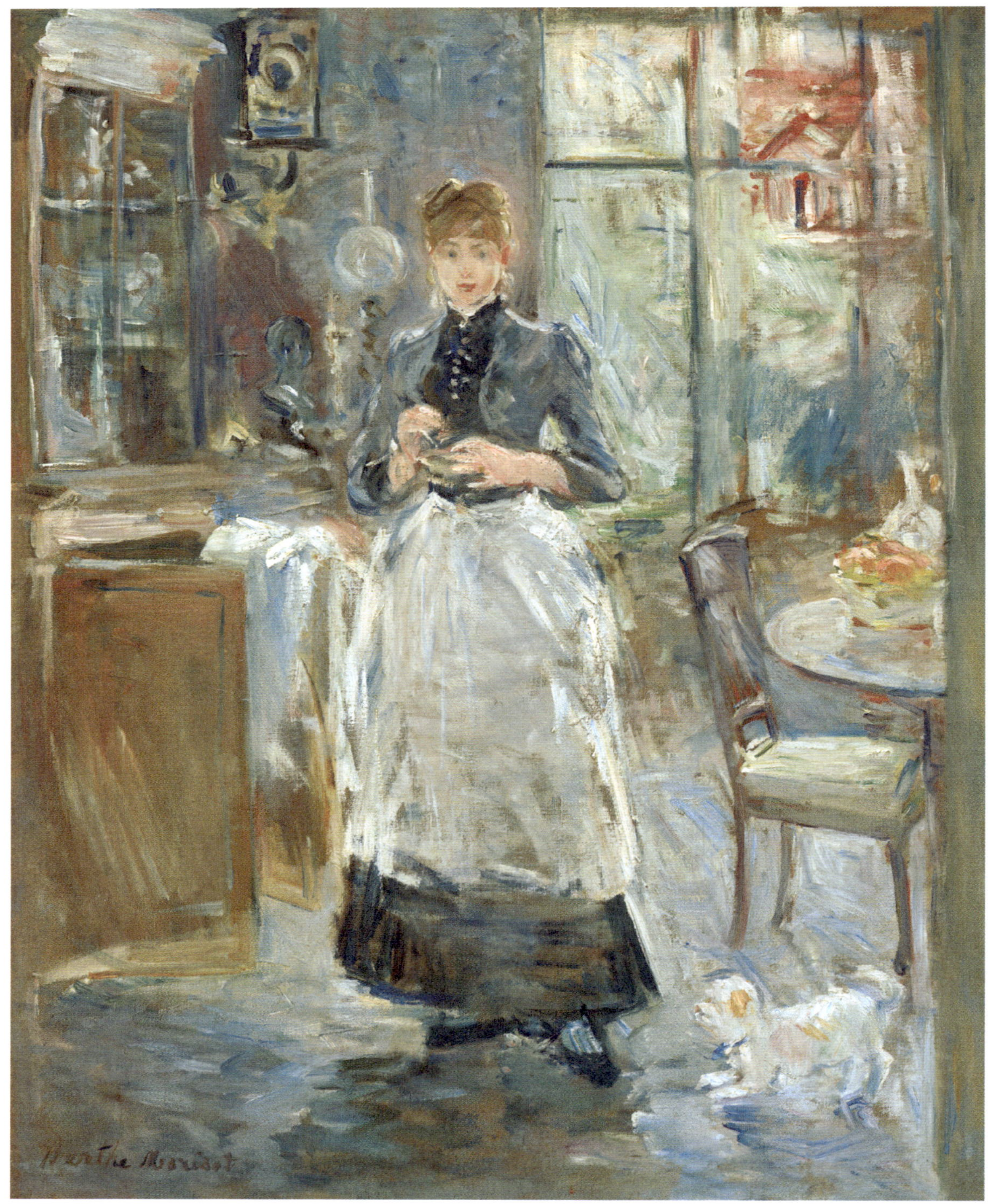

In the Dining Room, 1886
Oil on canvas, 61.3 x 50 cm (24⅛ x 19¹¹⁄₁₆ in)
• National Gallery of Art, Washington DC

Here a housemaid is caught in mid-task, rather like a photographic snapshot. This is a fleeting moment, caught with bold, rapid brushwork, but the composition is conventionally well balanced, with its principal subject centre-stage.

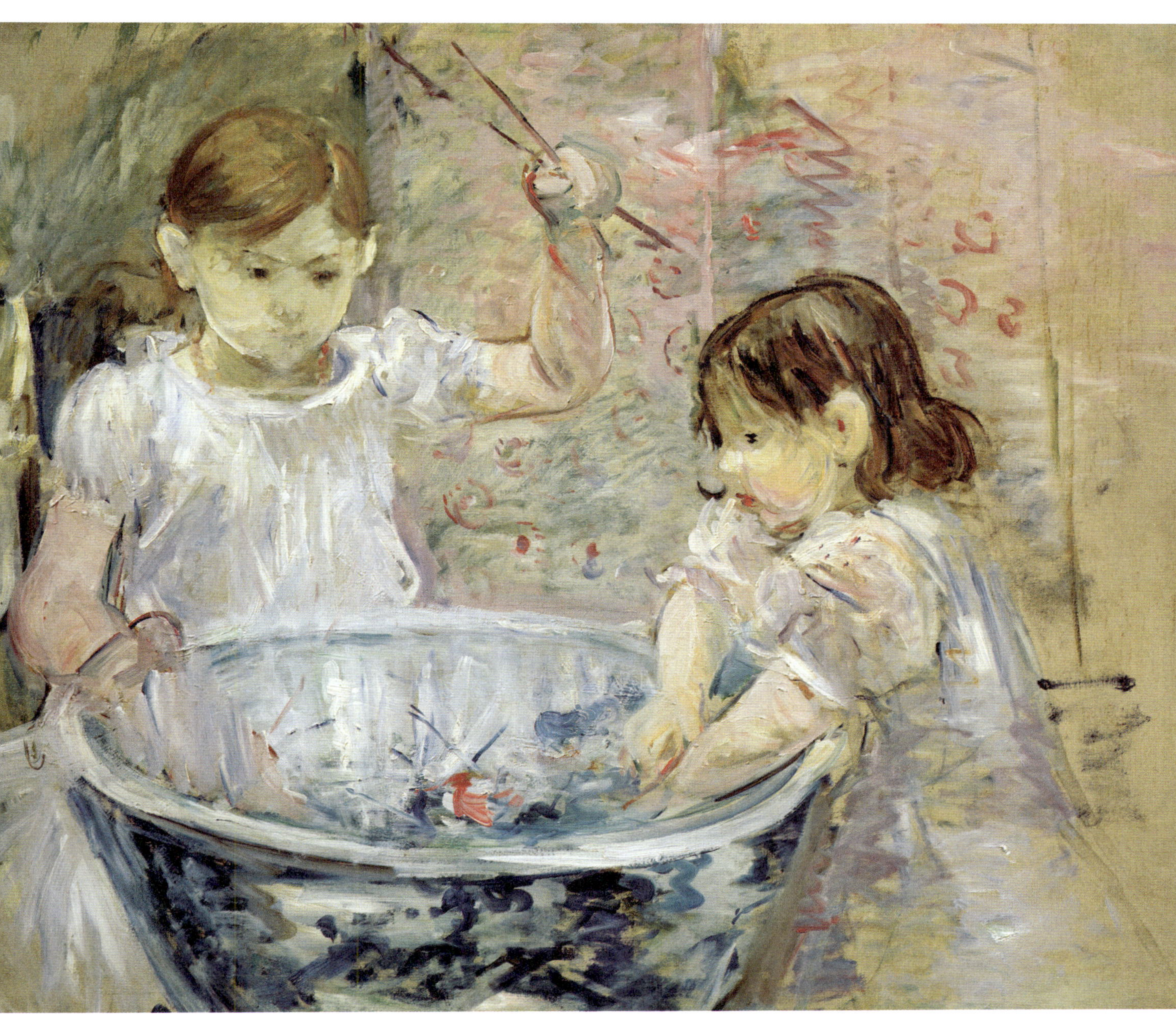

Children at the Basin, 1886
Oil on canvas, 73 x 92 cm (28¾ x 36¼ in)
• Musée Marmottan Monet, Paris

Featuring Julie and a little girl called Marthe, this was painted at Rue de Villejust.
The 'basin' in which they play at fishing is a blue-and-white Chinese porcelain vase
that was a gift from Edouard Manet.

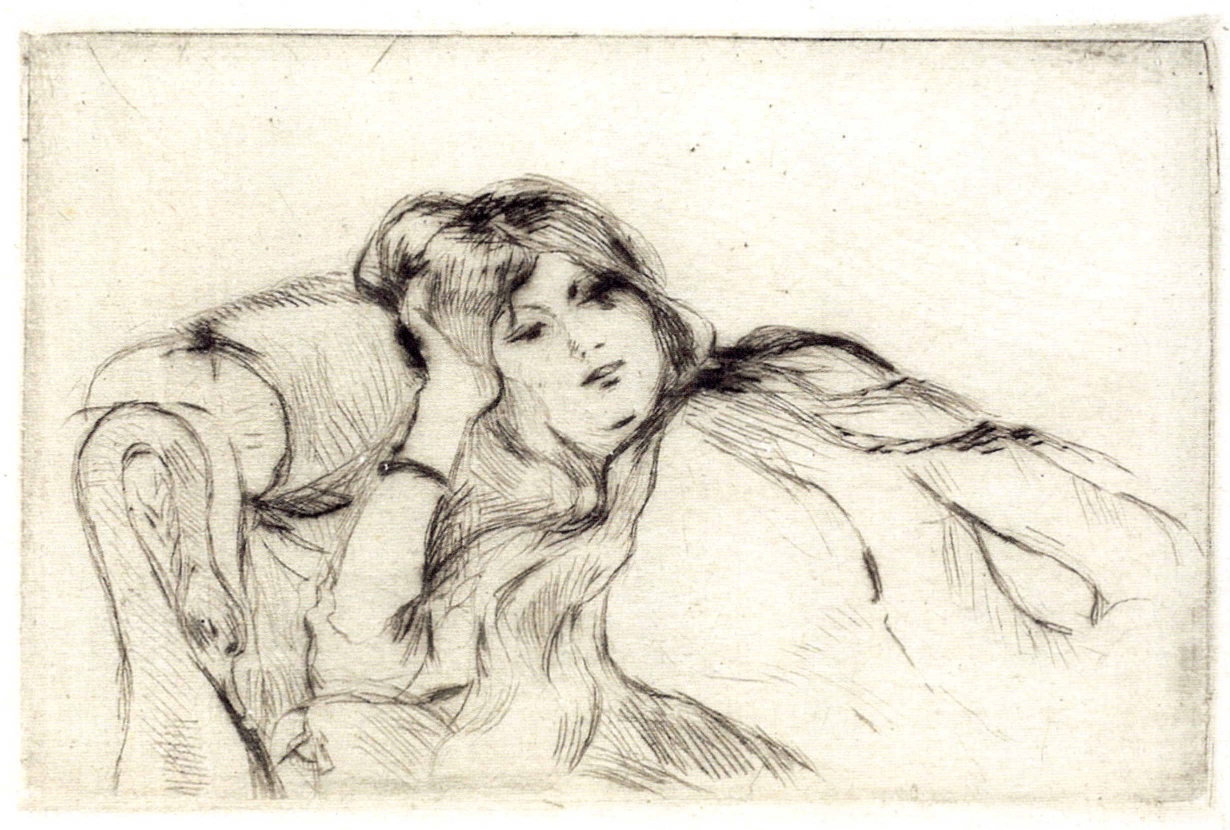

Young Woman at Rest, 1889

Drypoint in black on ivory laid paper, image: 7.8 × 11.6 cm (3 x 4½ in)

• The Art Institute of Chicago

A talented printmaker, Berthe was especially good with drypoint techniques, which can give a softer look rather like a pencil sketch. This image also appeared as a drawing and a painting.

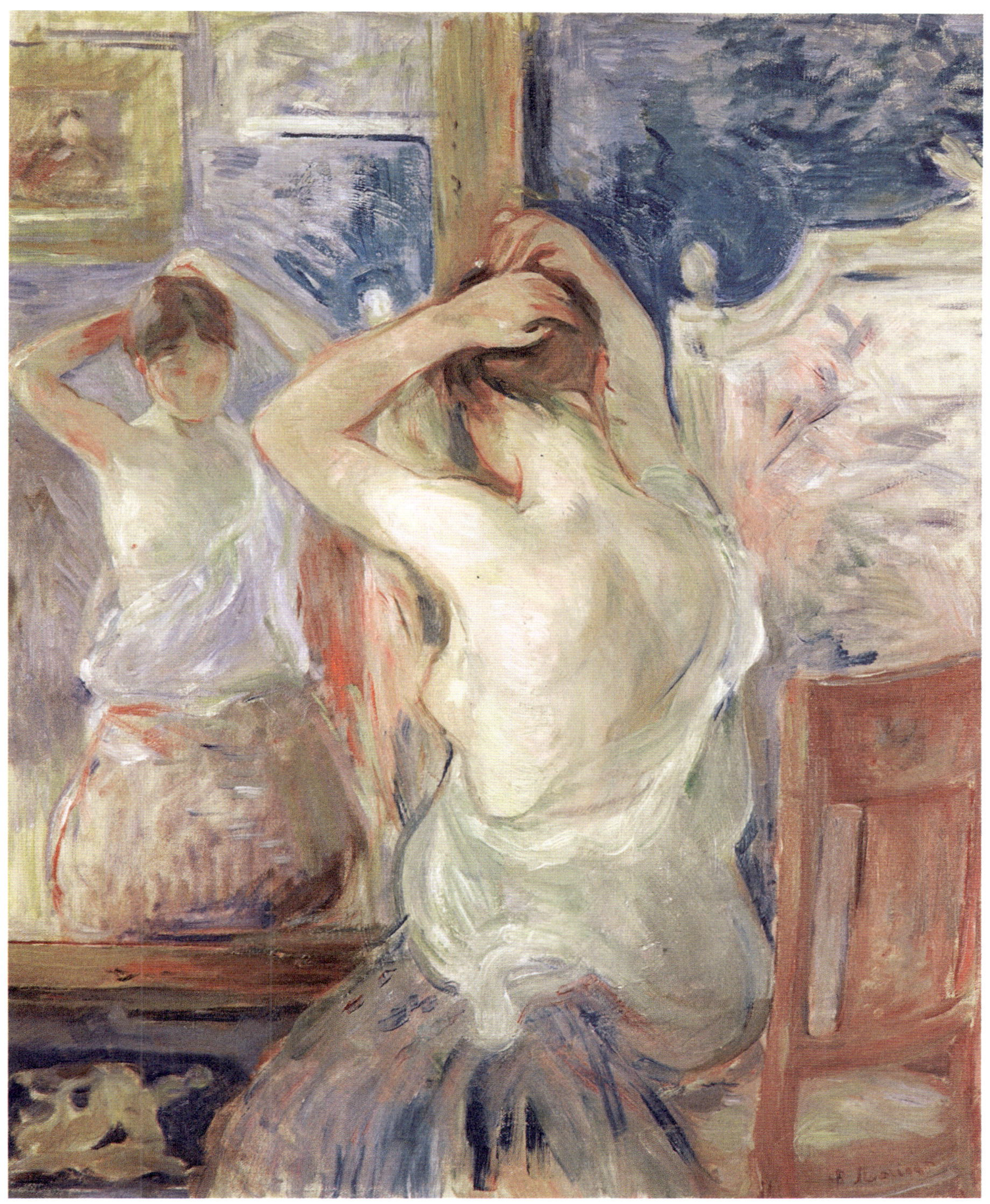

Before the Mirror, 1890
Oil on canvas, 55 x 46 cm (21⅔ x 18 in)
• Collection Fondation Pierre Gianadda, Martigny, Switzerland

Another wonderful play on light and reflections, details of body and face are obscured so that the figure becomes just another element in an artful arrangement of colours, shapes and brushstrokes.

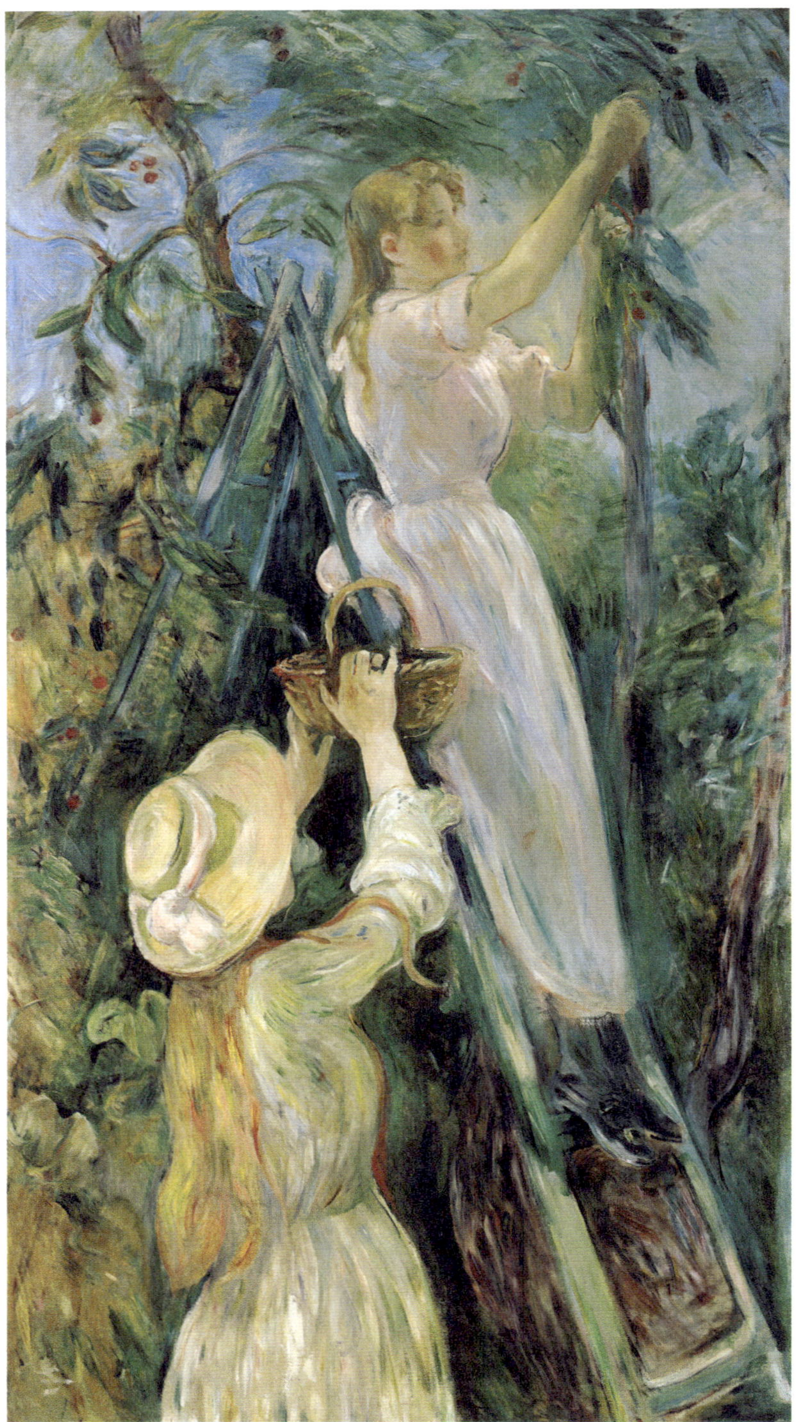

The Cherry Tree, 1891
Oil on canvas, 154 x 84 cm (60⅔ x 33 in)
• Musée Marmottan Monet, Paris

Berthe's tallest piece is often seen as her most ambitious. Several versions exist, plus many preparatory studies. Both Julie Manet and artists' model Jeanne Fourmanoir posed as the cherry-picker on the ladder while cousin Jeannie Gobillard was the model for the girl holding up the basket.

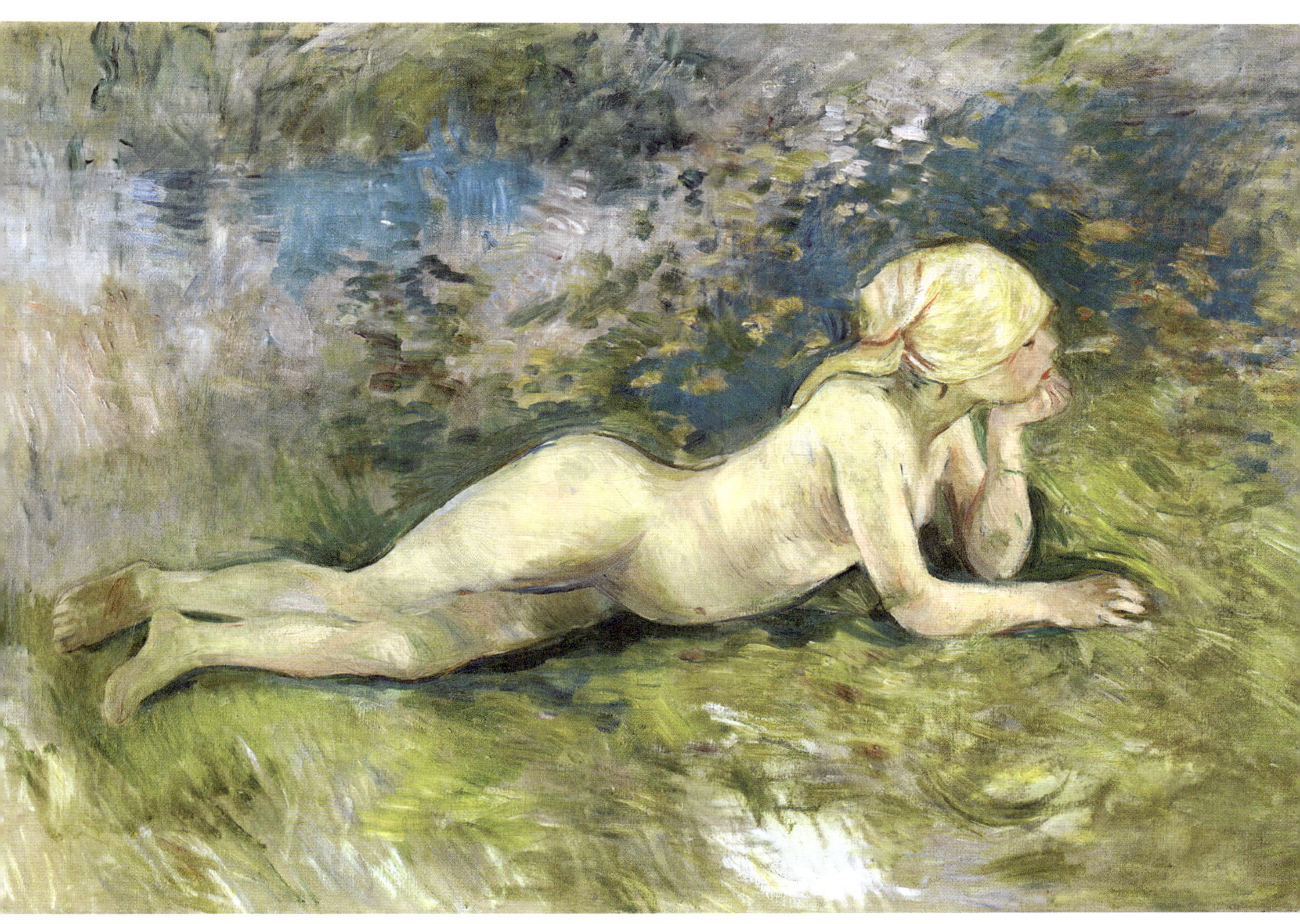

Reclining Nude Shepherdess, 1891
Oil on canvas, 57.5 × 86.4 cm (22⅔ x 34 in)
• Museo Nacional Thyssen-Bornemisza, Madrid

Berthe's mature period included interesting explorations of the nude. In 1890 and 1891, the family stayed at Mézy-sur-Seine, northwest of Paris, where a local girl named Gabrièlle Dufous posed for this work, and for the clothed version (*see* page 54).

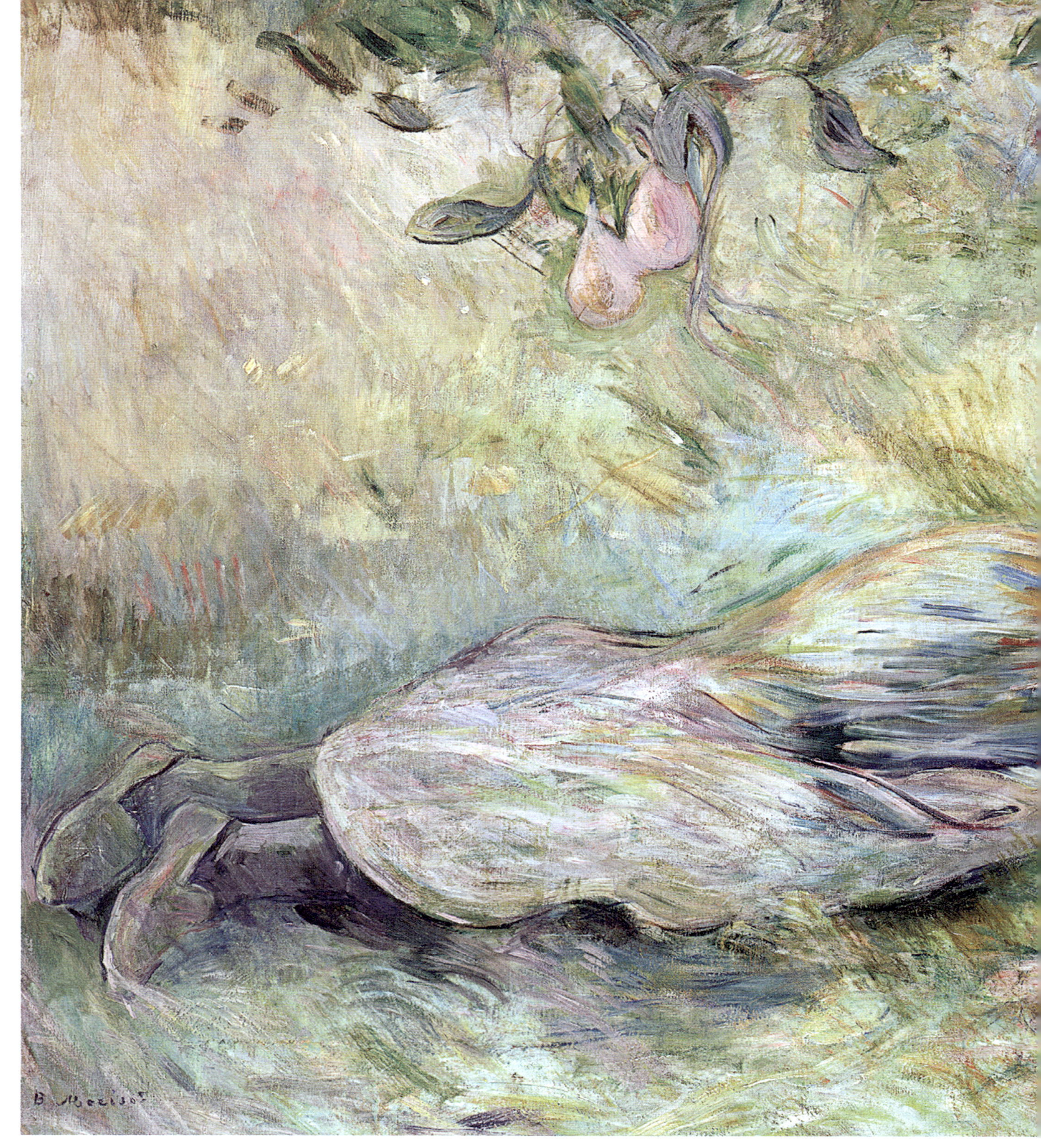

Reclining Shepherdess, 1891
Oil on canvas, 63 x 114 cm (24¾ x 45 in)
• Musée Marmottan Monet, Paris

Counterpart to the nude reclining shepherdess (*see* page 53), a goat has been added here.
Using a broader palette compared to the blue-green tones of the other image, Berthe fuses
vivid colours to make the image sing.

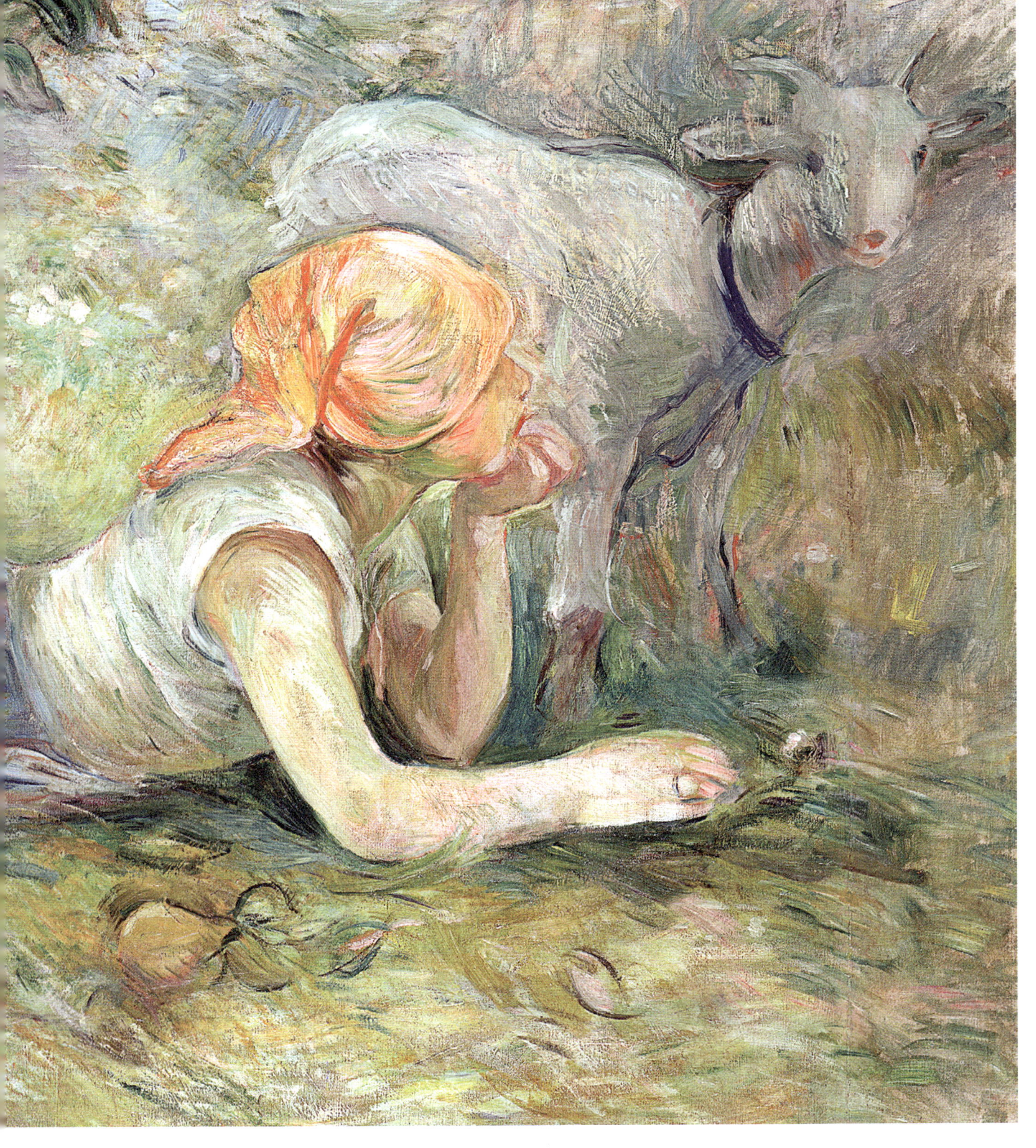

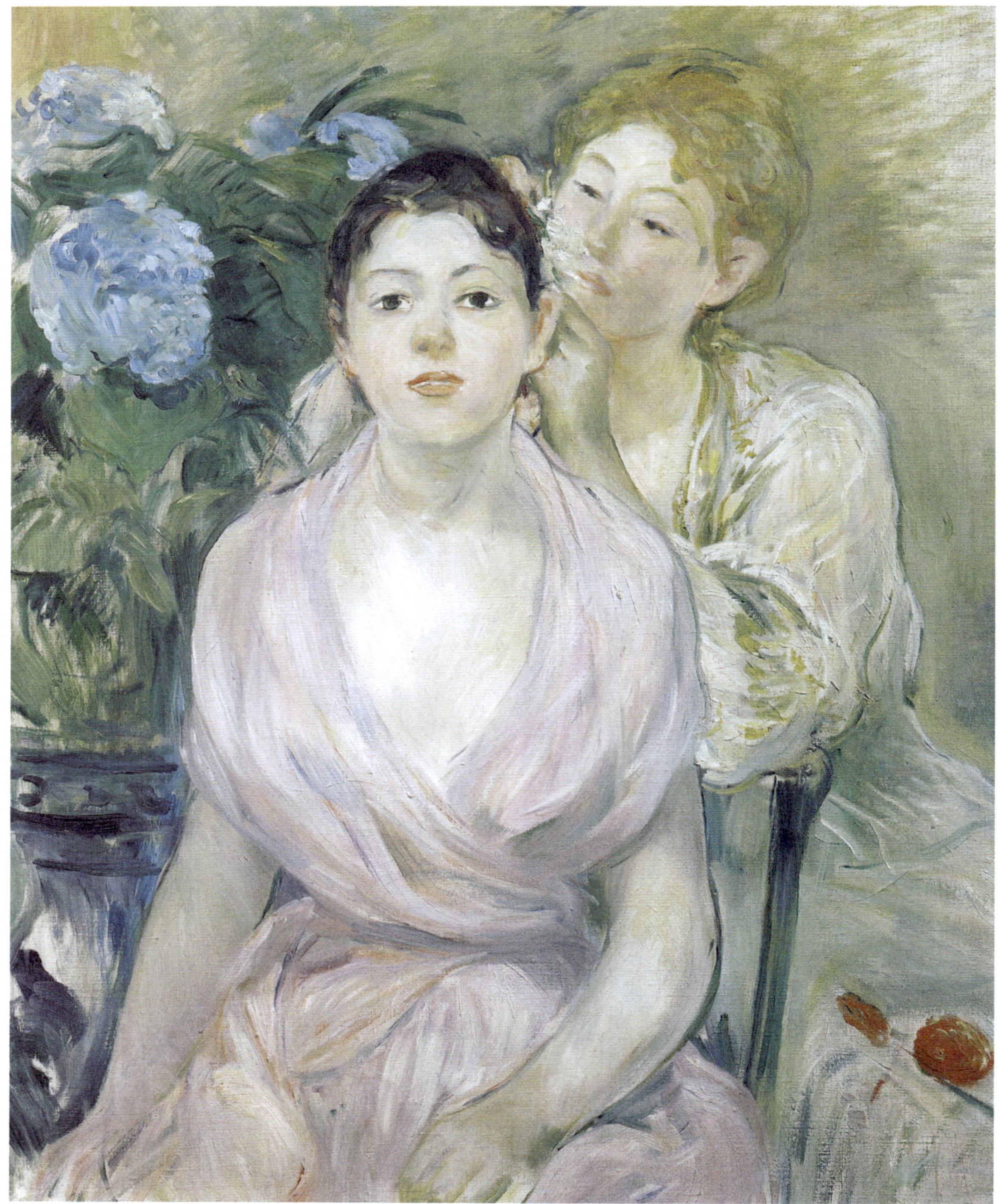

The Hortensia, 1894
Oil on canvas, 73 x 60.4 cm (28¾ x 23¾ in)
• Musée d'Orsay, Paris

Also called *The Two Sisters*, this is a skilled piece of design exploring shape and form – from swathes of soft fabric to the large, curvaceous vase and plant (a hortensia, or hydrangea) – with a glowing light on the girls' skin.

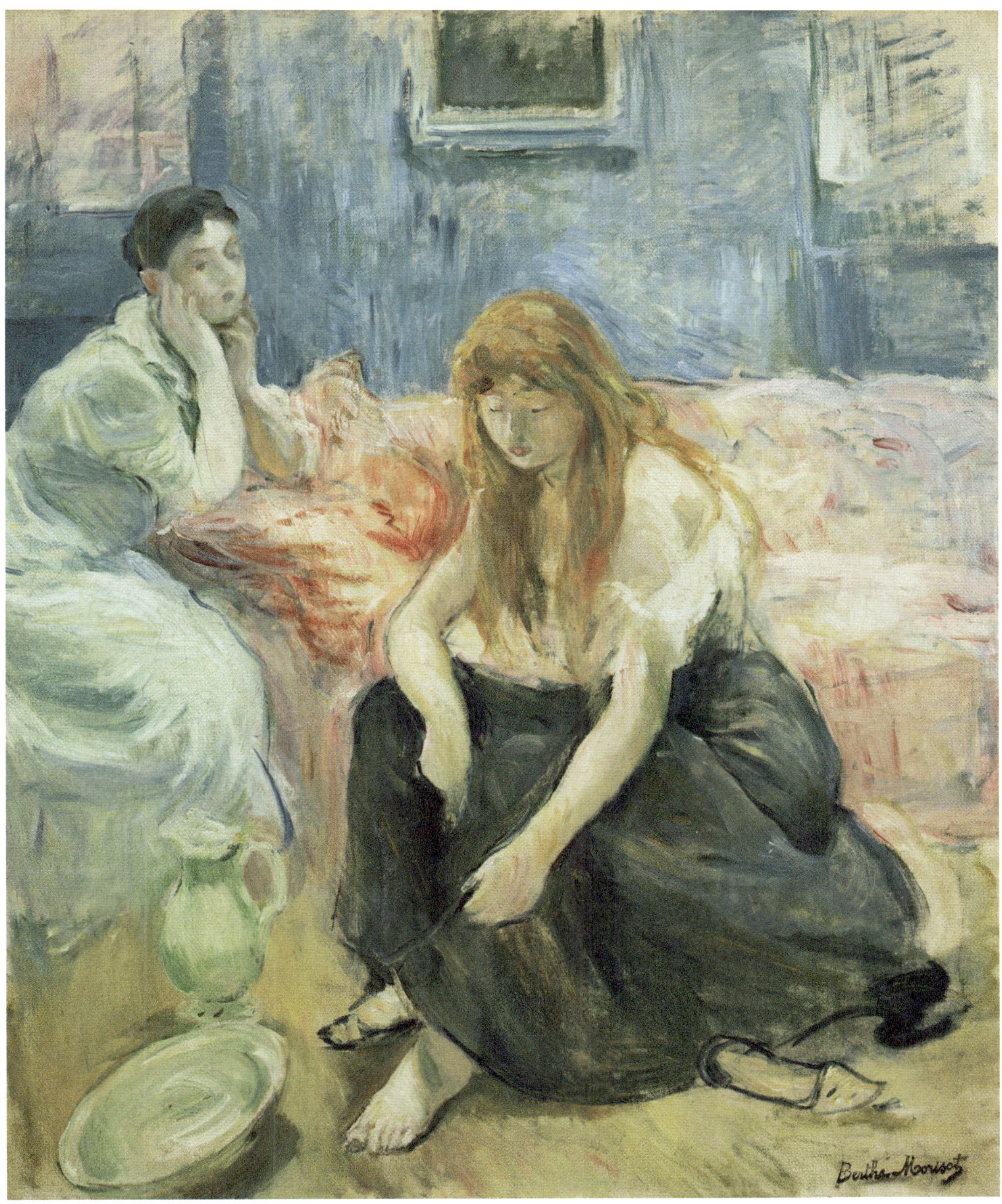

Two Girls, *c.* 1894
Oil on canvas, 65 x 54 cm (25⅔ x 21¼ in)
• The Phillips Collection, Washington DC

Painted at the end of her life, this foot-bathing scene typifies Berthe's very late style, featuring figures of some solidity that do not blend into their background. Unusual foreground perspectives suggest a highly modernist approach.

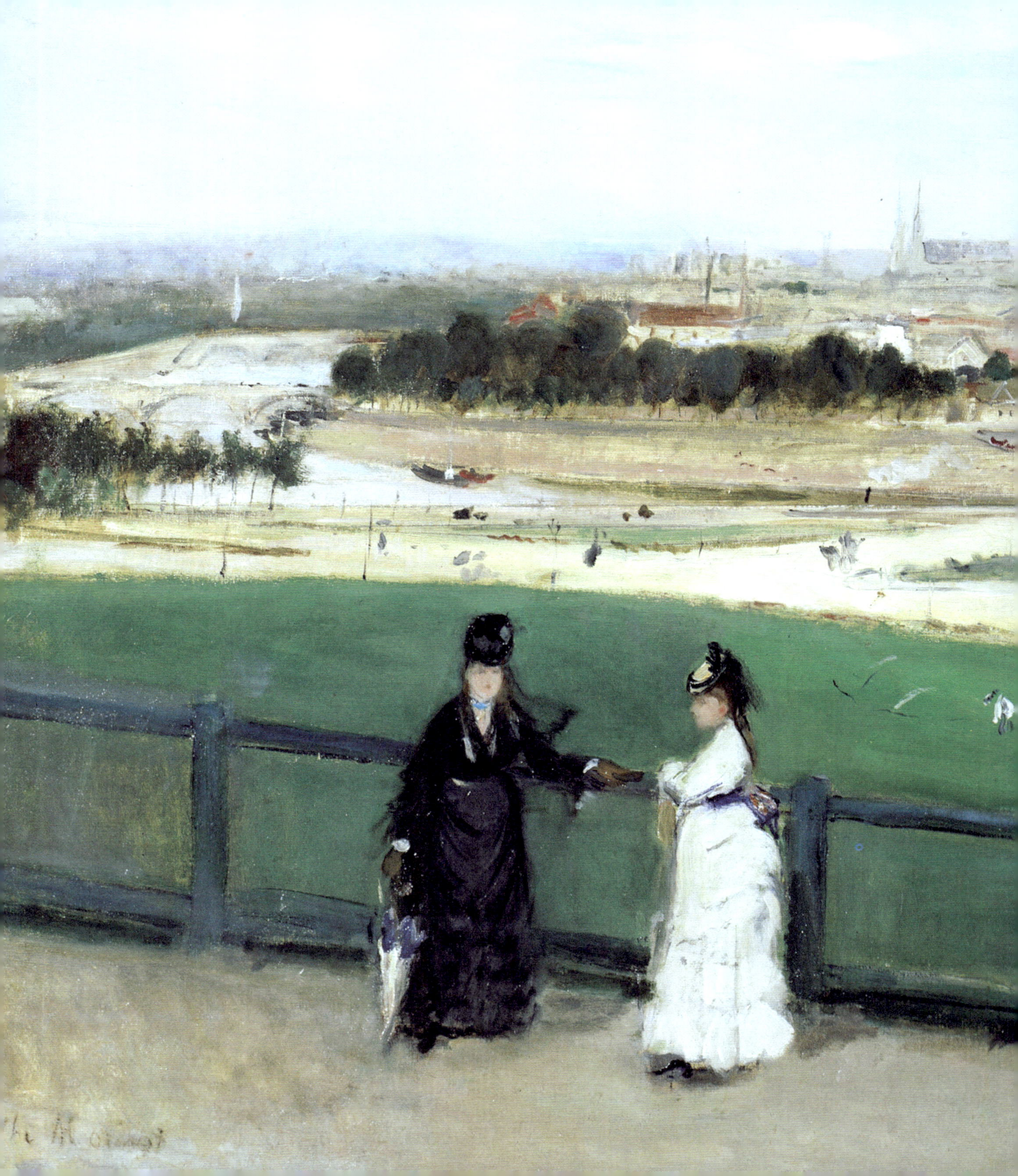

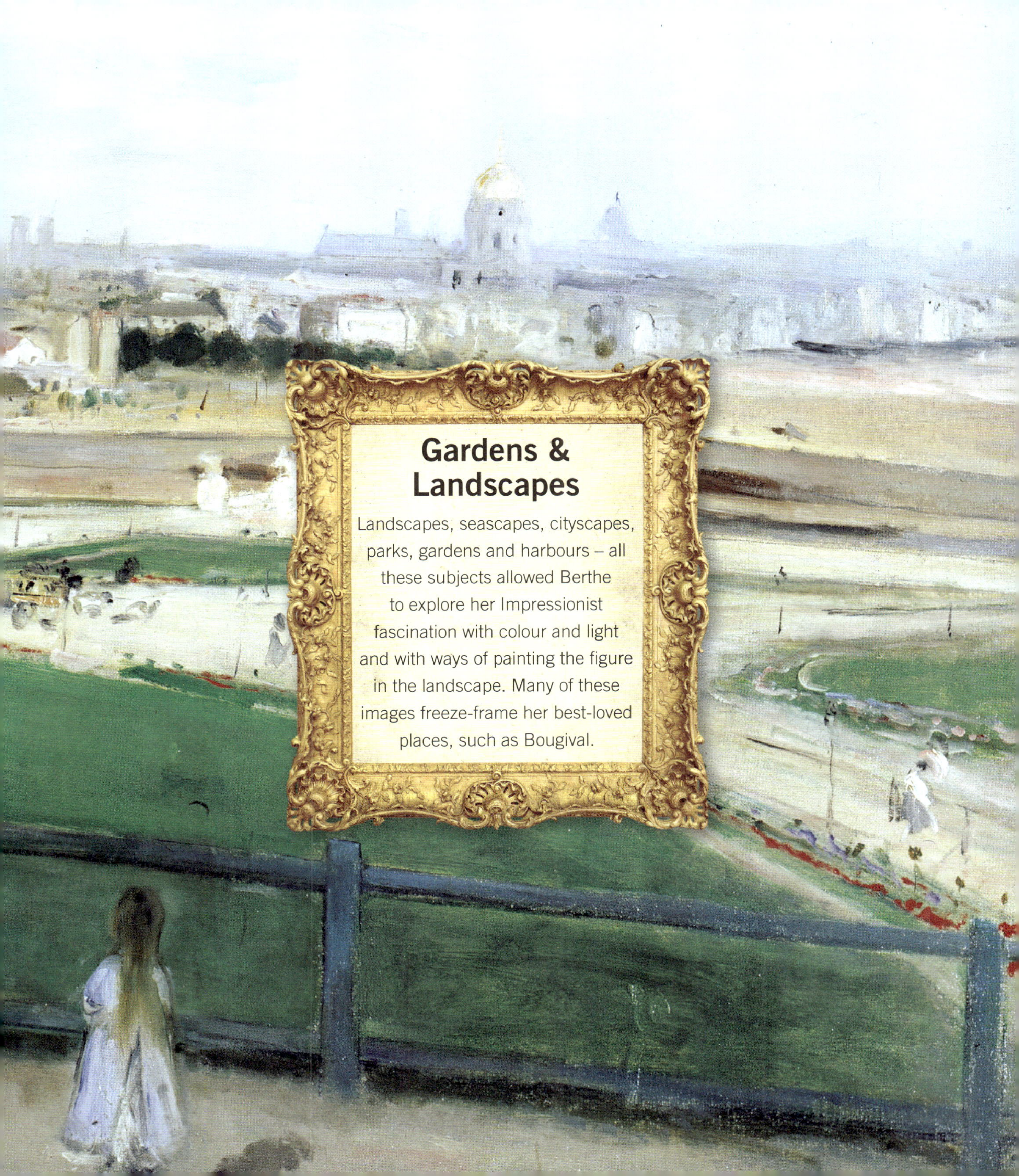

Gardens & Landscapes

Landscapes, seascapes, cityscapes, parks, gardens and harbours – all these subjects allowed Berthe to explore her Impressionist fascination with colour and light and with ways of painting the figure in the landscape. Many of these images freeze-frame her best-loved places, such as Bougival.

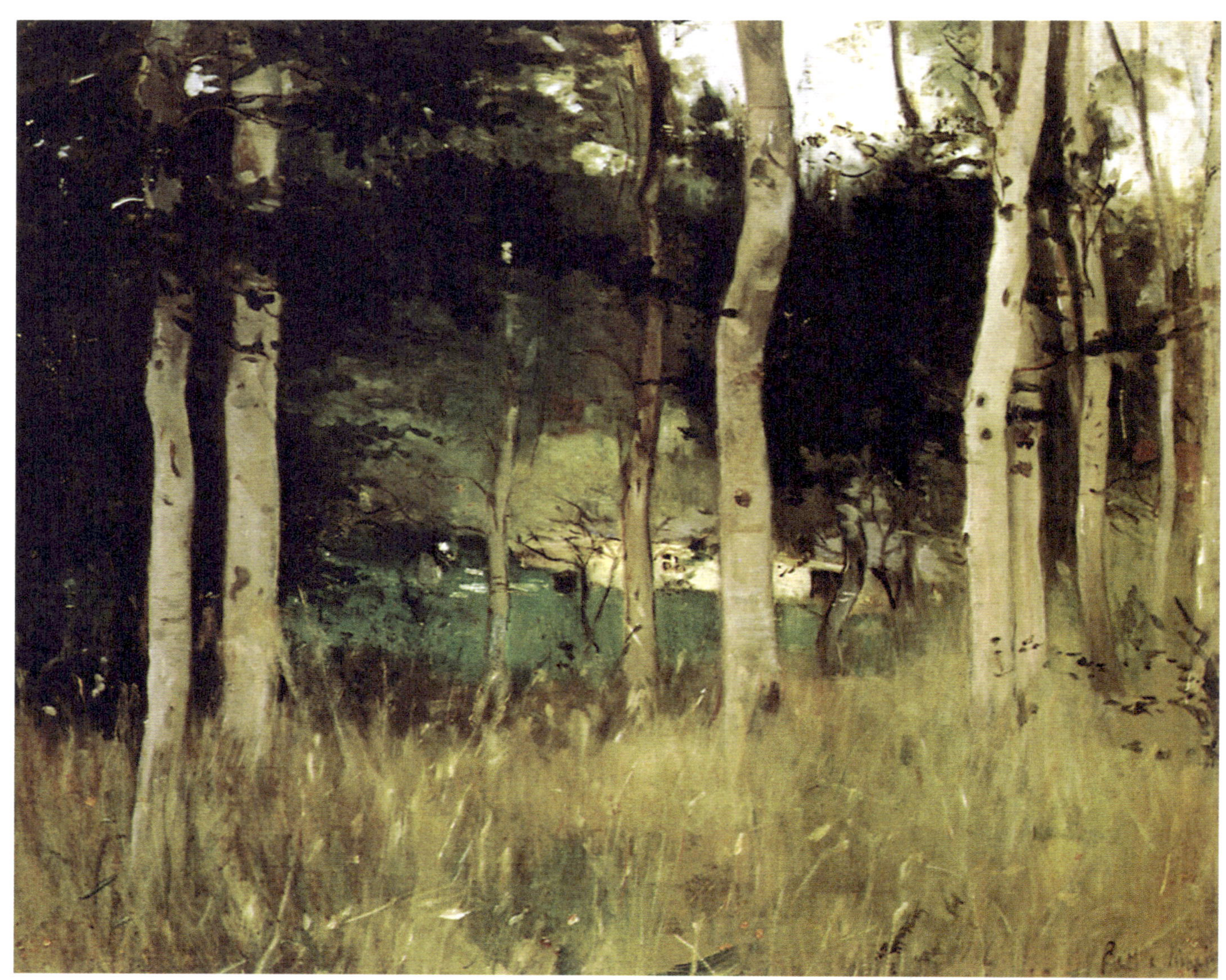

Thatched Cottage in Normandy, 1865
Oil on canvas, 46 x 55 cm (18 x 21¾ in) • Private Collection

Though immature in some ways, this early work is one of mood, mystery and stylistic cleverness. Light glances off the foreground grass while the tree trunks form an almost abstract pattern with a cottage glimpsed tantalizingly between them.

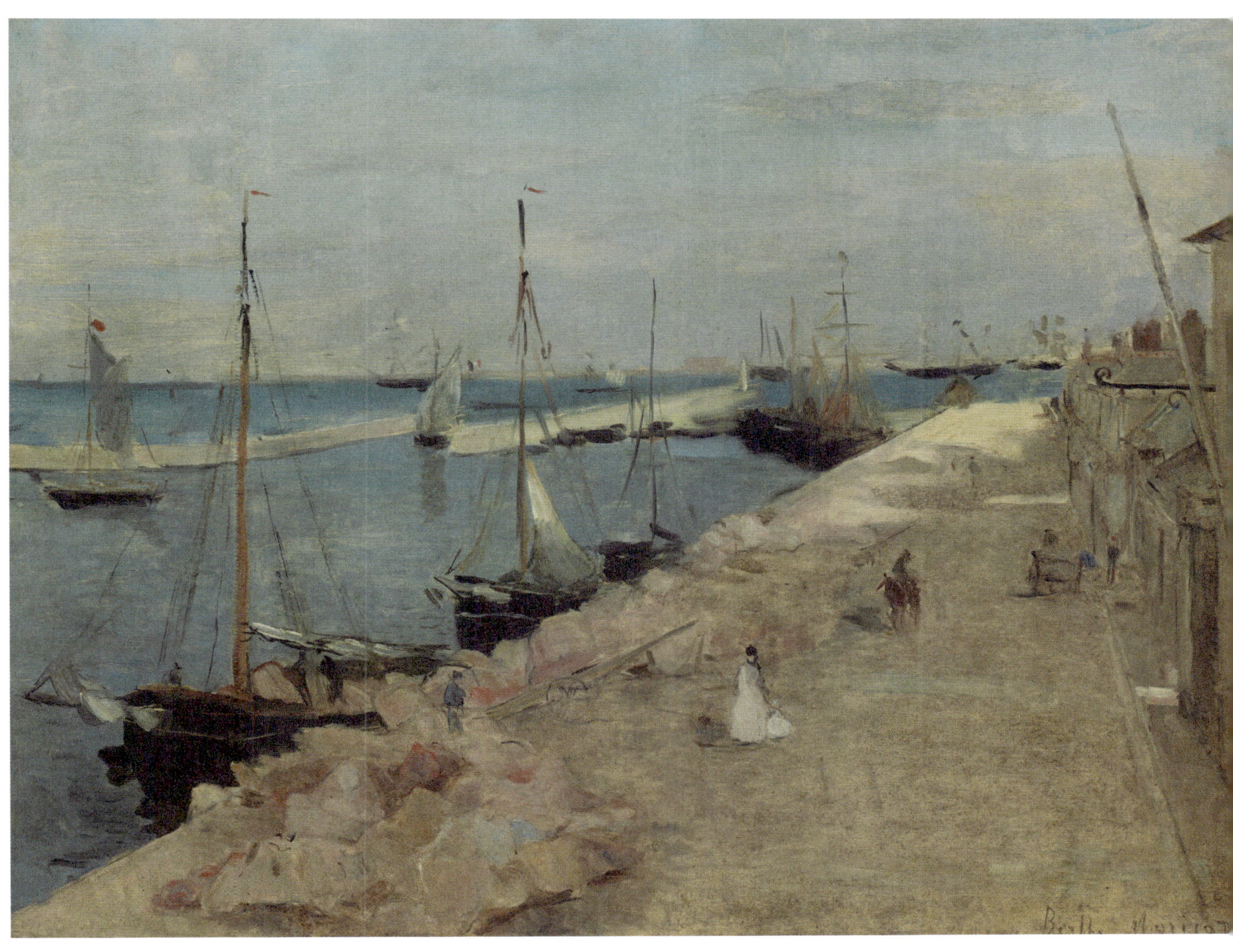

The Harbour at Cherbourg, 1871
Oil on canvas, 42 × 56.2 cm (16½ × 22 in)
• The Yale University Art Gallery, New Haven, Connecticut

Here the bold diagonal of the quayside slices the picture in two. The figures are barely suggested, a strong light rakes across the mid-ground and the ships' masts and rigging have a delicacy that echoes Turner's work.

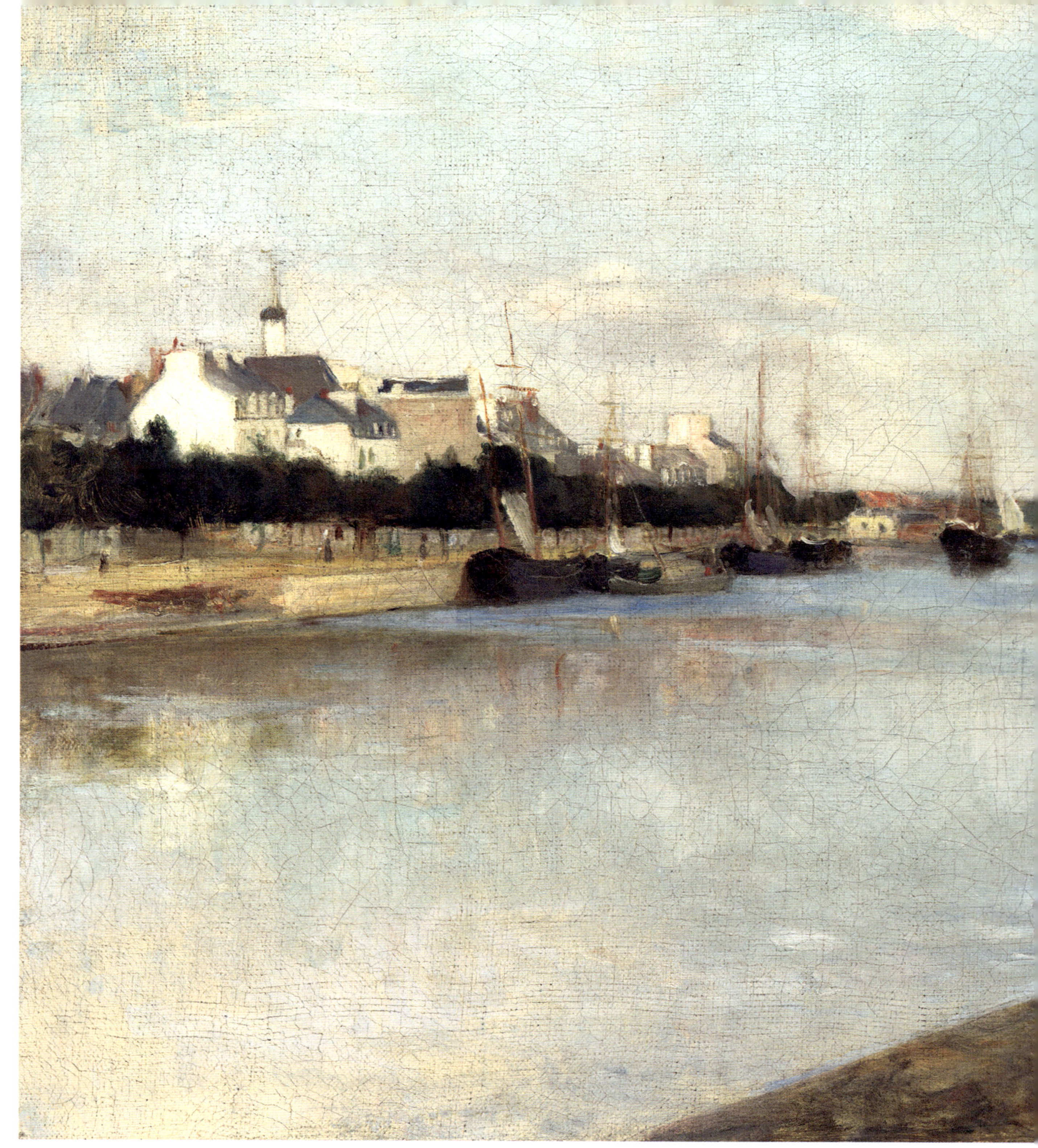

The Harbour at Lorient, 1869
Oil on canvas, 43.5 x 73 cm (17 x 28¾ in)
• National Gallery of Art, Washington DC

A mix of influences, this wide, tranquil view has its only figure (sister Edma) pushed to one edge, slightly chopped off. The warm, pearly glow, big sky and reflection-filled water echo Dutch Golden Age waterscapes by Albert Cuyp (1620–91).

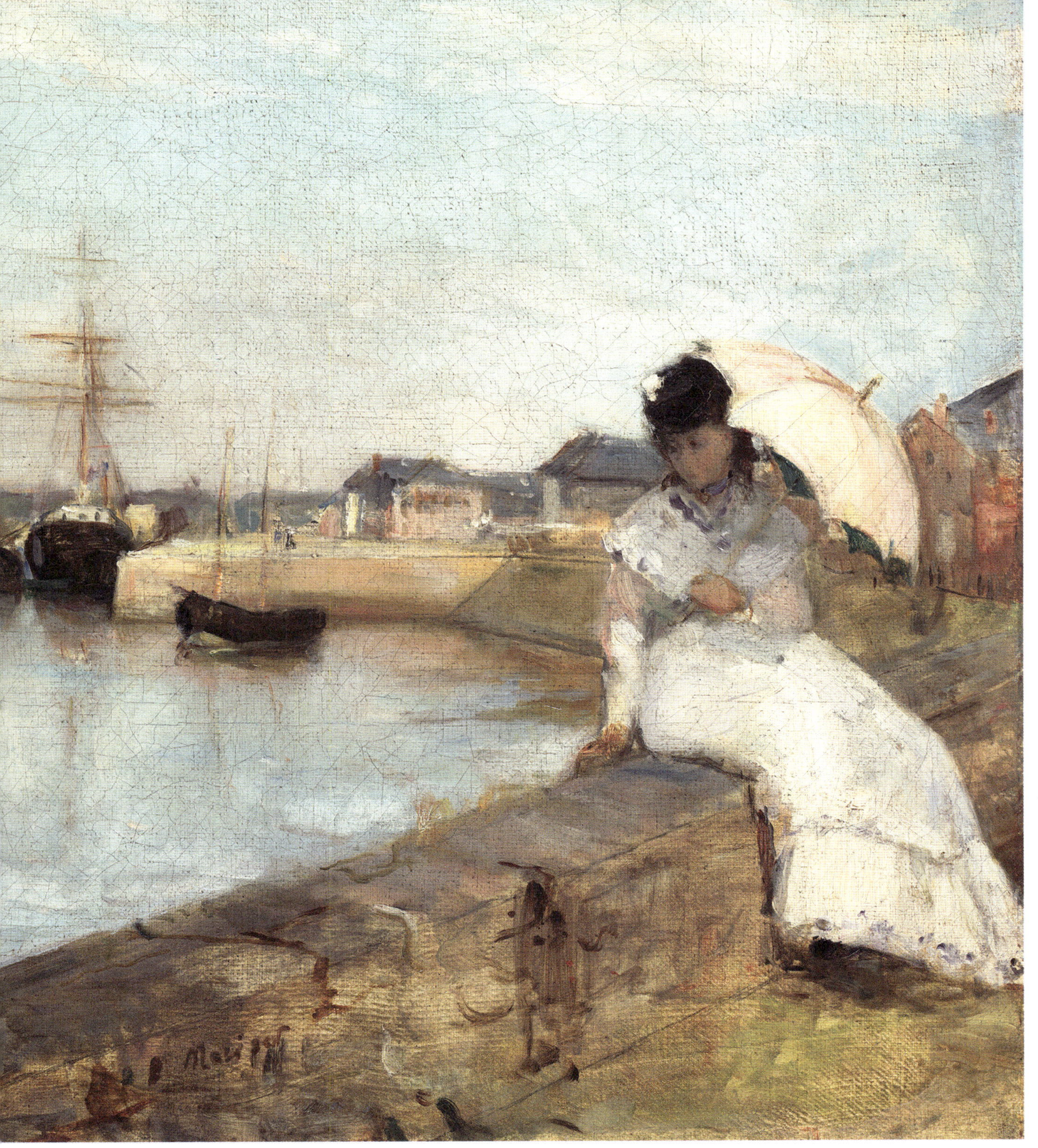

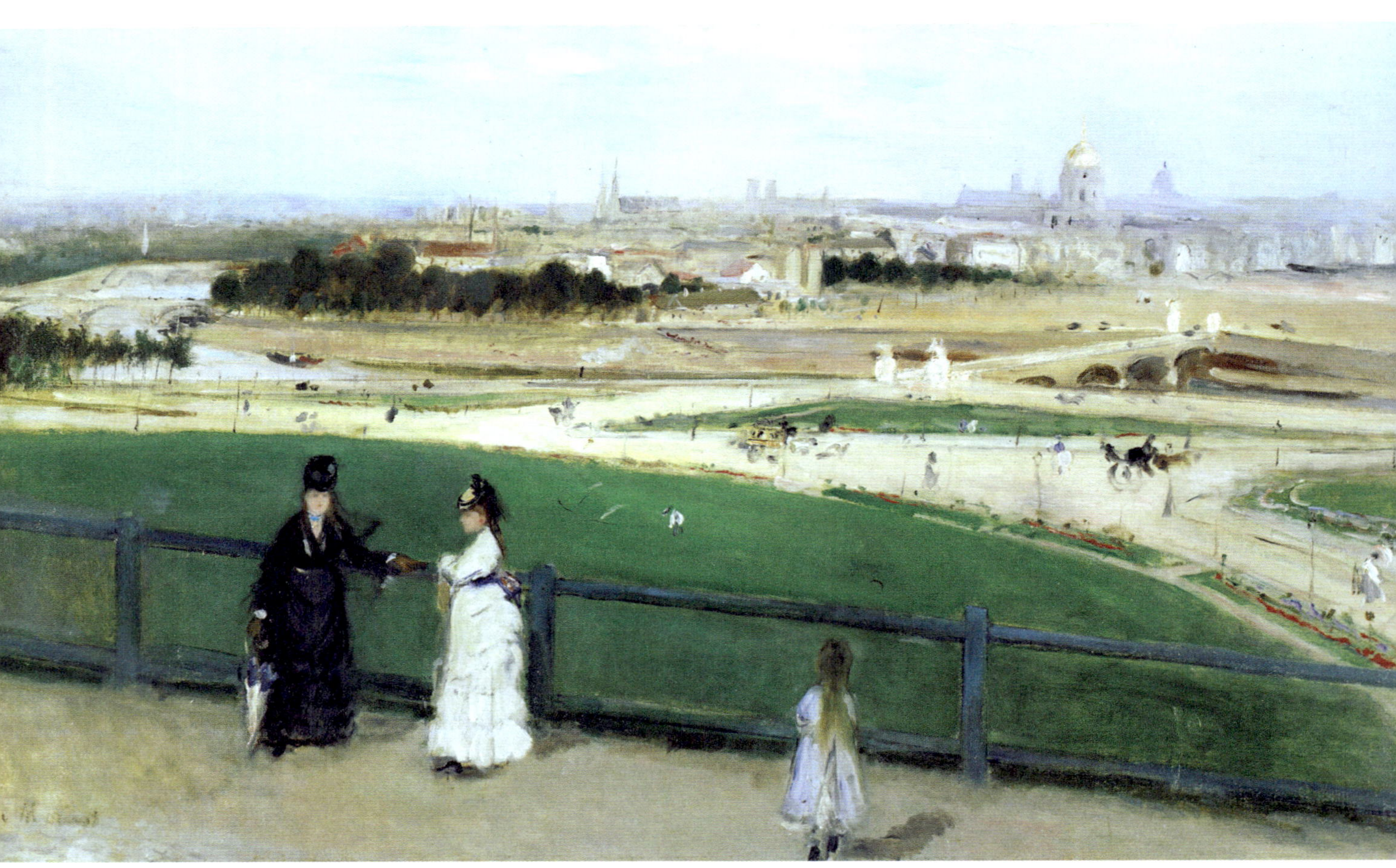

View of Paris from the Trocadéro, 1871–73
Oil on canvas, 46 x 81.6 cm (18 x 32 in)
• Santa Barbara Museum of Art, California

This ambitious panorama captures Paris in the midst of a great nineteenth-century project: the city's transformation into a grand modern city of straight, arterial boulevards, stately squares and green spaces by Baron Georges-Eugène Haussmann (1809–91).

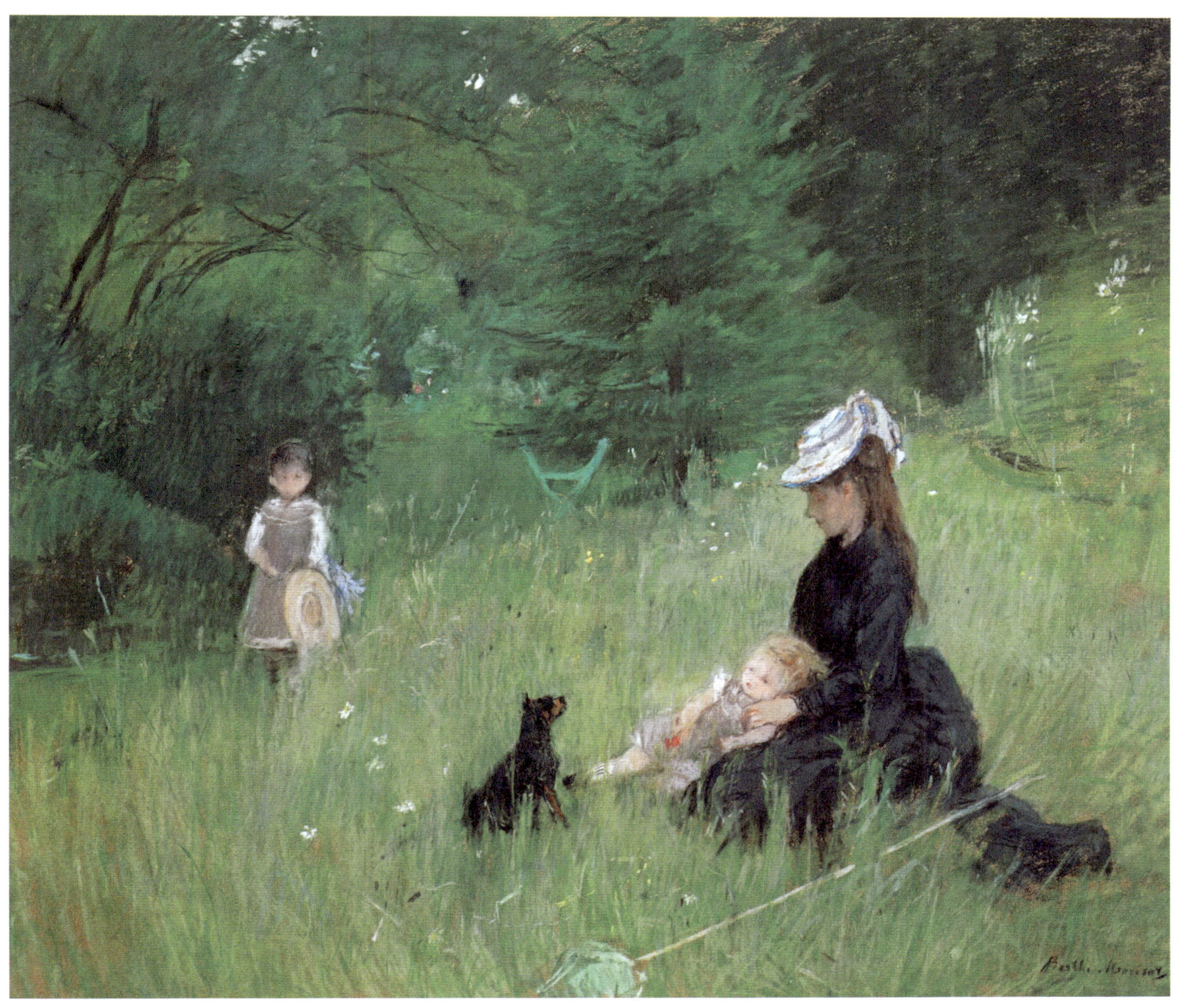

In a Park, *c.* 1874
Pastel on paper, 71 x 89 cm (28 x 35 in)
• Petit Palais, Musée des Beaux-Arts de la Ville de Paris

Here the velvety softness of pastels in limited, harmonious tones is put to perfect use in creating dense and lush greenery that almost seems to envelop the family enjoying a leisurely day out.

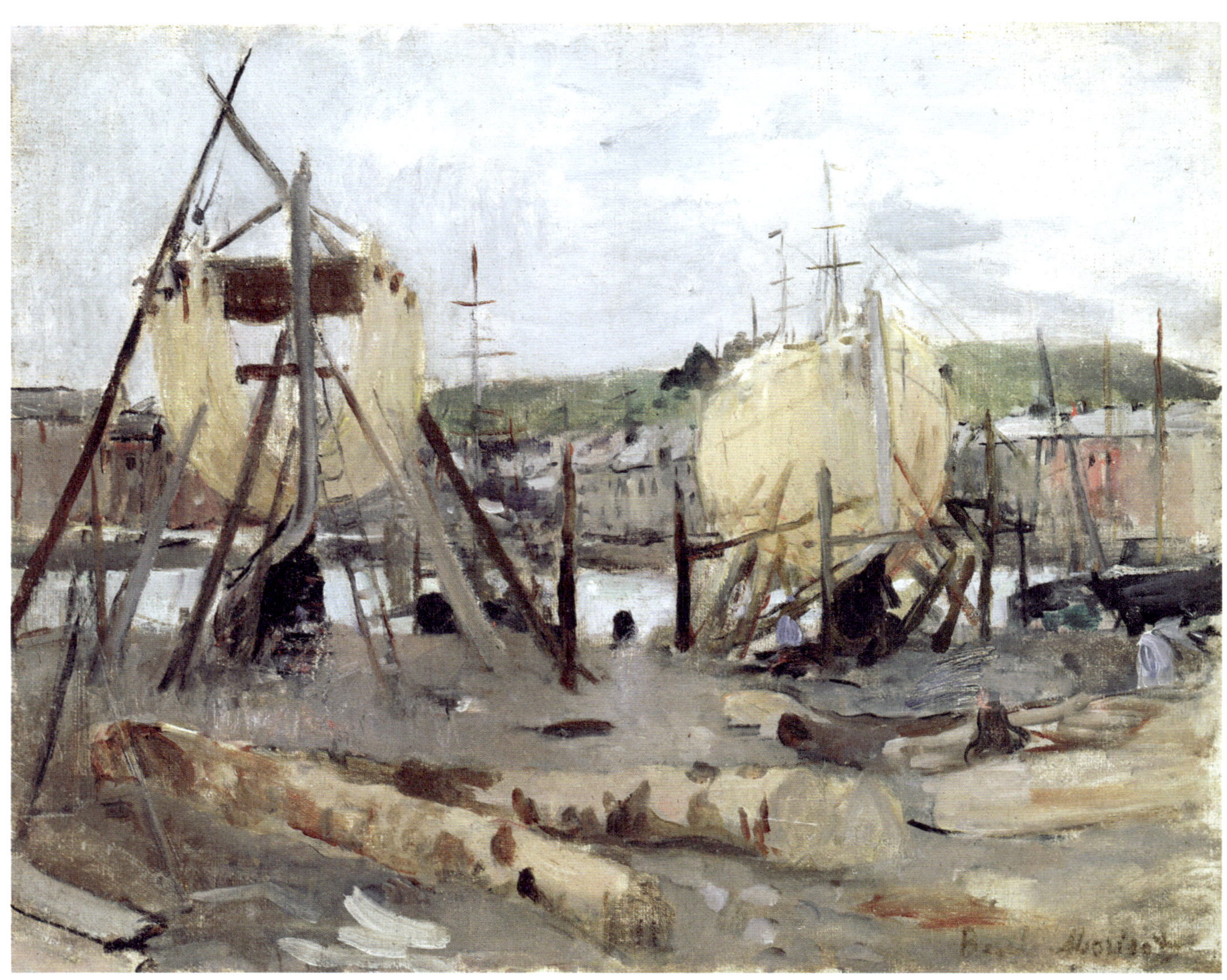

Boats Under Construction, 1874
Oil on canvas, 32 x 41 cm (12⅔ x 16 in)
• Musée Marmottan Monet, Paris

Summer 1874 found Berthe staying at Fécamp, on the Normandy coast, where she caught this scene in true sketchy *plein air* style. She passed time here with the Manets, watching the busy port and painting outdoors with Eugène, her future husband.

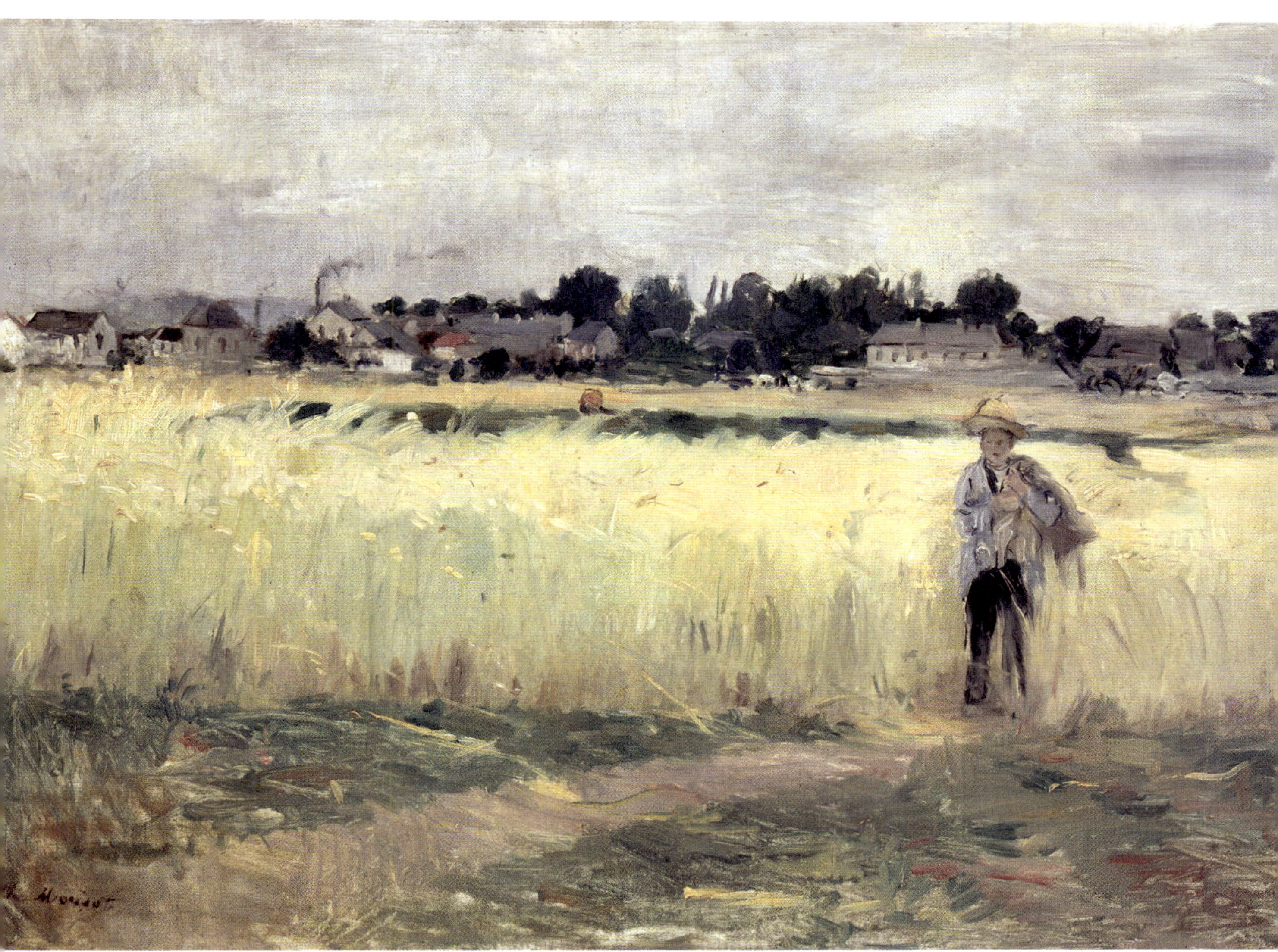

In the Wheatfields, 1875
Oil on canvas, 46.5 x 69 cm (18⅓ x 27 in) • Musée d'Orsay, Paris

This dates from spring 1875, when the newly married Berthe and Eugène visited Gennevilliers, on the outskirts of Paris. Her striking composition focuses on a direct response to nature, the wheat and the play of light across it.

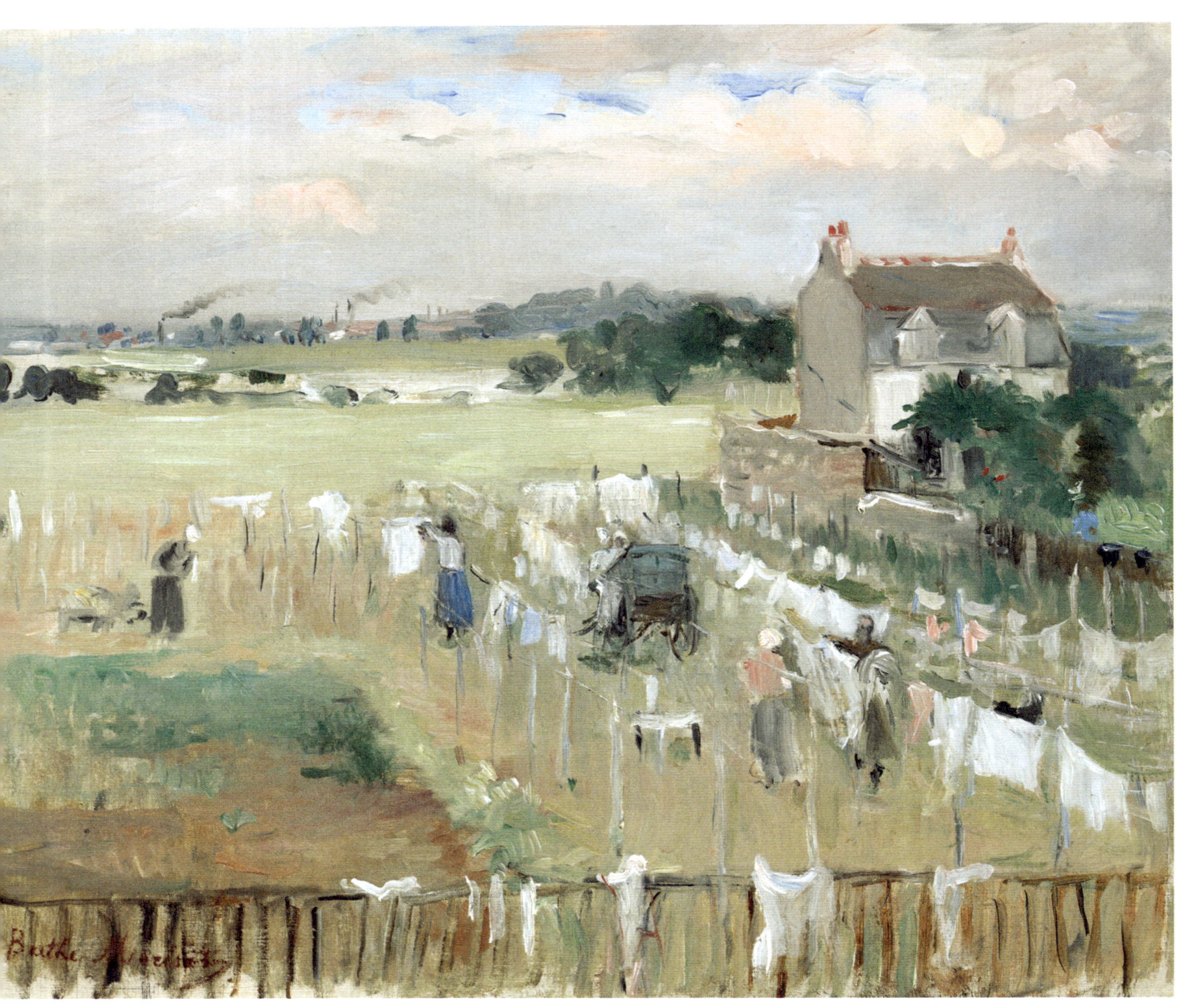

Hanging the Laundry out to Dry, 1875
Oil on canvas, 33 x 40.6 cm (13 x 16 in)
• National Gallery of Art, Washington DC

Viewed up close, it is clear that Berthe has created a head from one or two paint splodges, a leg from a couple of swift, long strokes. Pulling back, however, reveals an easily read scene with a truly convincing sky.

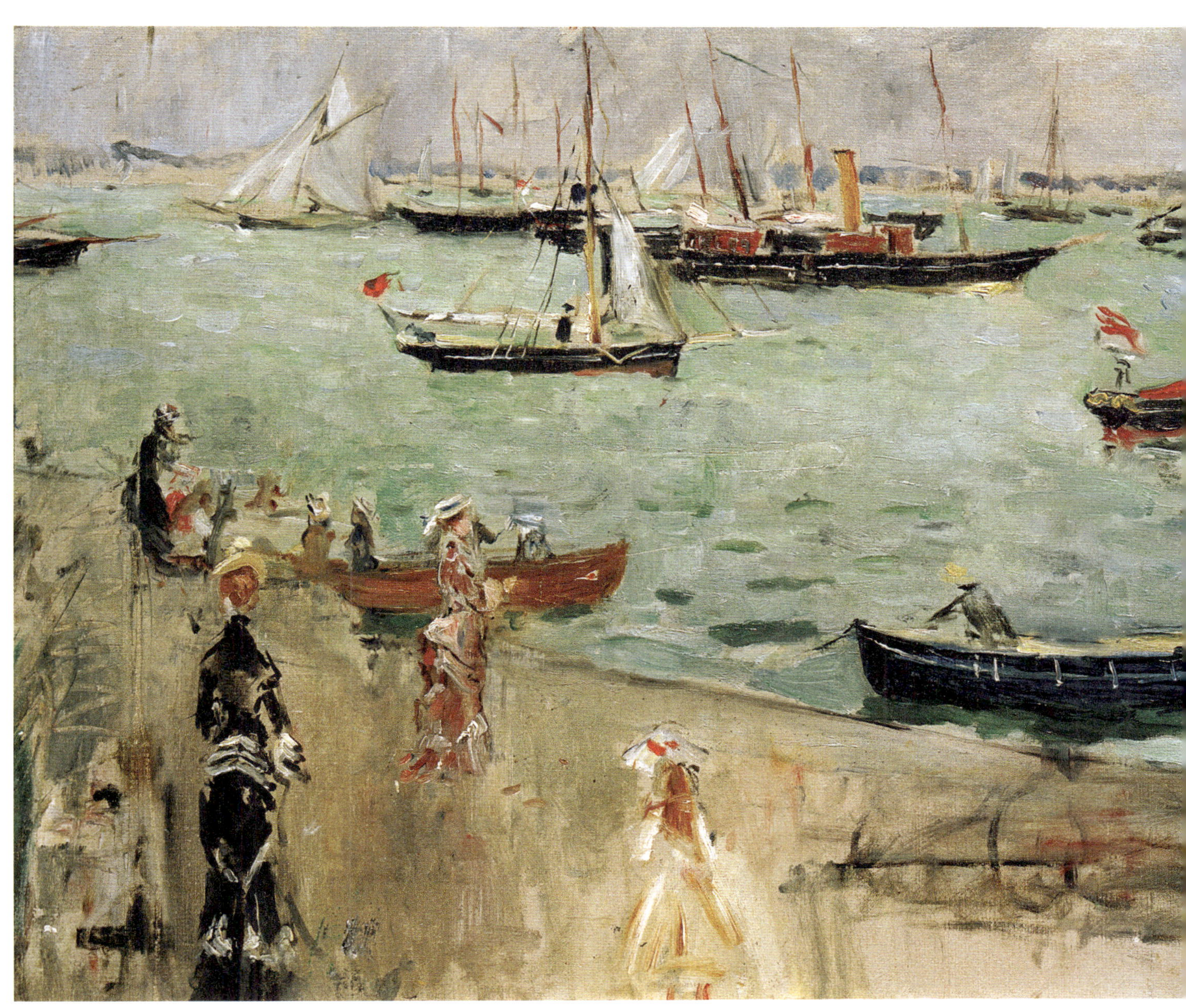

Harbour Scene, Isle of Wight, 1875
Oil on canvas, 36 x 48 cm (14 x 19 in) • Private Collection

Berthe made quite a few marine scenes. This one, from her honeymoon visit to the Isle of Wight, captures the immediacy of painting out of doors and in places veers close to abstraction.

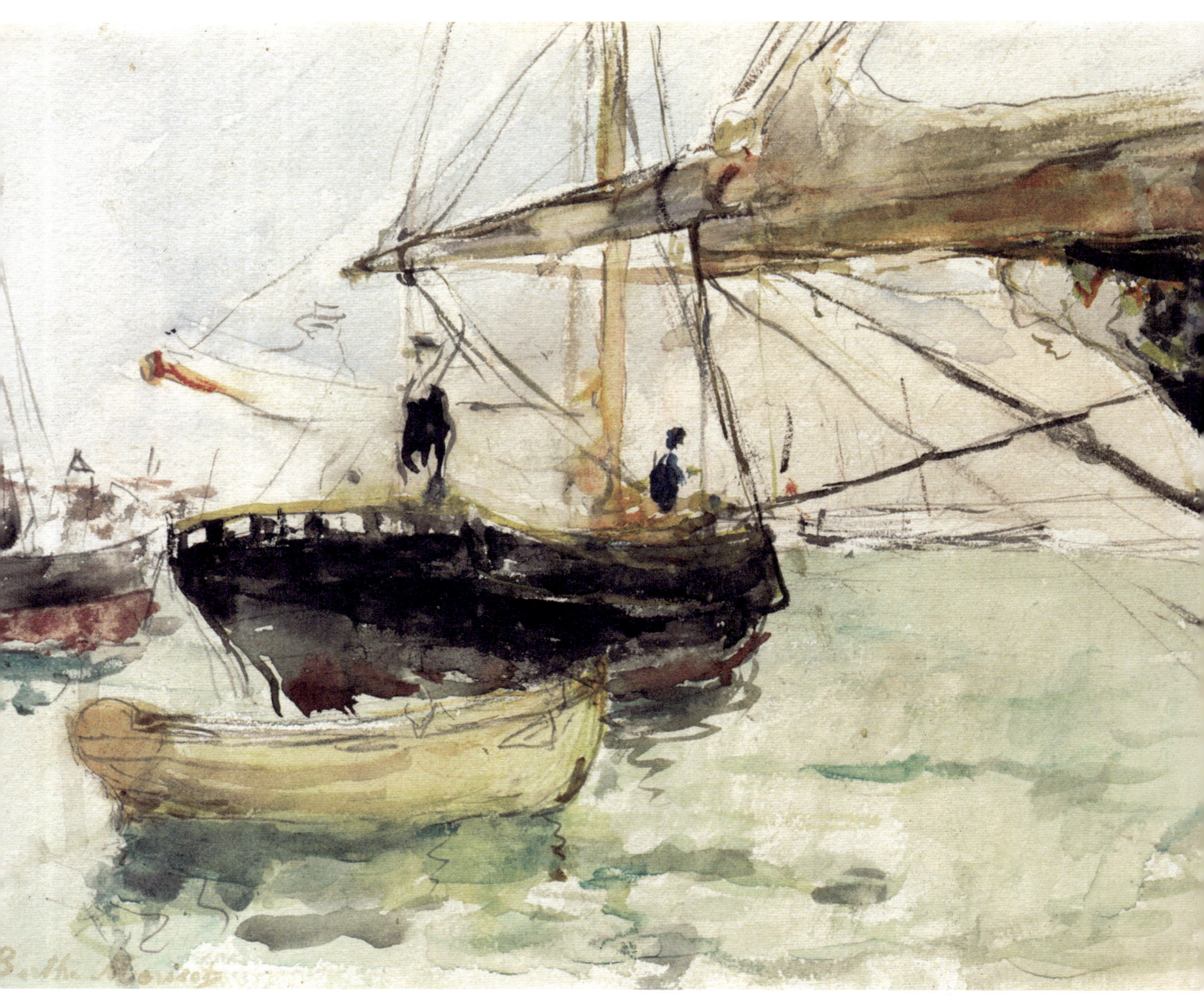

Before a Yacht, 1875
Watercolour over graphite on cream wove paper, 20.7 x 26.8 cm
(8 x 10½ in) • The Clark Art Institute, Williamstown, Massachusetts

This watercolour seascape shows confident bravura. Using a limited colour range, Berthe's swift brush delineates the scene's strong, essential forms. She creates prominent shapes coming in from the right-hand edge, which leads viewers into the picture.

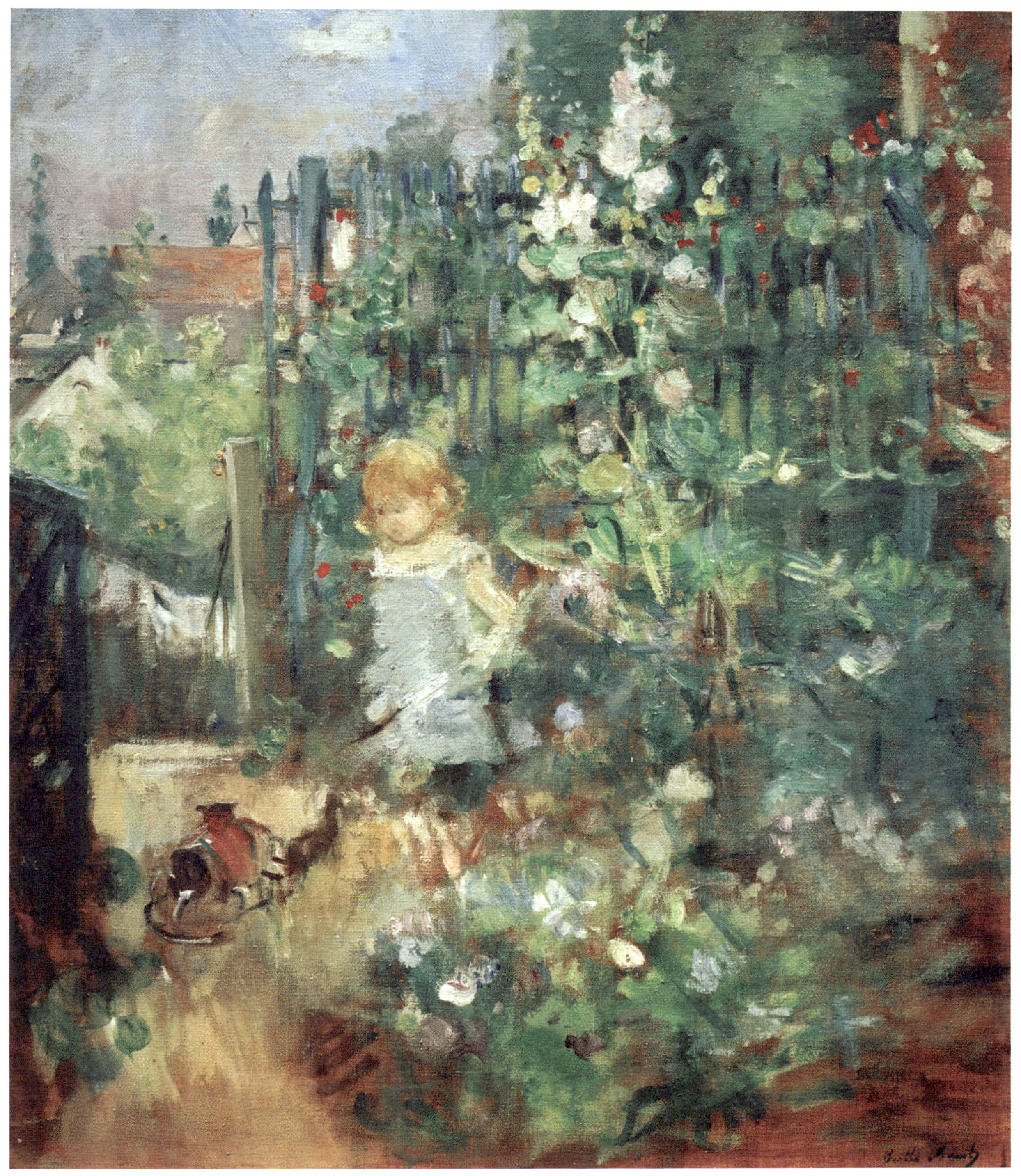

Child in the Hollyhocks, 1881
Oil on canvas, 50.6 x 42.2 cm (20 x 16⅔ in) • Private Collection

The 1880s were a period filled with garden pictures and with freely painted images where figure and surroundings melted into each other. Here the small child has almost disappeared among the lovely, tall blooms.

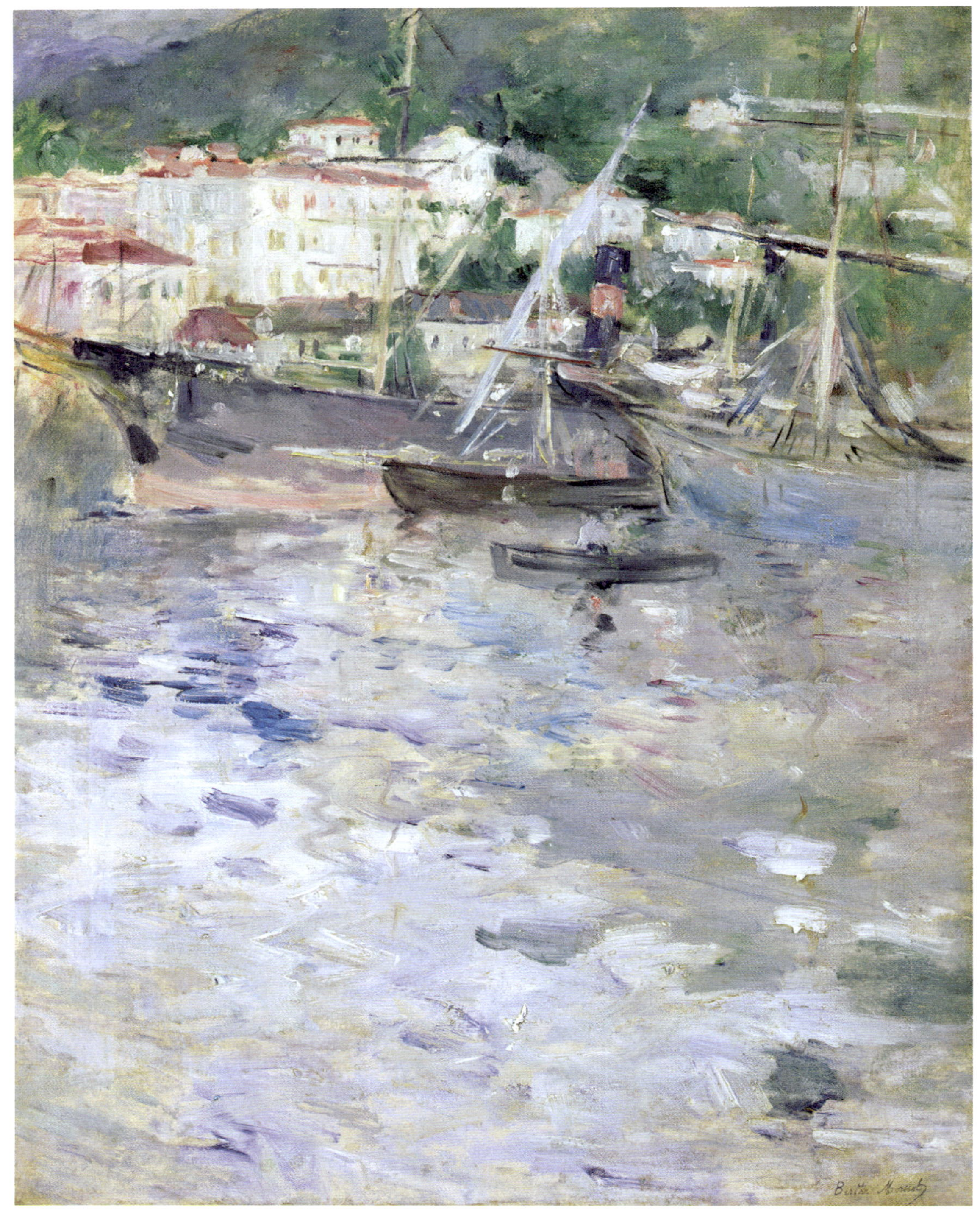

The Port of Nice, 1882
Oil on paper on canvas, 59 x 43 cm (23¼ x 17 in)
• Musée Marmottan Monet, Paris

Visiting Nice in 1882, Berthe painted while in a boat and produced images of great verve. The large foreground expanse of vividly lit, Monet-like water and the angled perspective make the viewer feel they are at sea themselves.

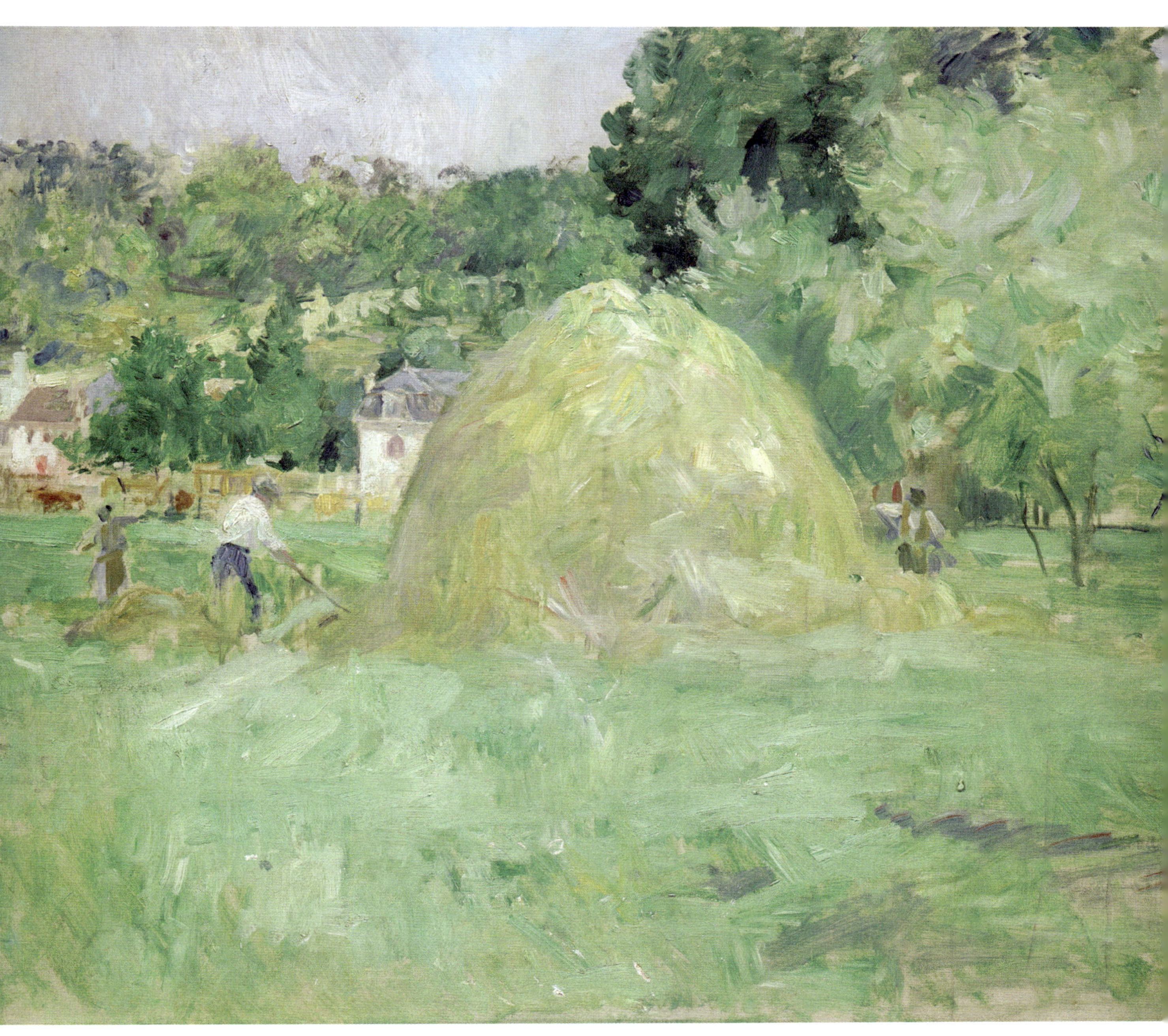

Haystacks at Bougival, 1883
Oil on canvas, 50 x 61 cm (19¾ x 24 in)
• Musée Marmottan Monet, Paris

On an 1883 trip to Bougival, Berthe and Eugène painted haymaking scenes together, outdoors. Berthe's versions pay close attention to light, season and time of day, bearing comparison with her friend Monet's later great 'Haystacks' series of 1890–91.

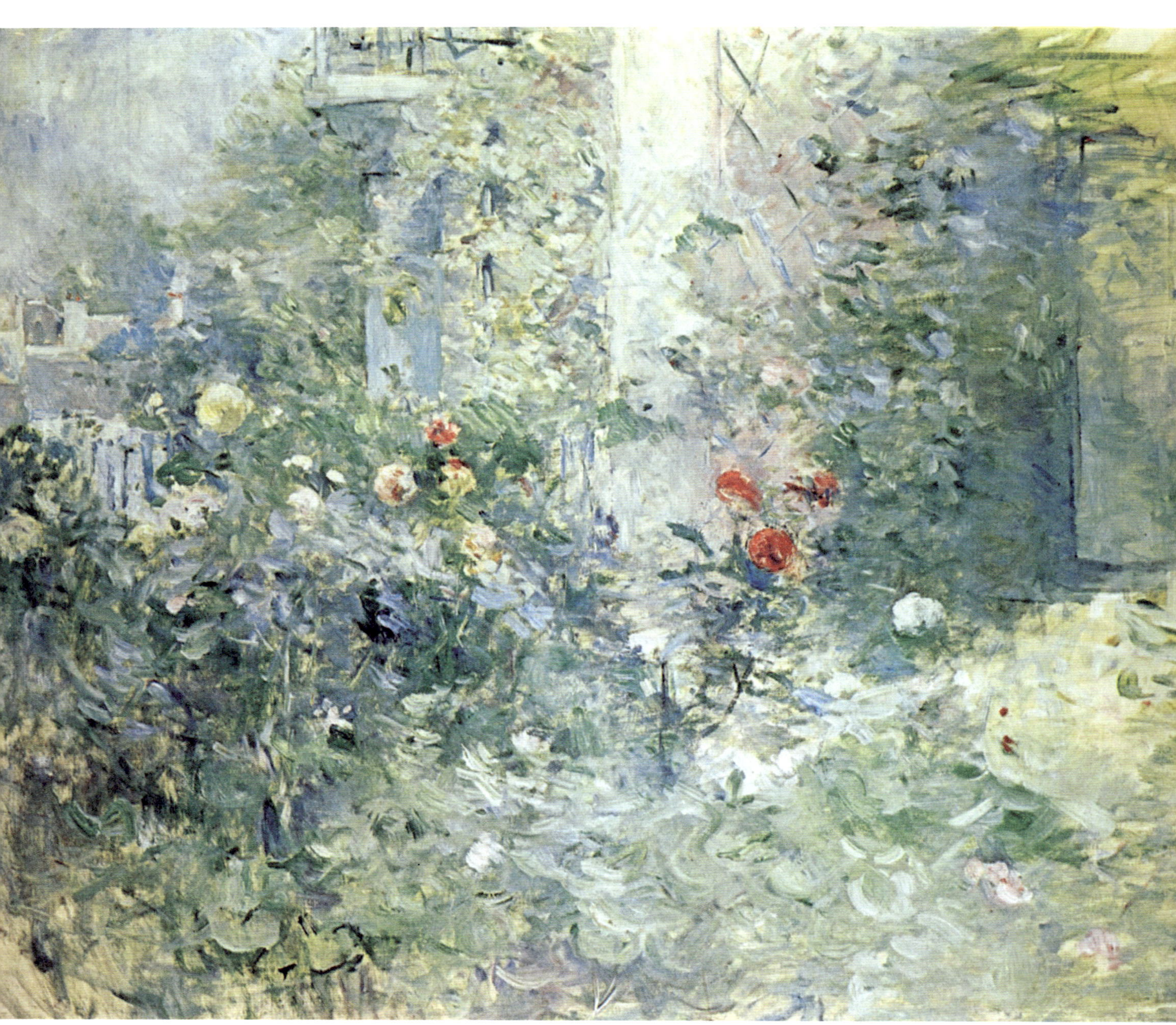

The Garden at Bougival, 1884
Oil on canvas, 73 x 92 cm (28¾ x 36¼ in)
• Musée Marmottan Monet, Paris

Painted the year they spent their last summer at much-loved Bougival, this image took just a few hours to paint. With fast, visible strokes, Berthe conjures up a floral confection of many colours, dissolving into glowing summer light.

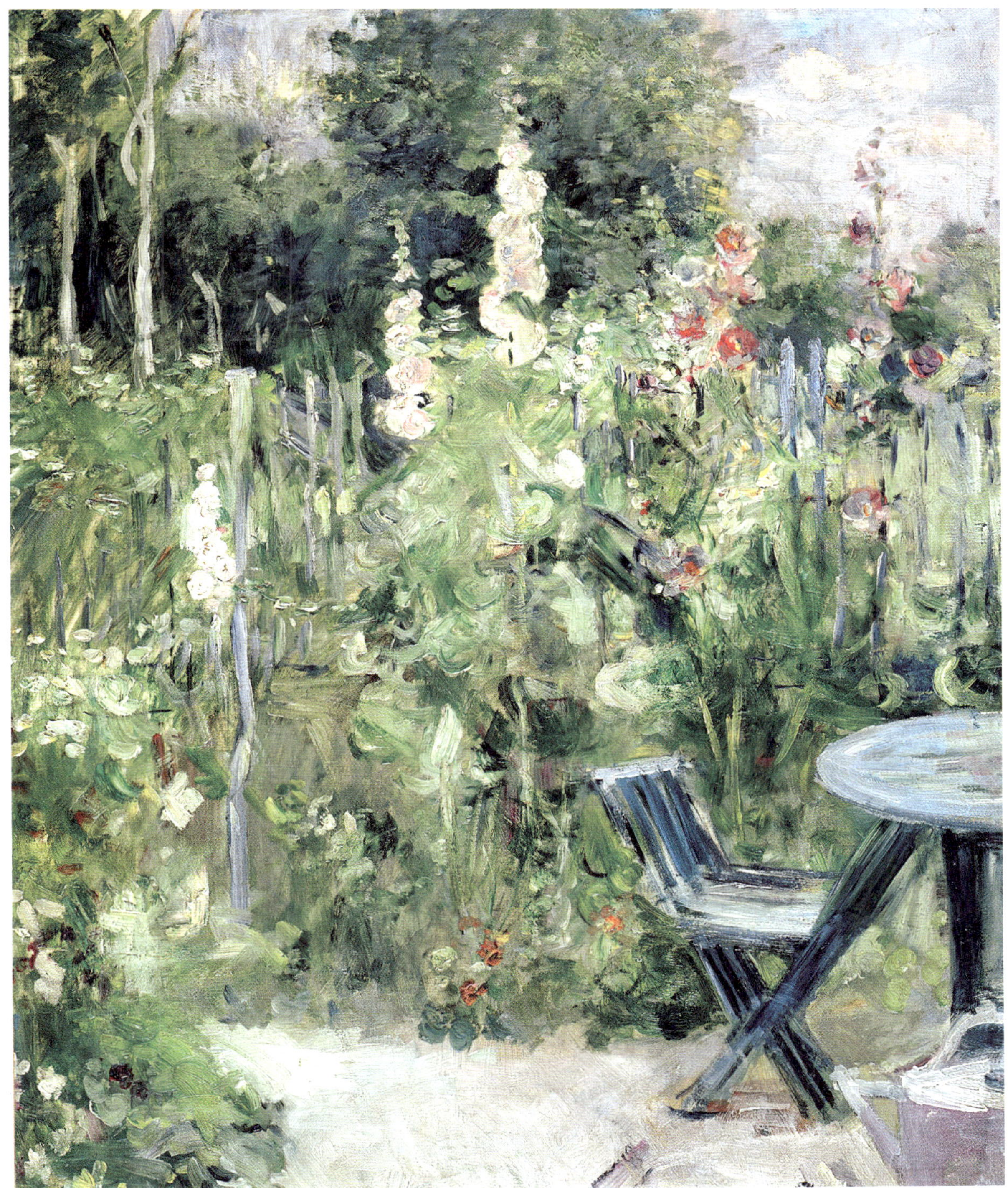

Hollyhocks, 1884
Oil on canvas, 65 x 54 cm (25⅔ x 21¼ in)
• Musée Marmottan Monet, Paris

Celebrating the lovely garden at Bougival, this is a perfect example of Berthe's use of a cut-off composition coupled with her ability to convey a profusion of floral colour in all its glory.

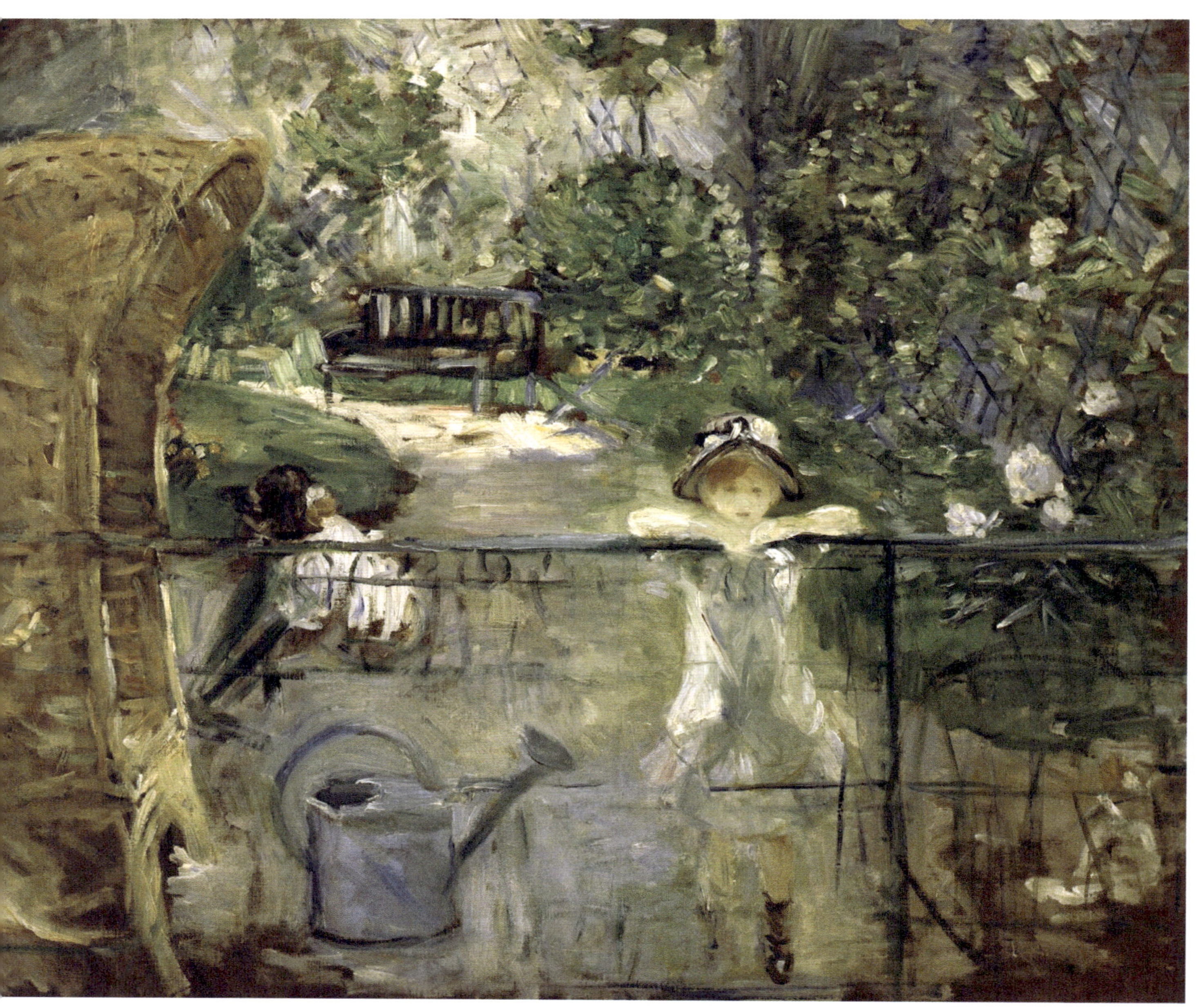

Little Girls in the Garden or The Basket Chair, 1885
Oil on canvas, 61.3 x 75.6 (24 x 29¾ in)
• The Museum of Fine Arts, Houston, Texas

In a semi-abstract image that captures a passing moment, featuring choppy strokes and cross-hatching, a basket chair looms up in the left-hand foreground while a watering can hovers in space. The little girl staring out invites viewers into the picture.

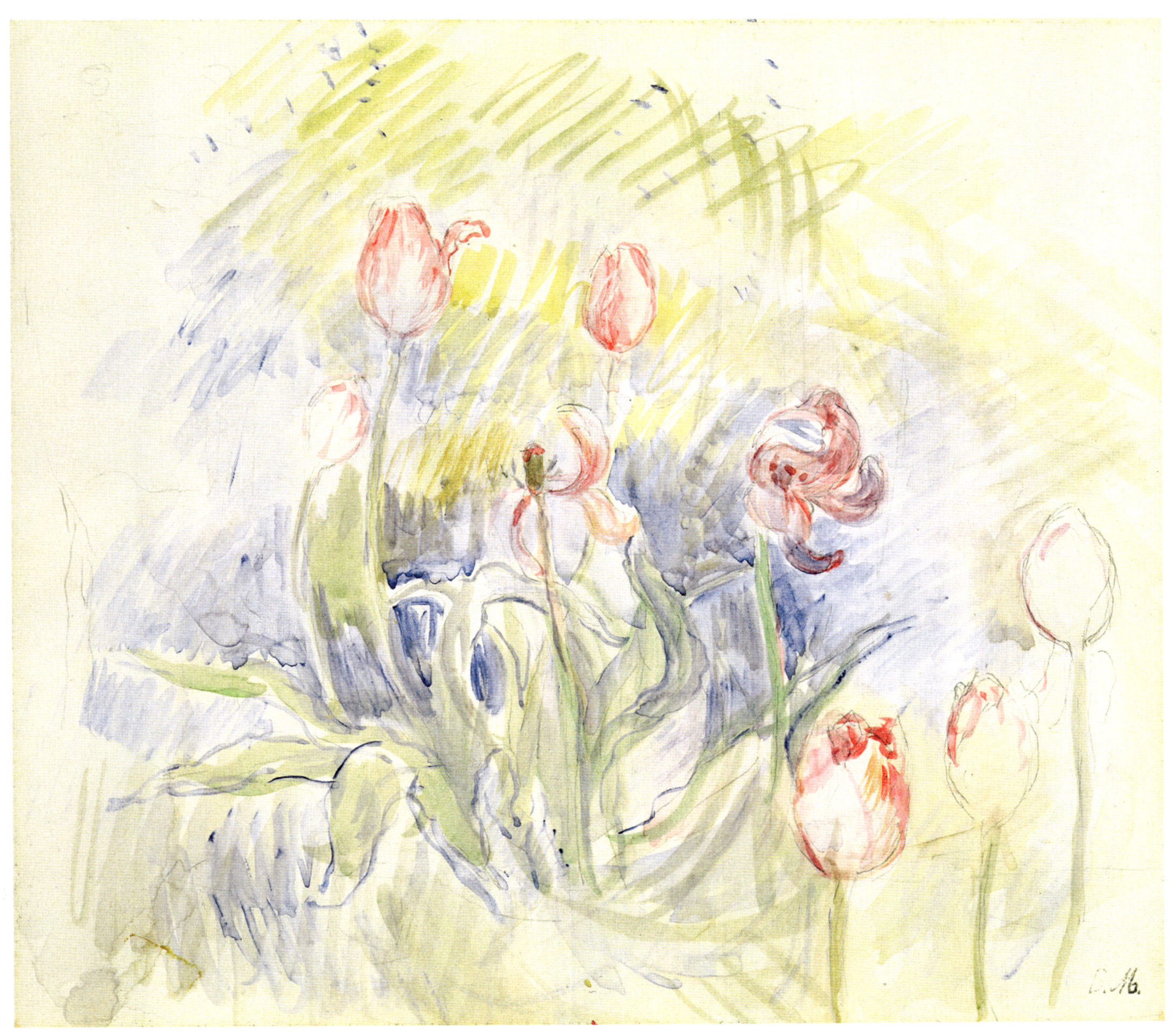

Tulips, 1890
Watercolour on paper, 31 x 36 cm (12¼ x 14¼ in)
• Musée Marmottan Monet, Paris

This late work shows how the pastel-coloured hues, brightness and glowing light effects produced by having white paper shine through watercolours also informed Berthe's works in oil. Her alternative versions of oils and preparatory studies were often in watercolour.

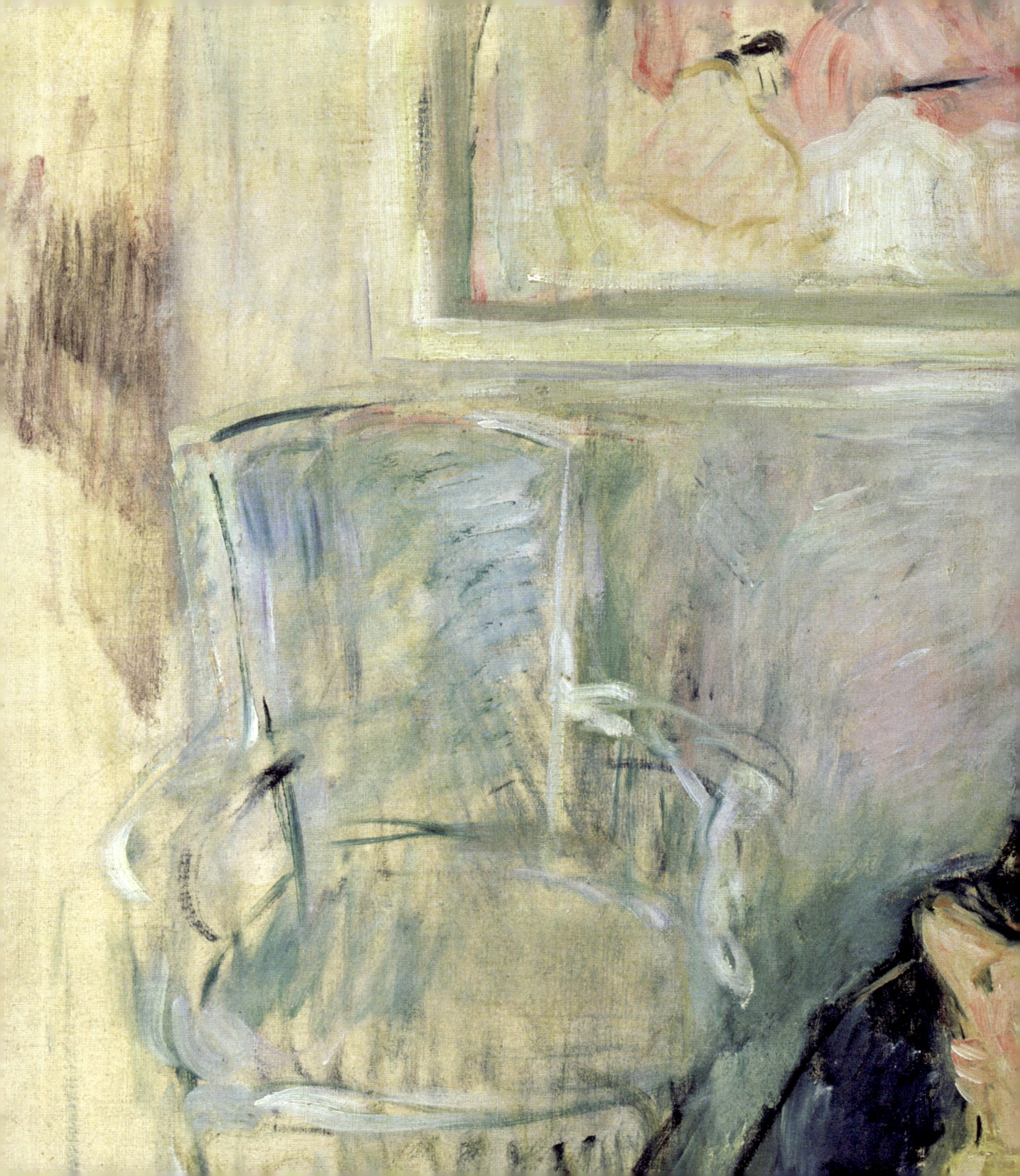

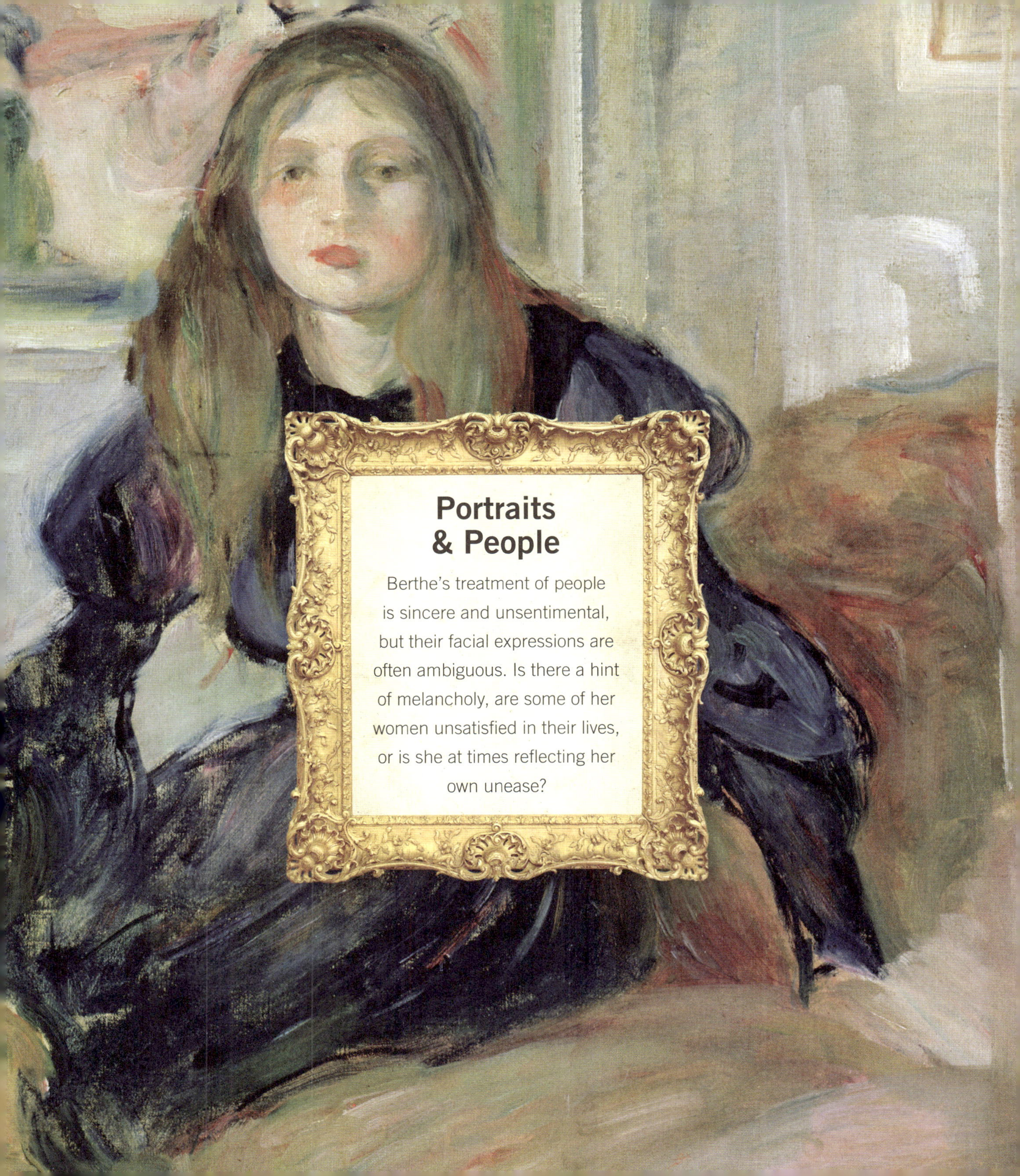

Portraits & People

Berthe's treatment of people is sincere and unsentimental, but their facial expressions are often ambiguous. Is there a hint of melancholy, are some of her women unsatisfied in their lives, or is she at times reflecting her own unease?

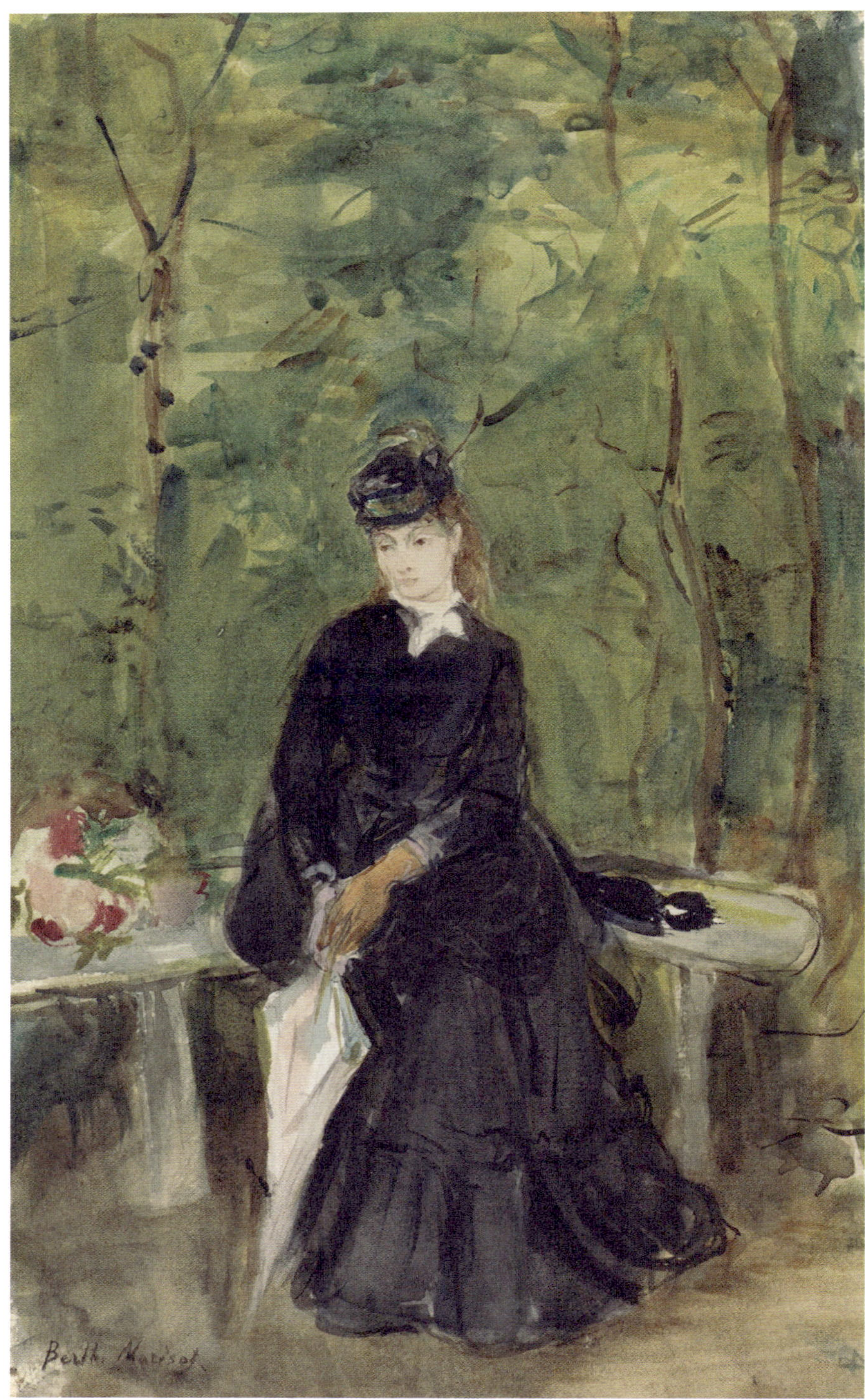

The Artist's Sister Edma Seated in a Park, 1864
Watercolour, 25 x 15 cm (9¾ x 6 in)
• National Gallery of Art, Washington DC

This dark representation of Edma comes from the early days when Berthe's figures were highly influenced by Manet; enveloping her in blue-green vegetation is more of a Berthe trademark. White paper showing through helps to create the pale parasol.

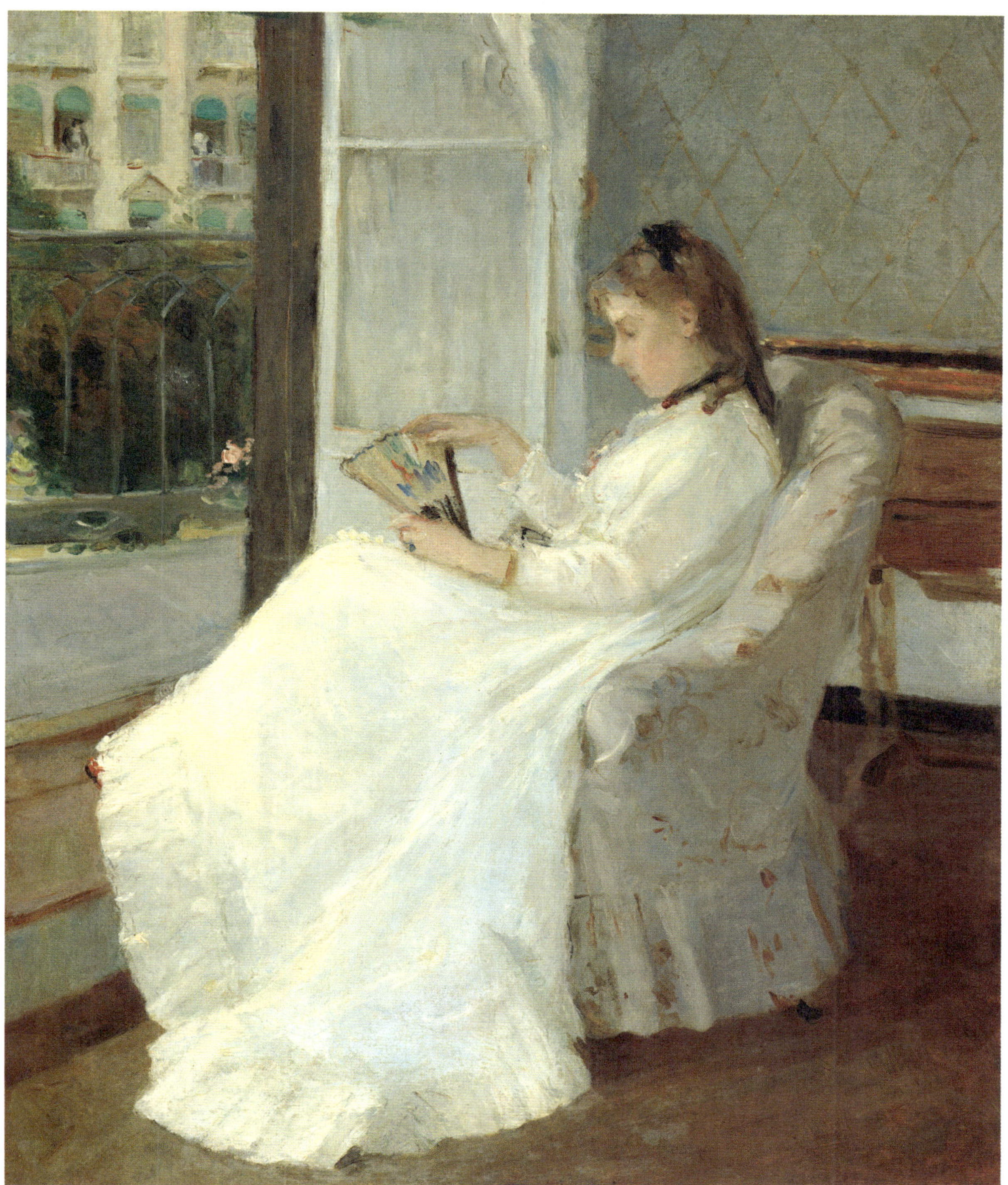

The Artist's Sister at a Window, 1869
Oil on canvas, 54.8 x 46.3 cm (21⅔ x 18¼ in)
• National Gallery of Art, Washington DC

Berthe's depiction of her sister Edma, who became Madame Pontillon in the year it was painted, is dominated by the beautifully luminous pale block of her dress. This and the sideways pose echo the work of Whistler.

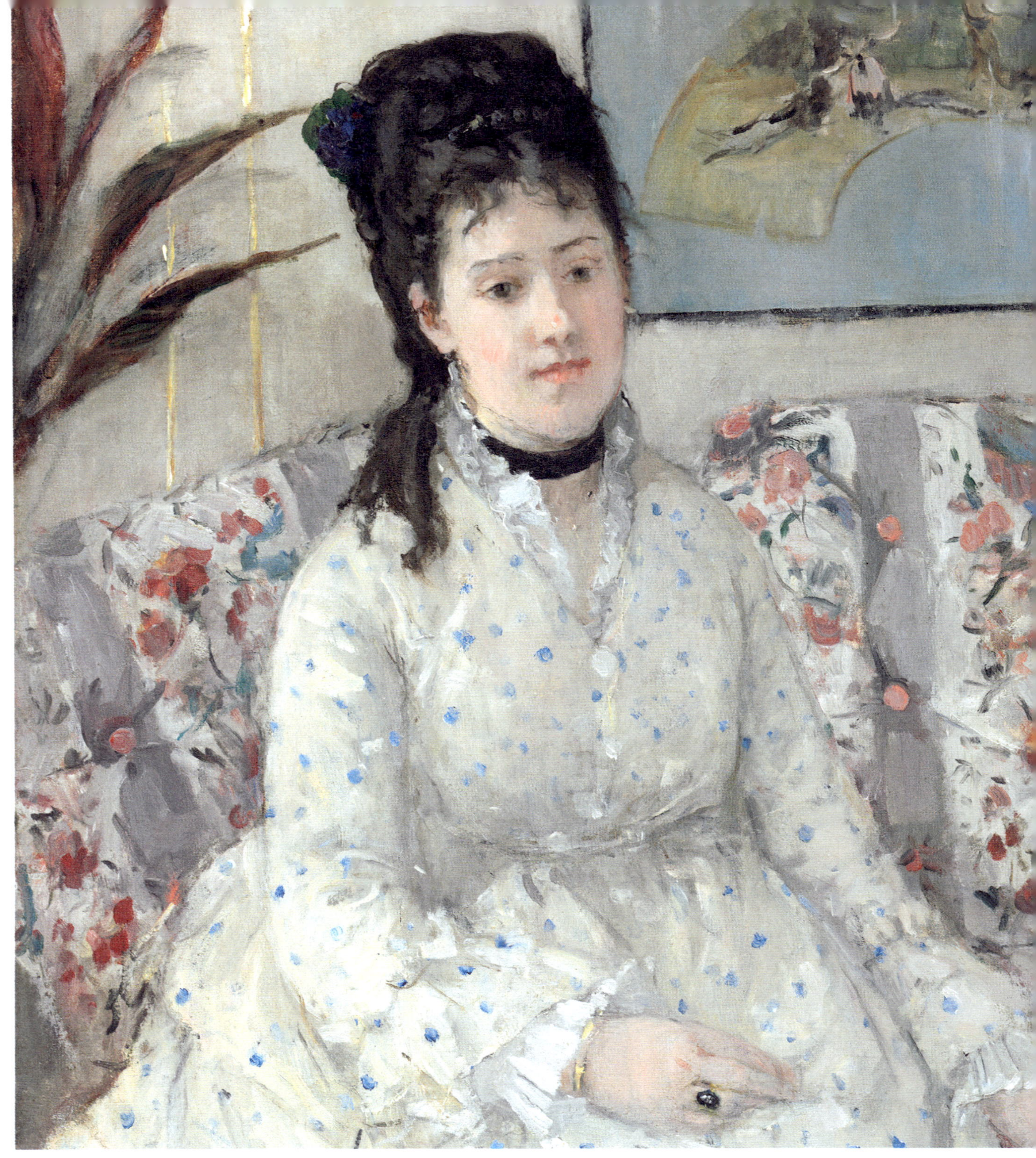

The Sisters (Two Sisters on a Sofa), 1869
Oil on canvas, 52 x 81.3 cm (20½ x 32 in)
• National Gallery of Art, Washington DC

Here both sitters, whose identities are disputed, stare mysteriously in different directions.
Berthe included actual artworks in some pictures: the fan-shaped piece on the wall is Degas'
Spanish Dancers and Musicians (1868–69), a gift to her from the artist.

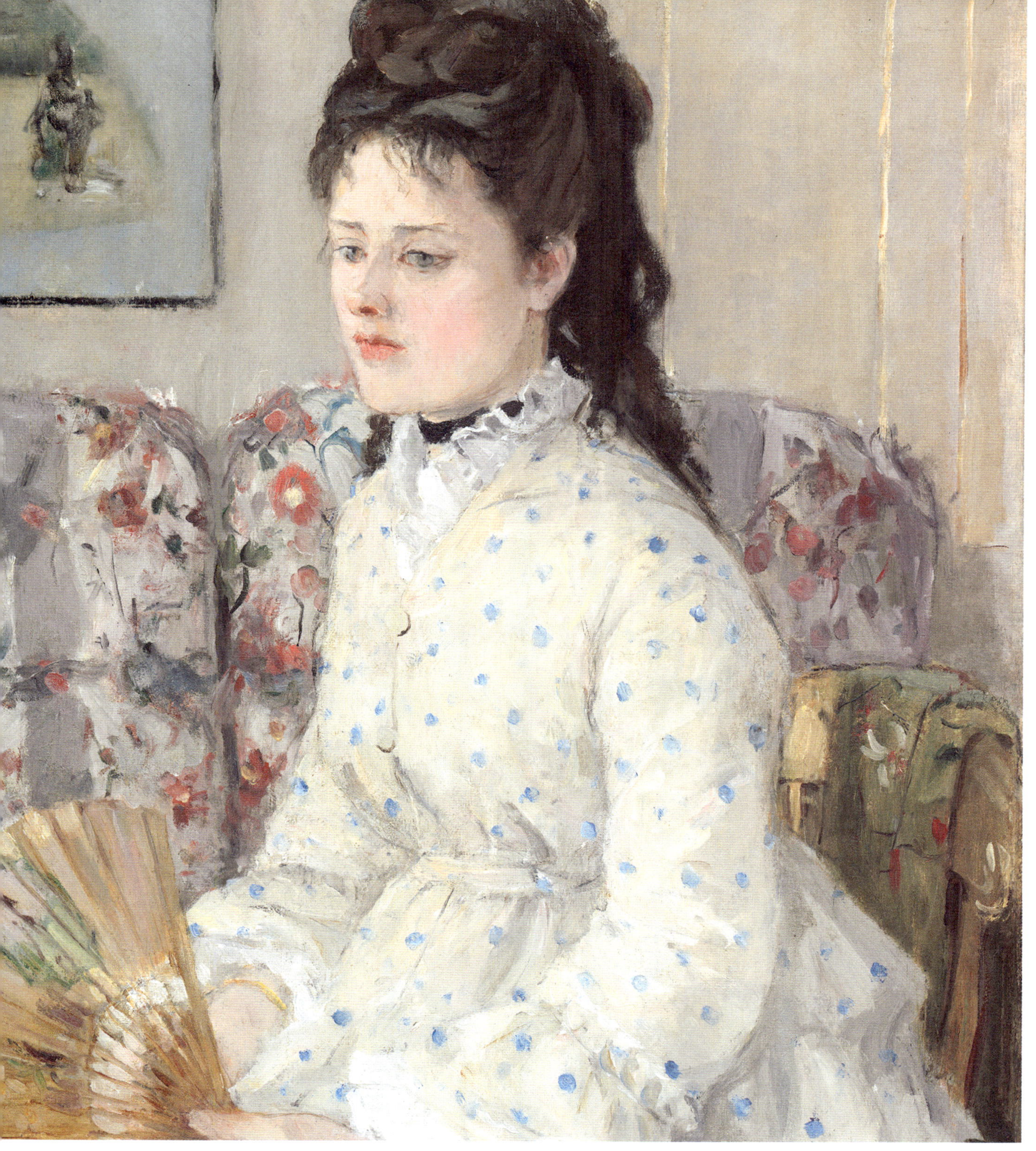

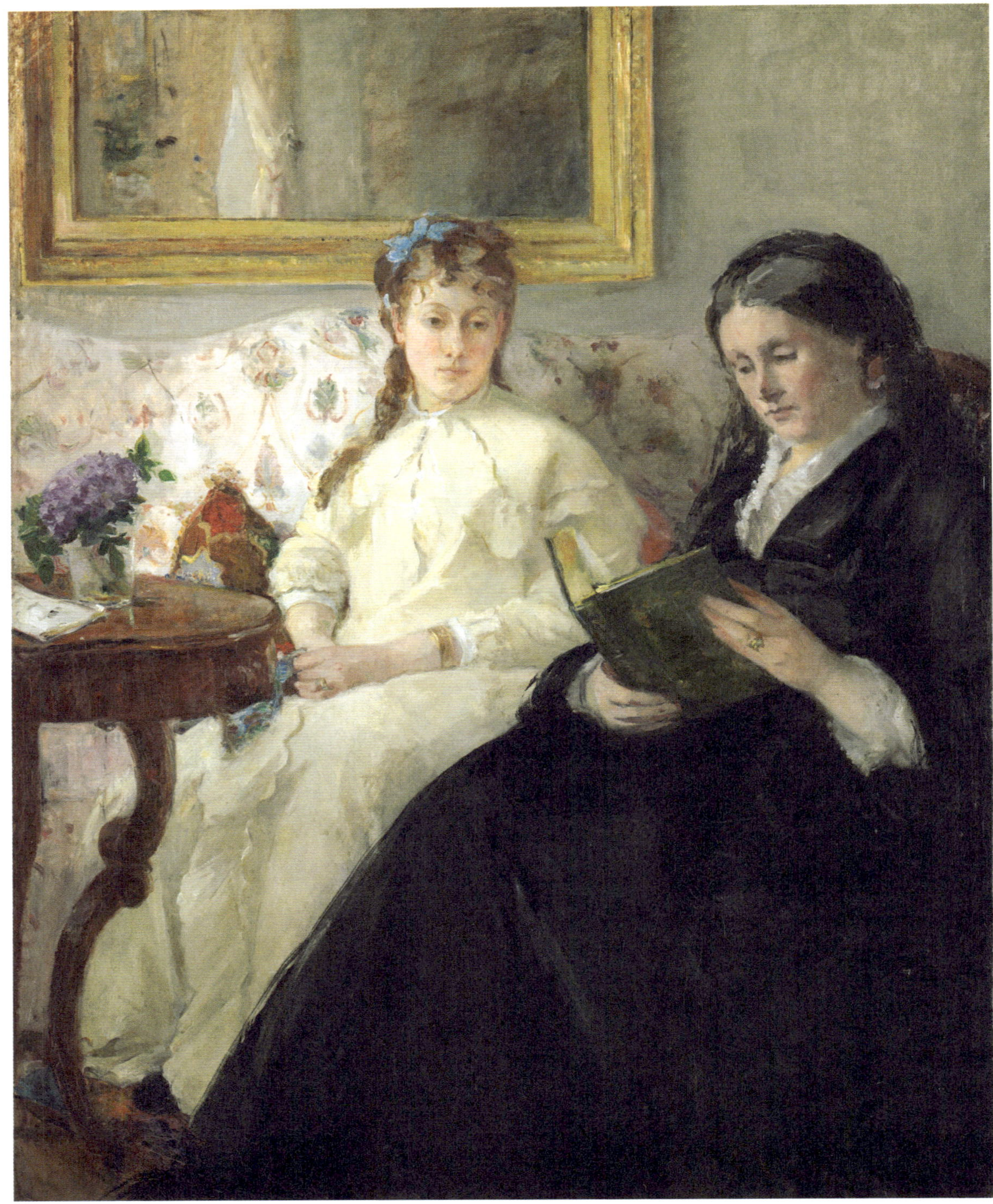

The Mother and Sister of the Artist, 1869–70
Oil on canvas, 101 x 81.8 cm (39¾ x 32³⁄₁₆ in)
• National Gallery of Art, Washington DC

This is among Berthe's biggest canvases. Edma is painted in a more delicate style than that of her mother. Berthe sought Manet's advice on the picture and he undertook considerable repainting work on Madame Morisot.

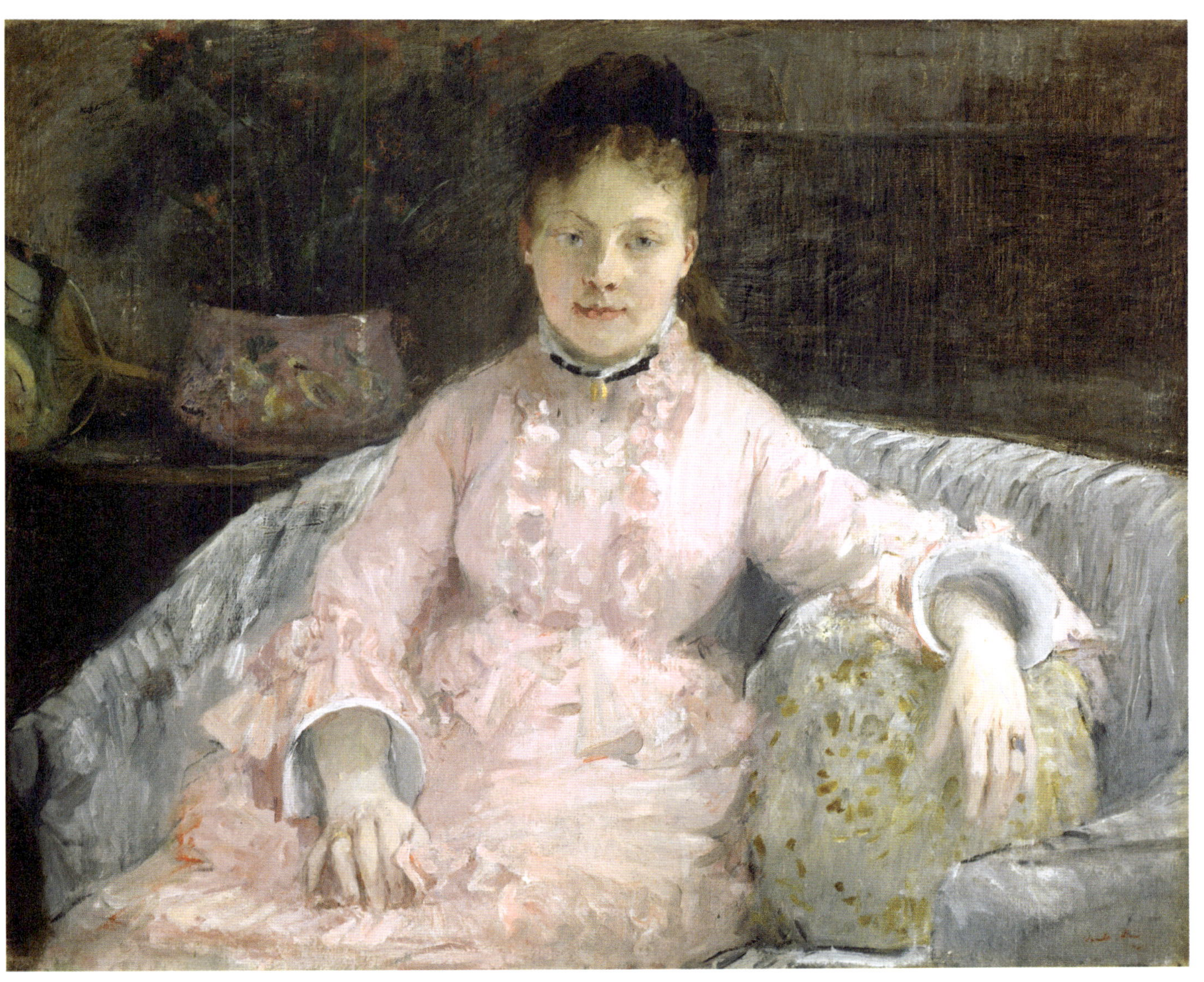

The Pink Dress, *c.* **1870**
Oil on canvas, 54.6 x 67.3 cm (21½ x 26½ in)
• The Metropolitan Museum of Art, New York

One of few works to survive from Berthe's early career, this depicts a teenaged Albertie-Marguerite Carré, later Madame Ferdinand-Henri Himmes. Never satisfied, Berthe repeatedly painted over a session's work on the picture, and so multiple sittings were needed.

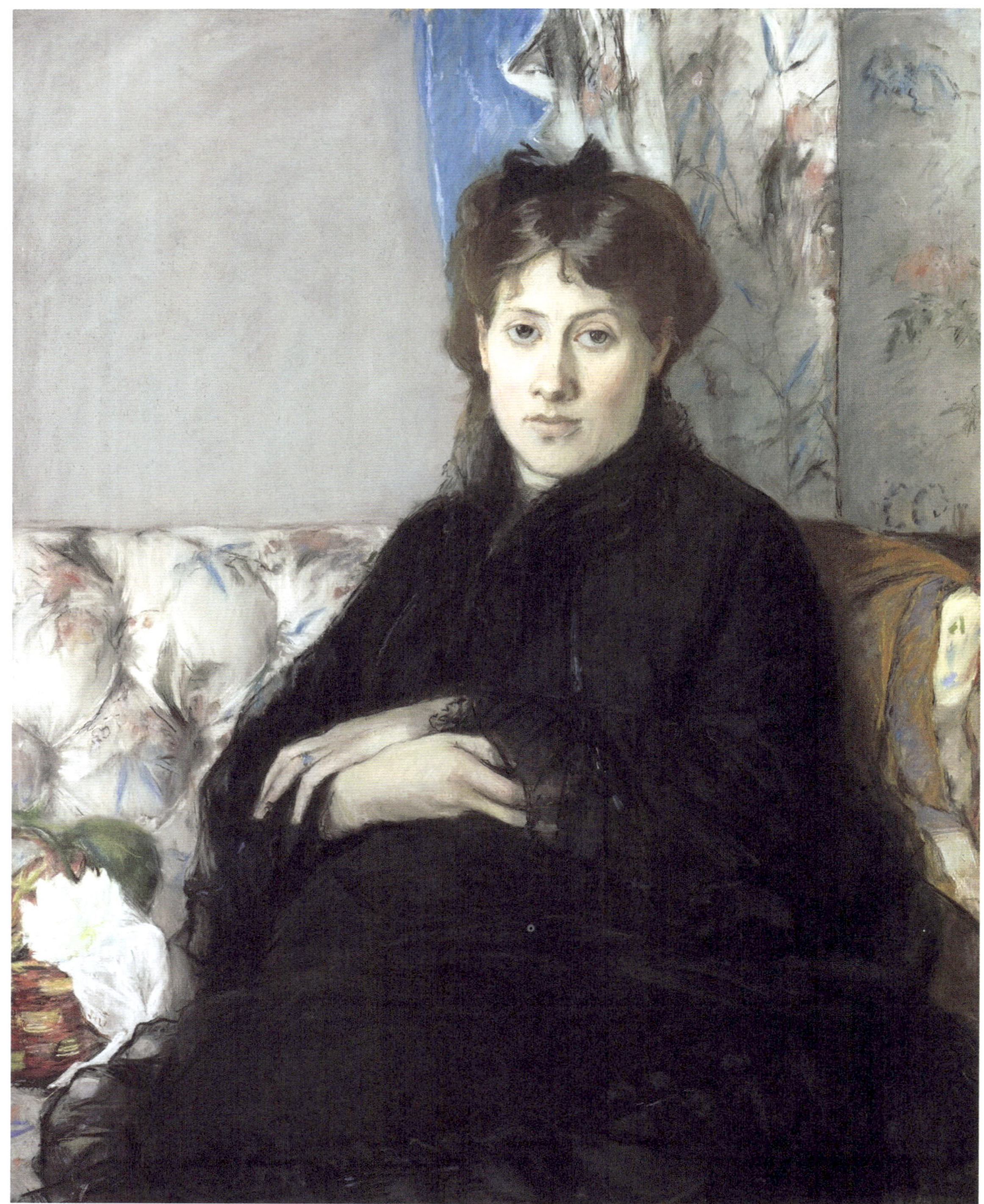

Portrait of Madame Edma Pontillon, 1871
Pastel on paper, 81.5 x 65.8 cm (32 x 26 in) • Musée d'Orsay, Paris

Edma's well-defined facial features and strong gaze, skin tones and black solidity owe much to Manet. The composition is an interplay of shapes; a bright blue central area draws viewers in while stretches of decorative soft furnishing suggest *Japonisme*.

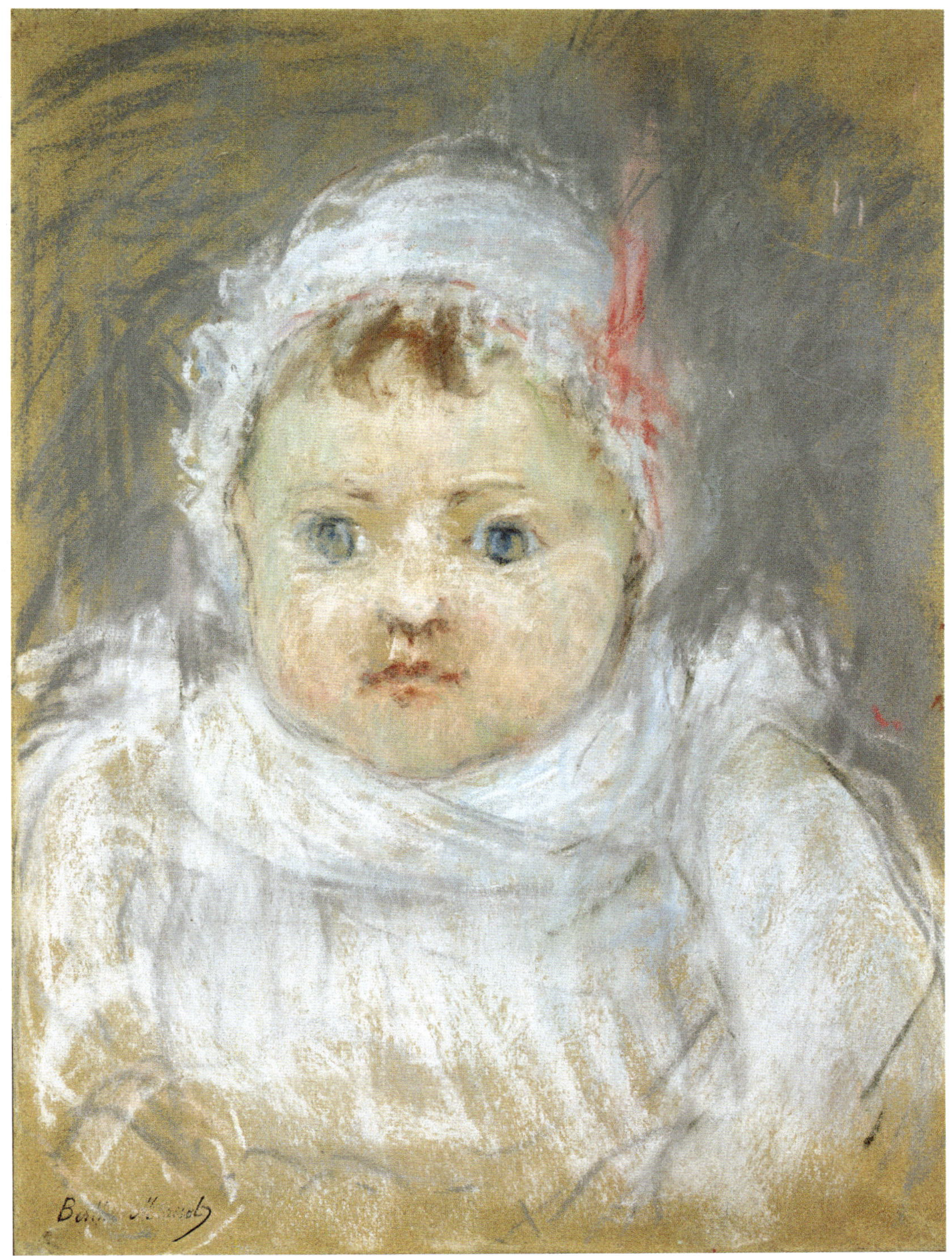

Blanche Pontillon as a Baby, 1872
Pastel on paper, 33 x 24.5 cm (13 x 9⅔ in) • Private Collection

Edma's daughter Blanche is shown here with pastels that perfectly capture the soft bloom of her cheeks. She looks sweet but with a distinctive personality. Blanche also modelled for the baby in *The Cradle* (1872, *see* page 30).

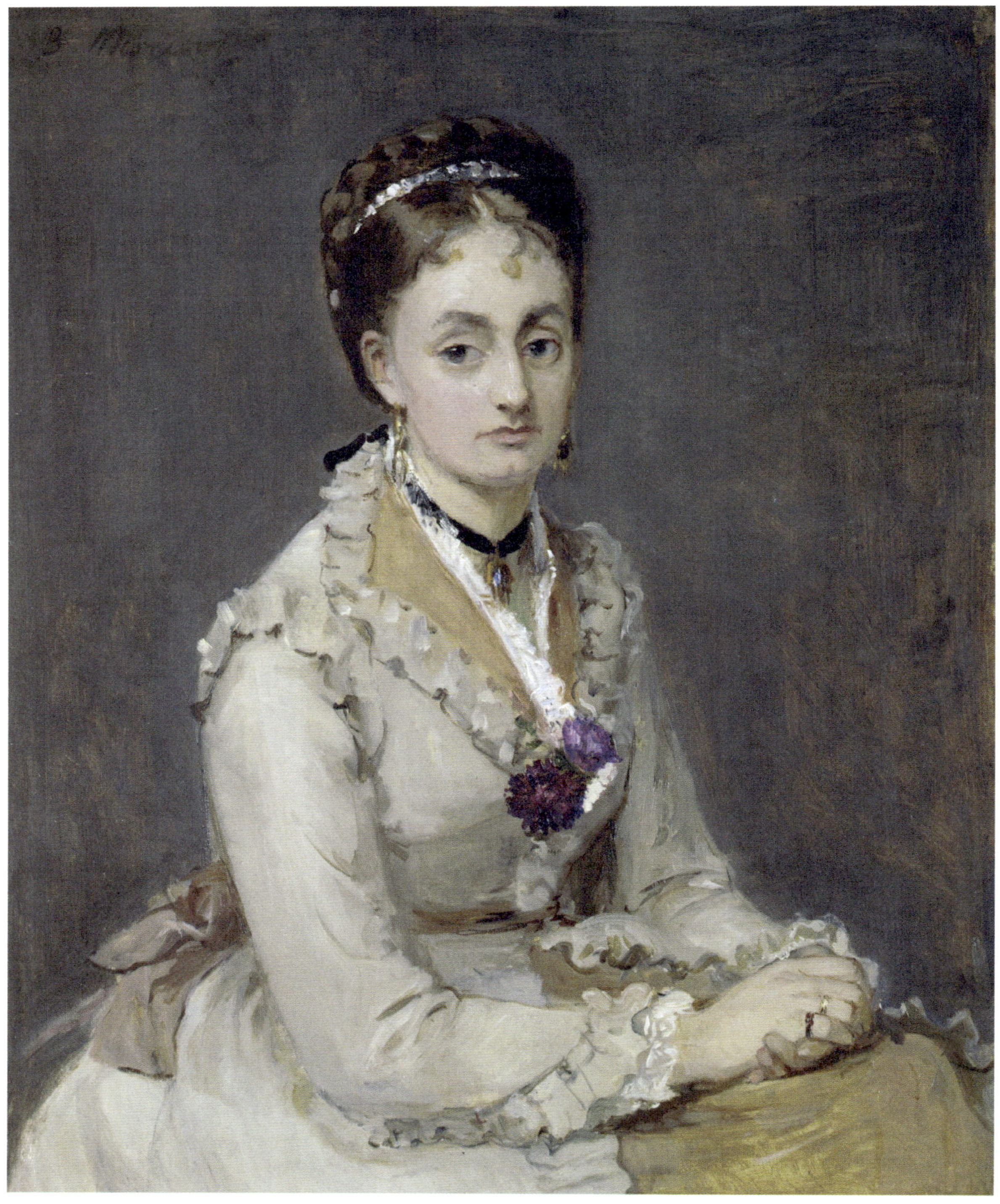

Portrait of a Woman, 1872–75
Oil on canvas, 56 x 46 cm (22 x 18 in)
• The Courtauld Gallery, London

In many ways this is a fairly conventional Salon-style portrait (probably of Edma). However, the facial expression is less idealized than many traditional portraits of the day and the mood is rather hard to gauge, as with so many works by Berthe.

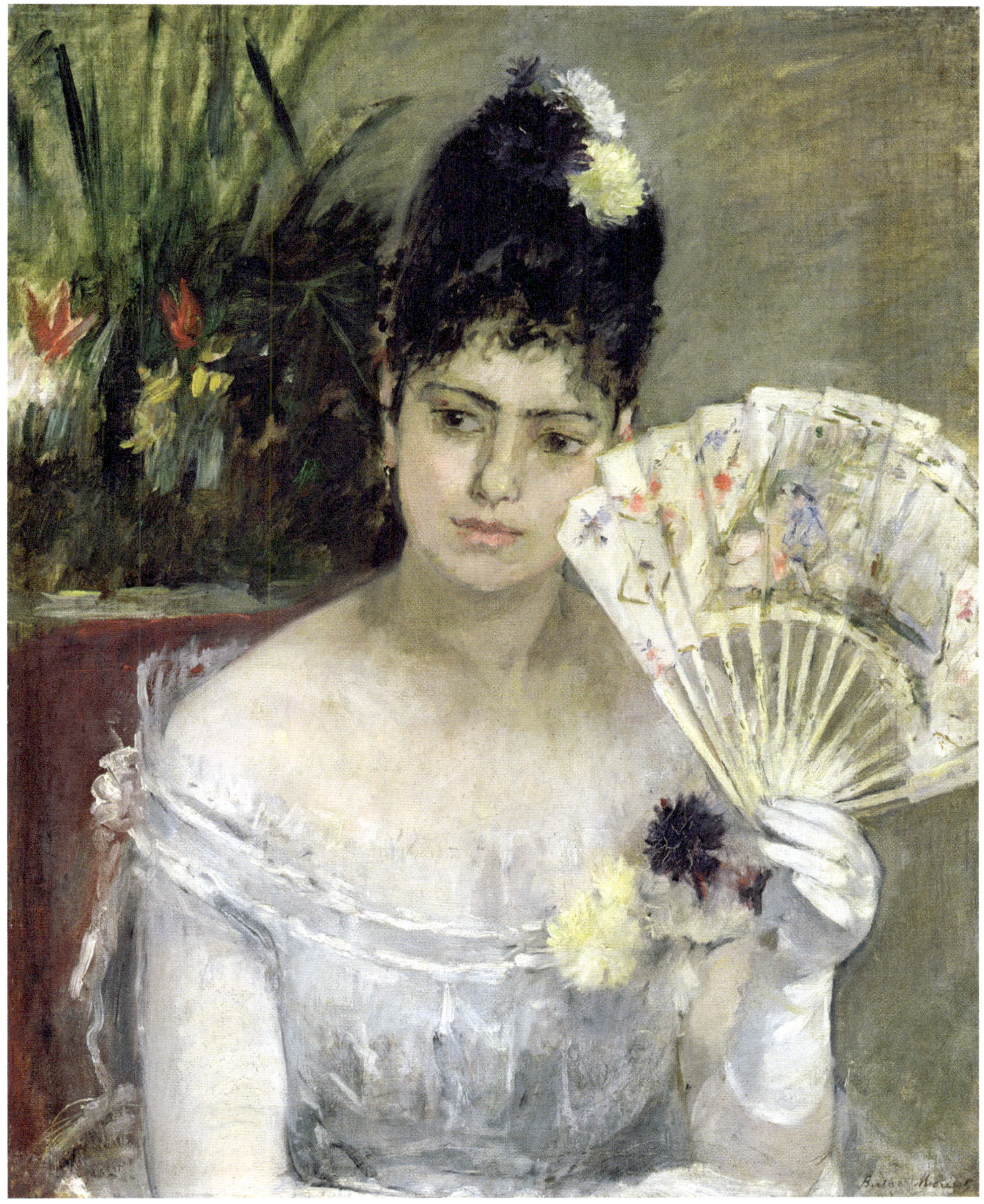

At the Ball, 1875

Oil on canvas, 62 x 52 cm (24½ in x 20½ in)

• Musée Marmottan Monet, Paris

It is not known who modelled for this portrait. The brushwork here is quite bold, but the splashes of colour and frivolous air have a Rococo feel; Berthe may have been descended from the leading French Rococo artist Jean-Honoré Fragonard.

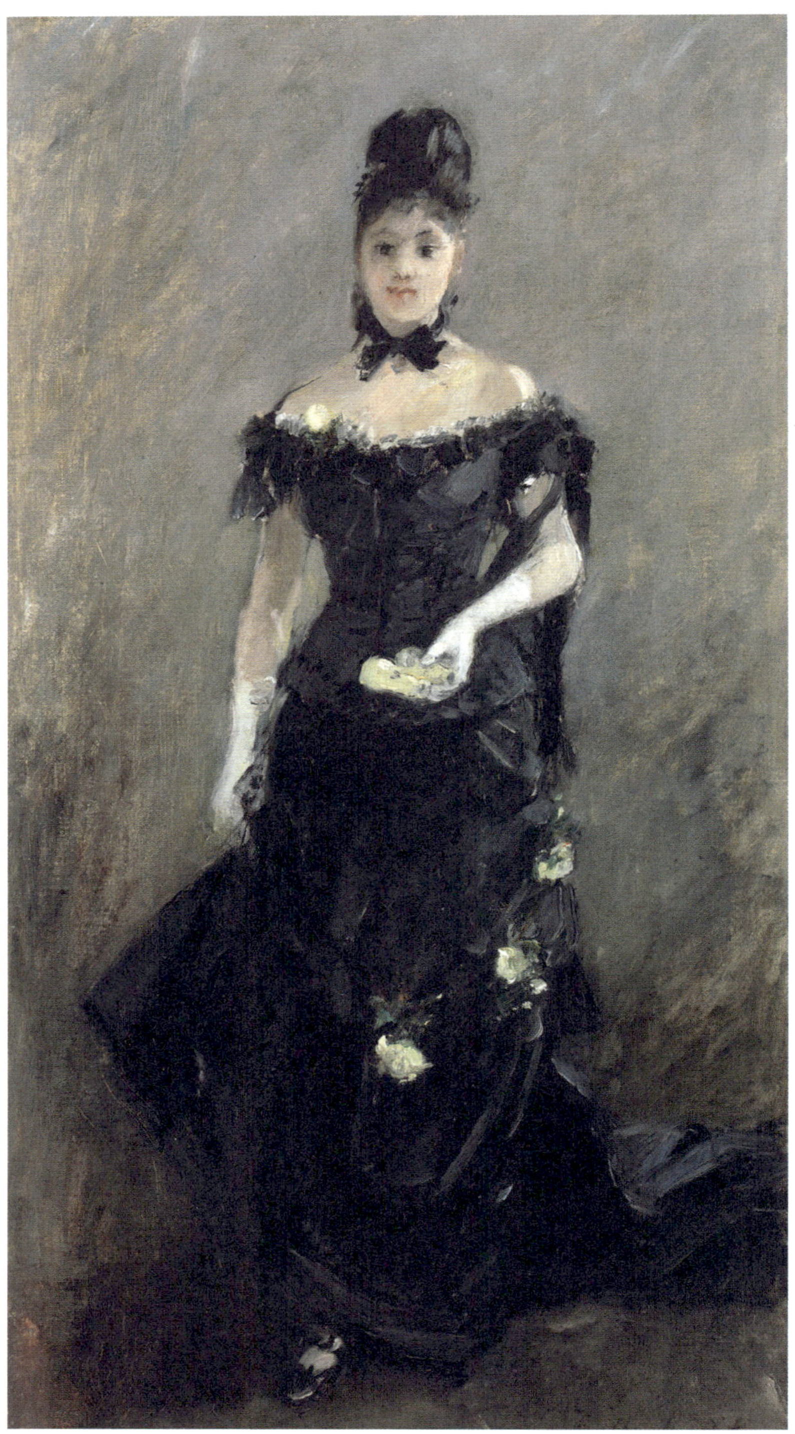

Woman in Black (Before the Theatre), 1875
Oil on canvas, 57.3 x 30.7 cm (22½ x 12 in)
• The National Museum of Western Art, Tokyo

One of few full-length portraits by Berthe, this has more than a dash of Manet about it. She has given it an irresistible brio that instantly communicates that this is a stylish modern Parisian woman about town.

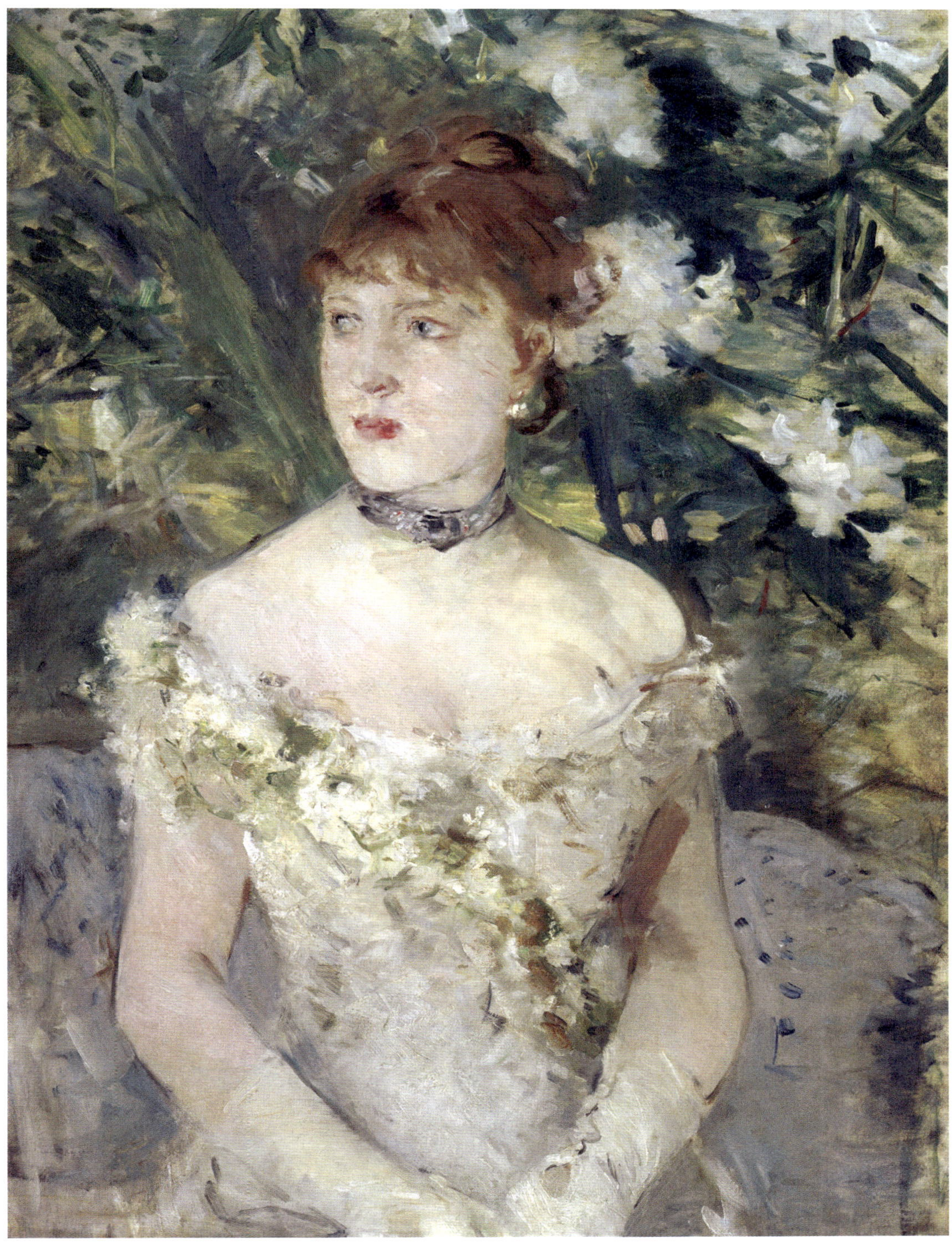

Young Woman in a Ball Gown, 1879
Oil on canvas, 71 x 54 cm (27 x 21¼ in) • Musée d'Orsay, Paris

This is a skilled essay in tonal harmonies. So different to the kind of formal portrait that traditionally found success at the Paris Salon, this appears free and spontaneous, with the delicate flowers of the woman's surroundings echoed on her dress.

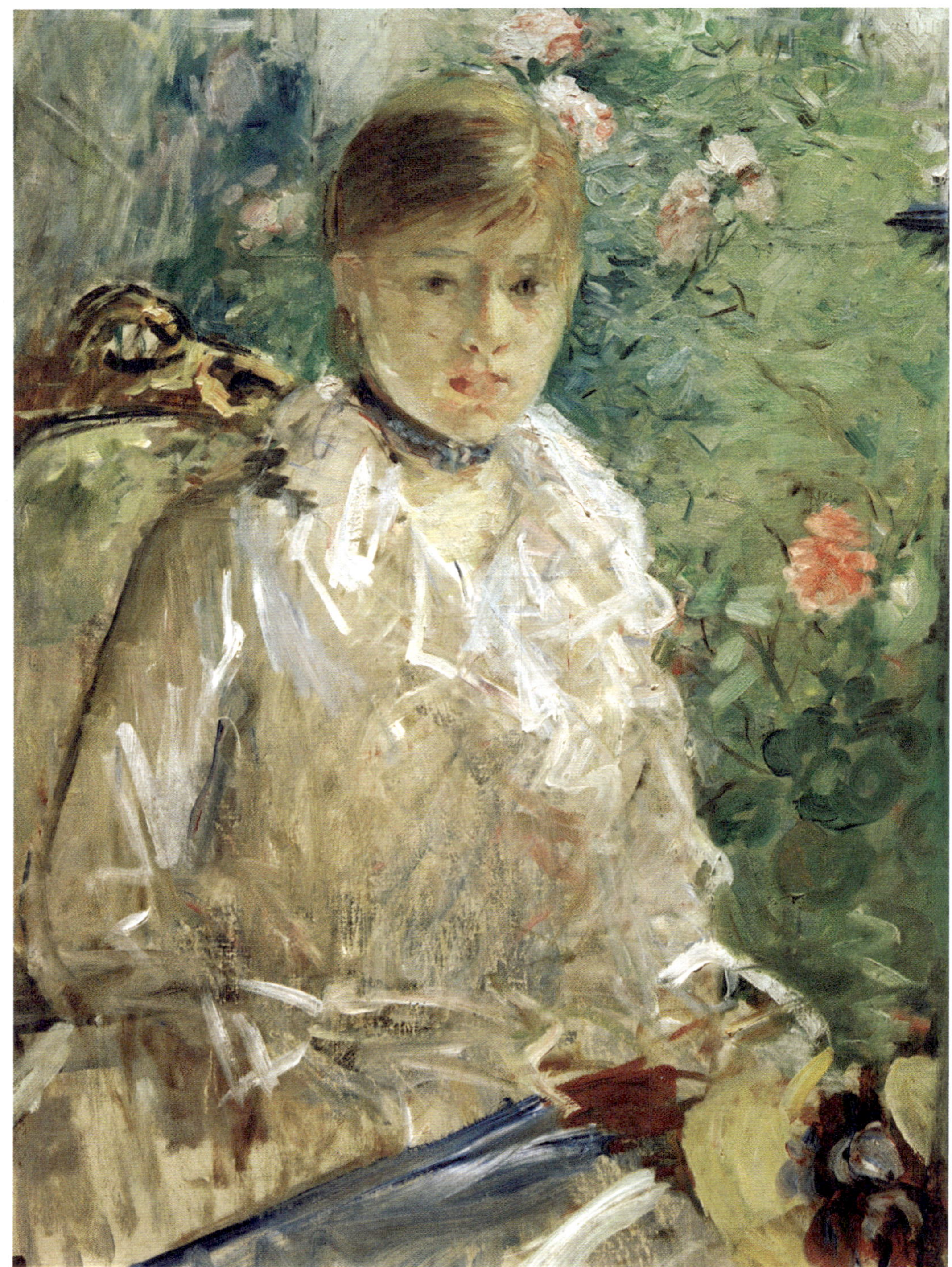

Summer, 1879

Oil on canvas, 76 x 61 cm (30 x 24 in) • Musée Fabre, Montpellier

Representing the seasons as women was an established Rococo tradition (*see* also *Winter*, opposite). Figure and surroundings join in a beautiful pattern here, rather like a decorative Japanese screen, while the base of the image dissolves into abstraction.

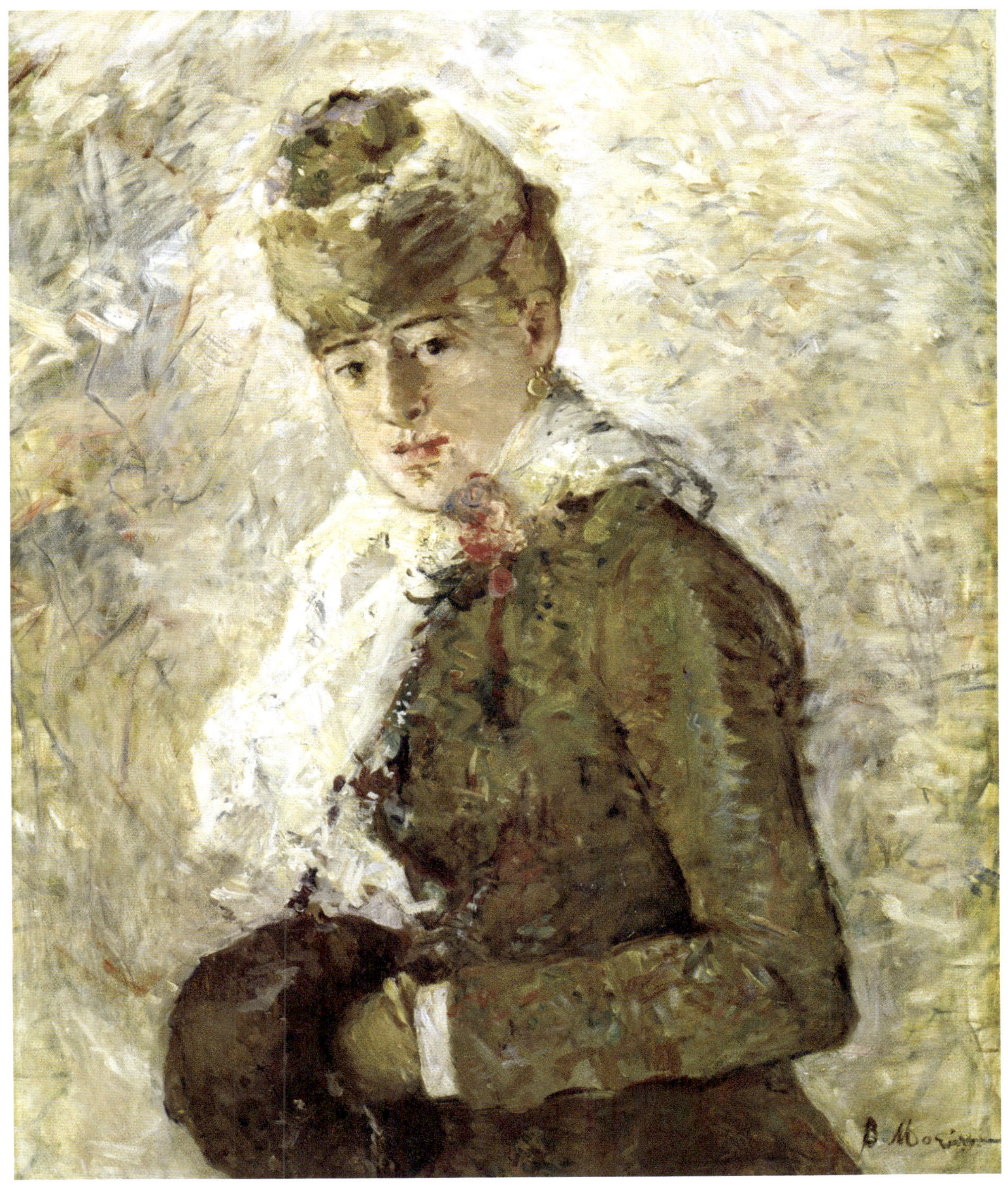

Winter, 1880
Oil on canvas, 75 × 61.6 cm (29½ × 24¼ in)
• Dallas Museum of Art, Texas

This image, whose model is unknown, is a counterpart to *Summer* (*see* opposite). Berthe's energetic flurry of varied strokes and dabs, where costume and snowy background mirror each other, create a clever visual blending of many different colours.

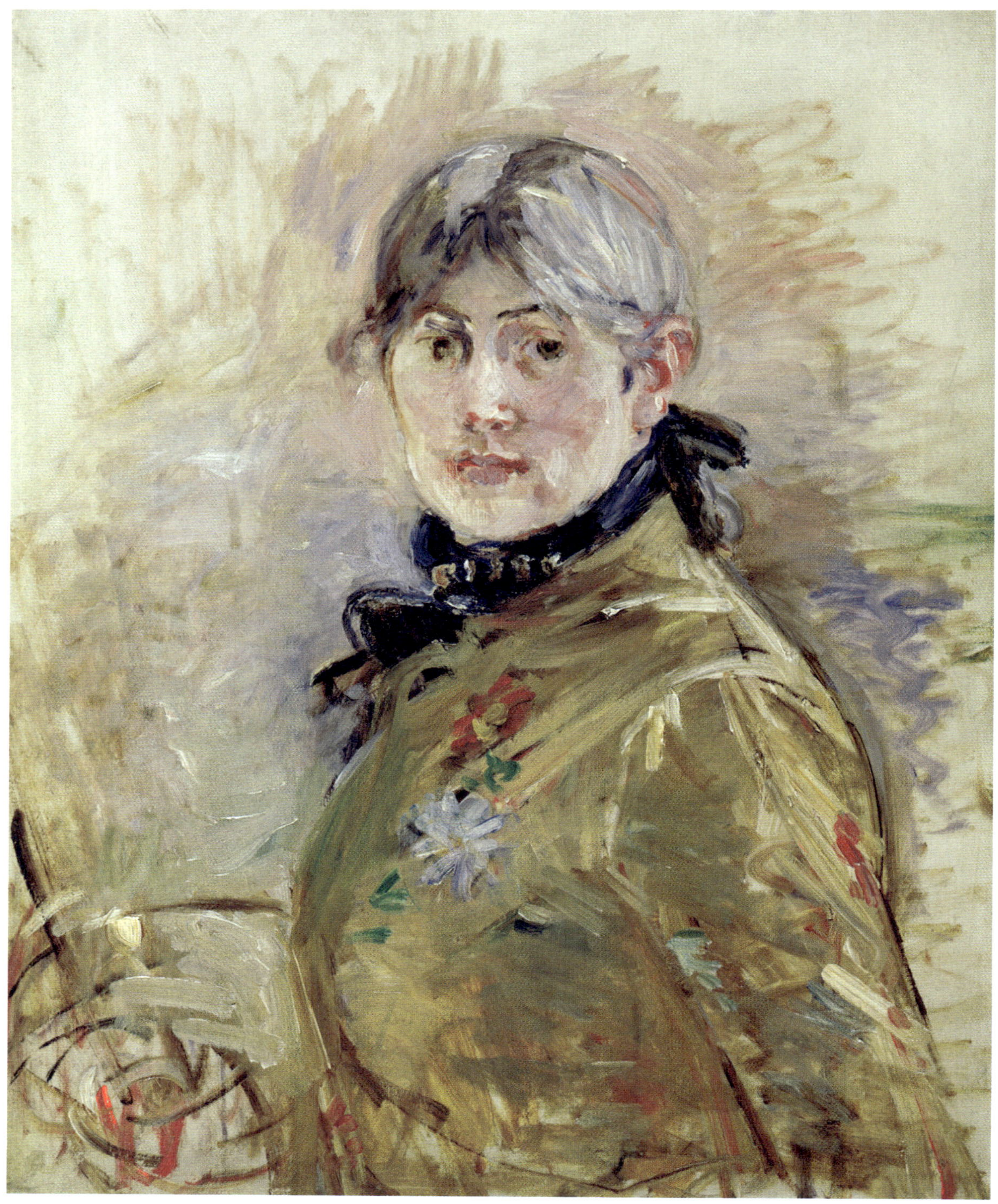

Self-Portrait, 1885
Oil on canvas, 61 x 50 cm (24 x 19¾ in)
• Musée Marmottan Monet, Paris

Here Berthe aligns herself with her male colleagues by creating a traditional artist's self-portrait: an upper-body view where she turns to look confidently towards the viewer, the tools of her trade – brush and palette – in her hand.

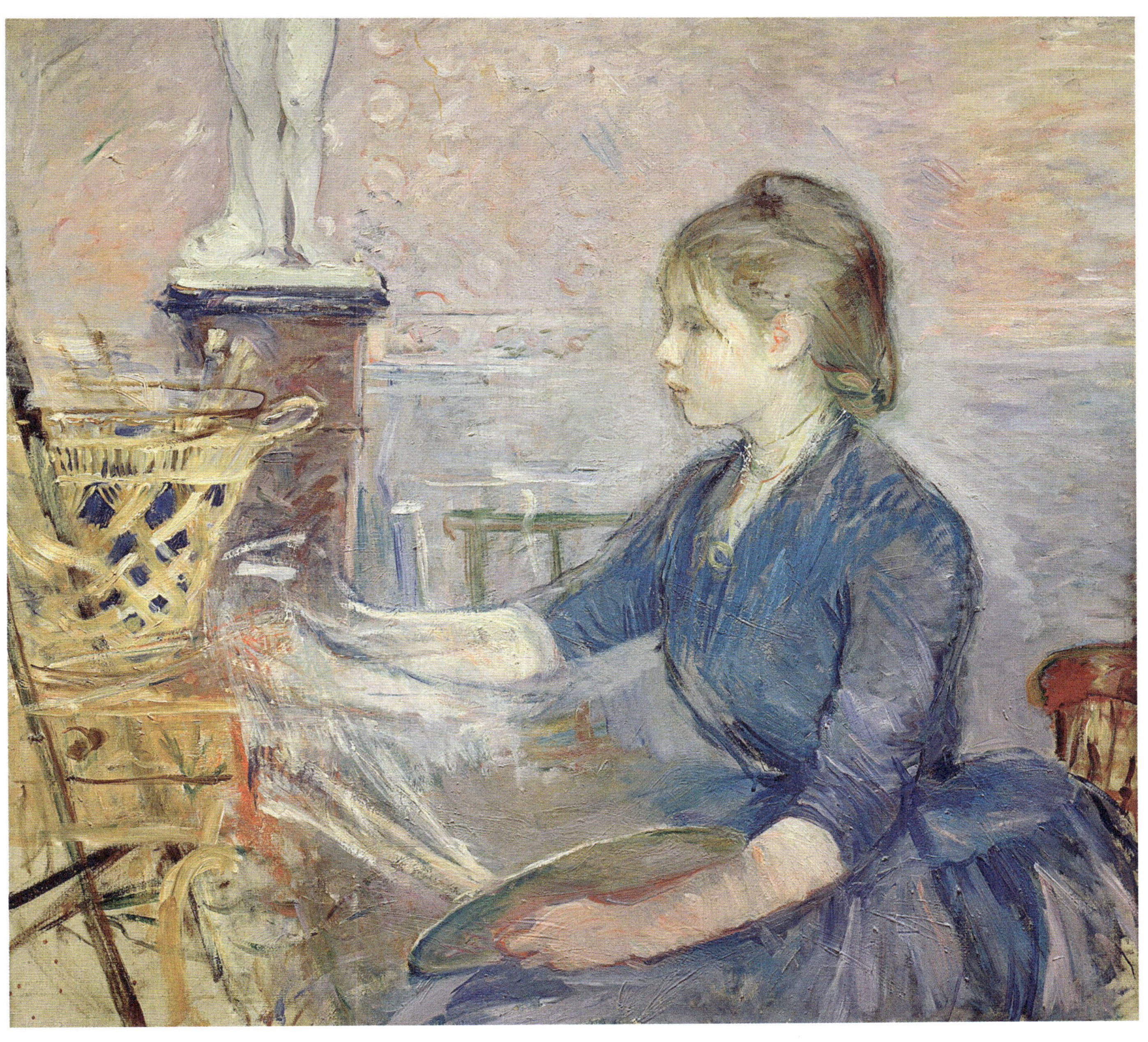

Paule Gobillard Painting, 1887
Oil on canvas, 86 x 94 cm (33¾ x 37 in)
• Musée Marmottan Monet, Paris

Berthe's eldest niece, Paule, was a keen painter. The 20-year-old modelled for this picture in Berthe's salon at Rue de Villejust. It probably marks her achievement in 1886 of gaining her own official permit to work as a Louvre copyist.

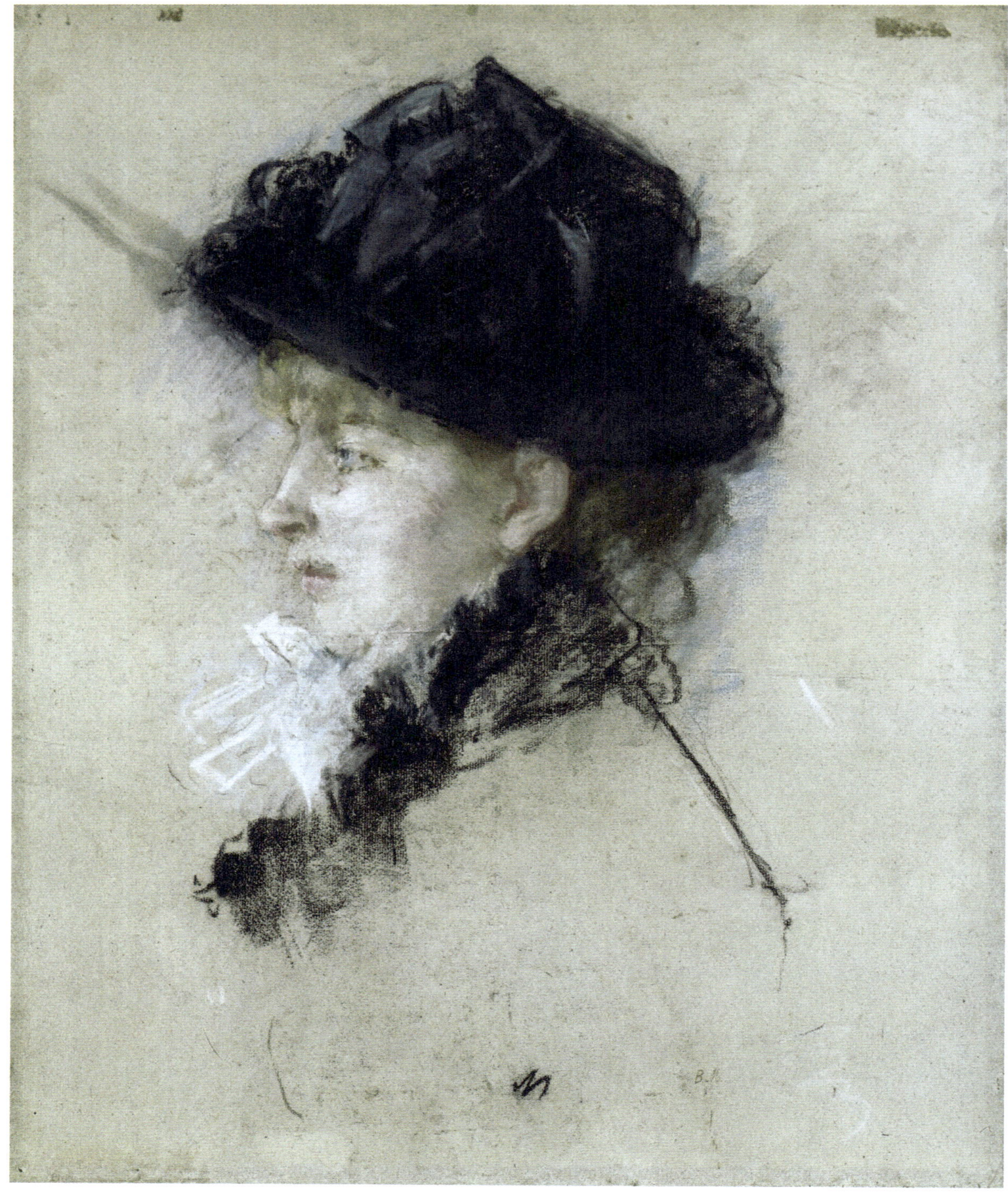

Mlle Louise Riesener, 1888
Charcoal and pastel on paper, 56 x 47 cm (22 x 18½ in)
• The Cleveland Museum of Art, Ohio

This stunning work is indebted to Manet's spontaneous pastel portraits. Using a limited palette, Berthe brings her friend Louise alive with subtle modelling and modulated colouring on the face and velvety rich blacks in her hat.

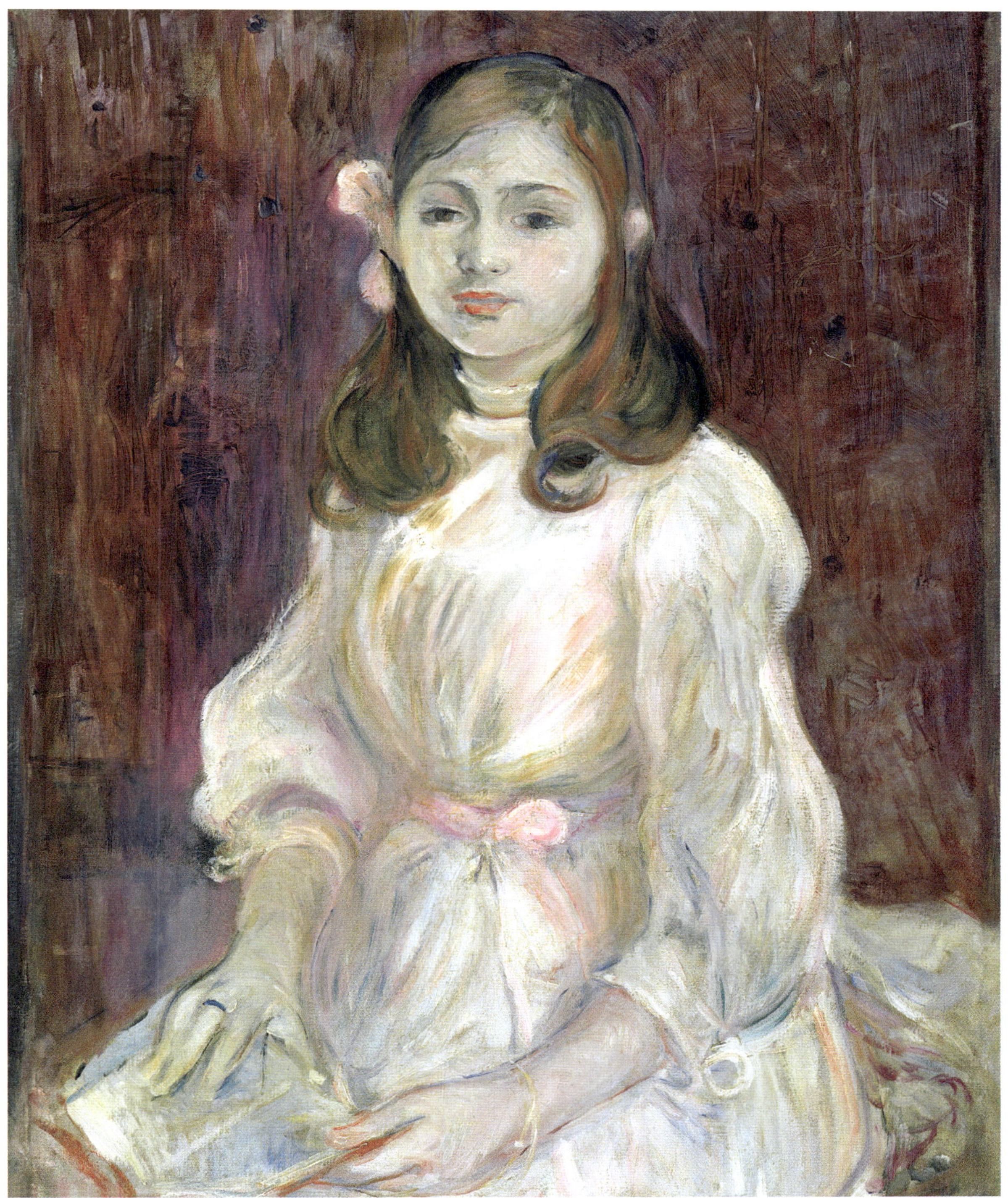

Portrait of Julie Manet Holding a Book, 1889
Oil on canvas, 65 x 54 cm (25⅔ x 21¼ in) • Private Collection

This portrait shows the increased fluidity of shape and stroke and the greater definition of figure that marked Berthe's very late work. However, her beautiful way with colour and light are still very much in evidence.

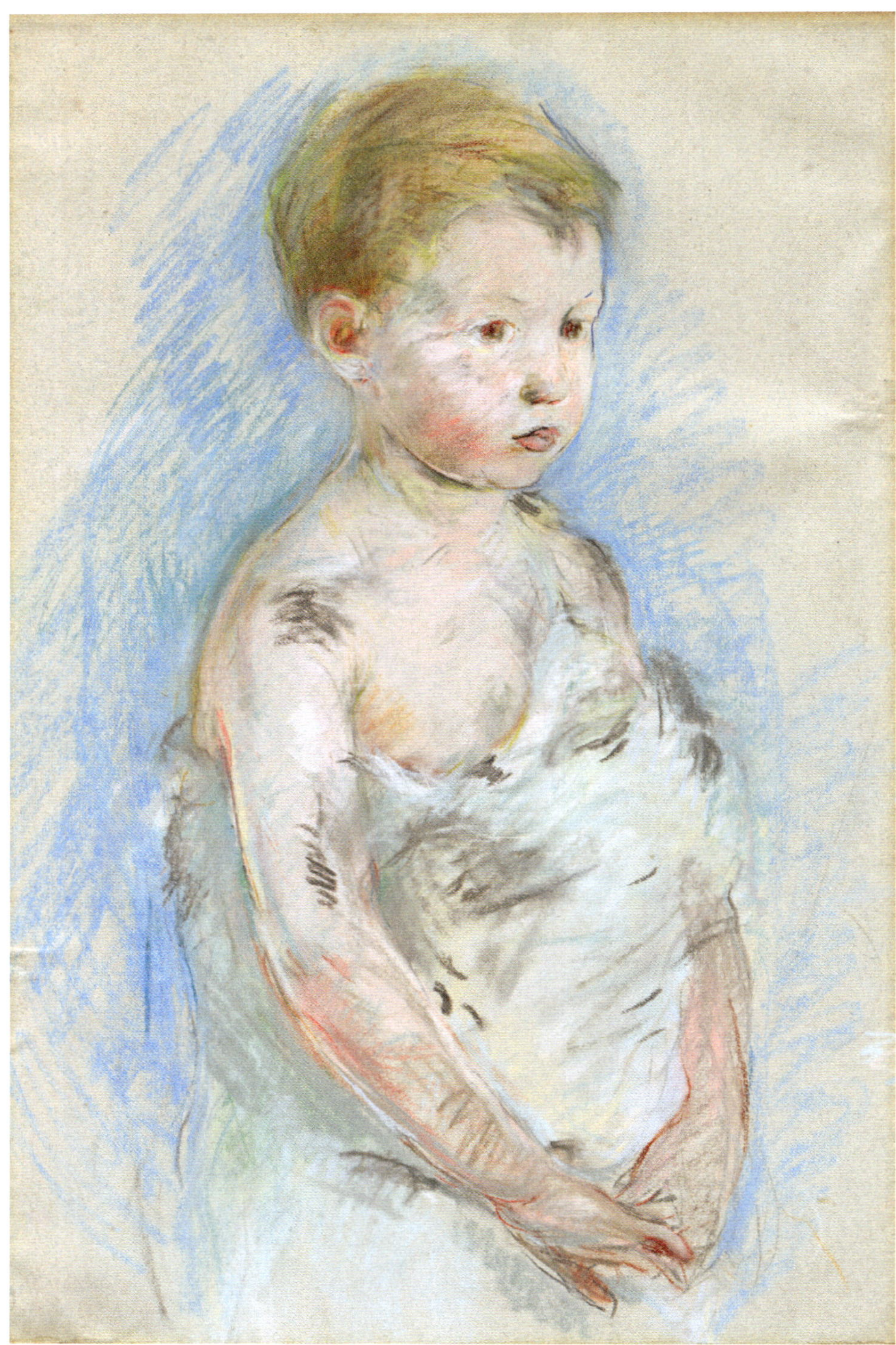

Little Saint John, 1890
Pastel, 58 x 38 cm (22¾ x 15 in)
• The Cleveland Museum of Art, Ohio

This lovely study, for a lost painting, dates from a stay in a rented country house outside Paris at Mézy-sur-Seine. A local boy posed, swathed in a sheepskin, and the pastel was done in the property's barn.

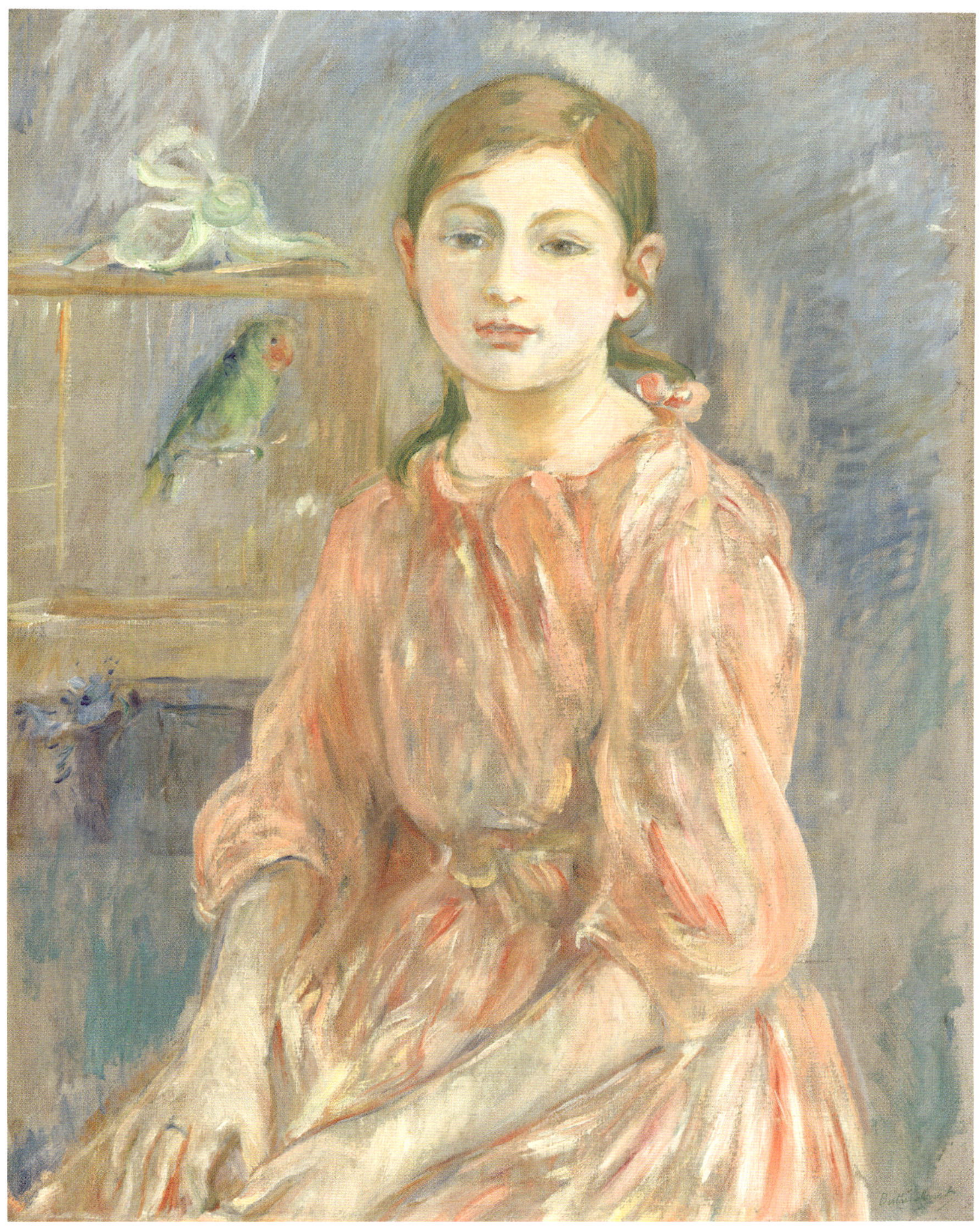

The Artist's Daughter with a Parakeet, 1890
Oil on canvas, 65.6 x 52 cm (25¾ x 20½ in)
• National Gallery of Art, Washington DC

With a similar feel to *Portrait of Julie Manet Holding a Book* (1889, *see* page 97), here fluid strokes create beautifully blended skin tones. The parakeet provides a burst of complementary colour to that of the dress.

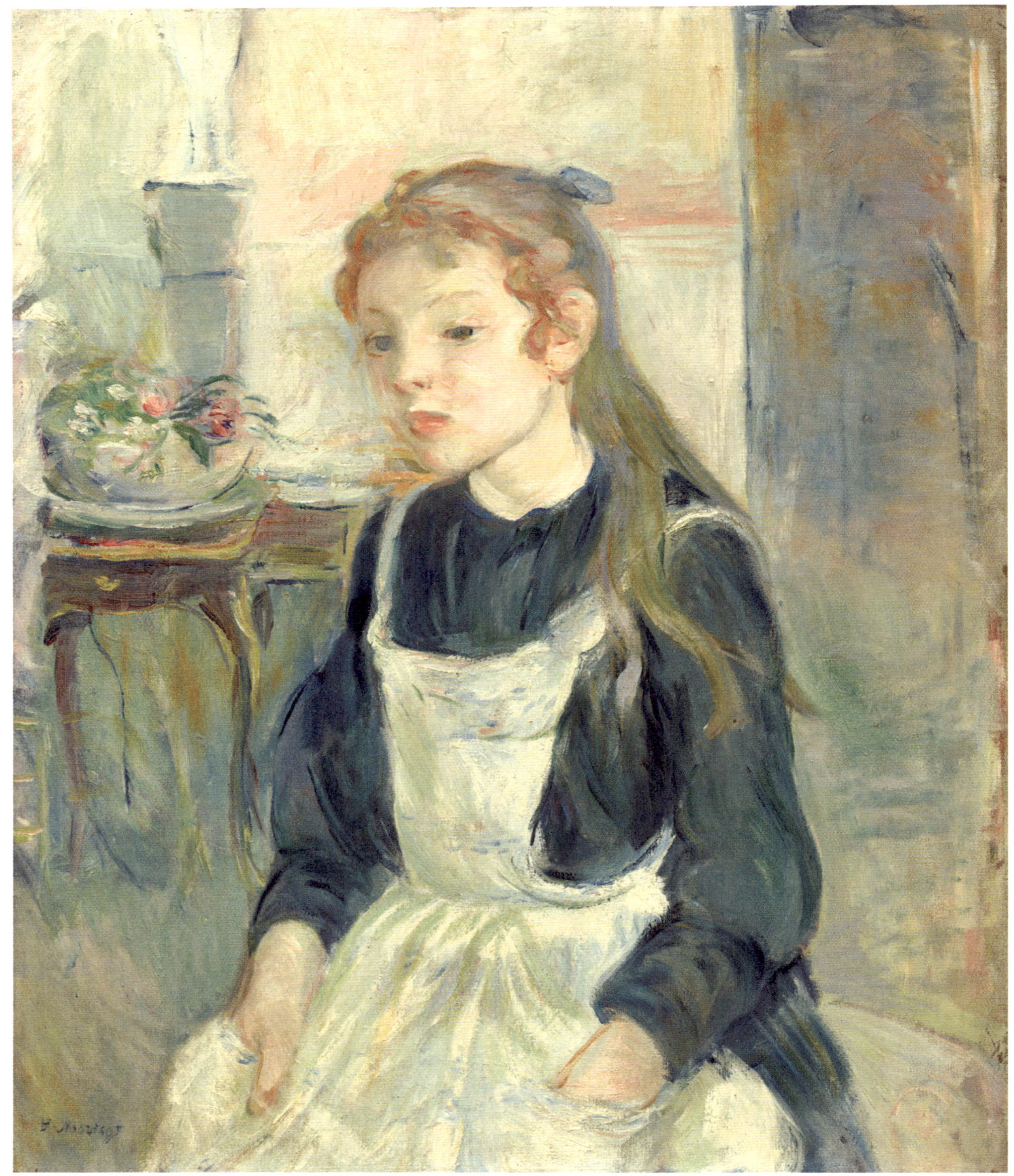

Young Girl with an Apron, 1891
Oil on canvas, 65 x 54.6 cm (25⅔ x 21½ in)
• National Gallery of Art, Washington DC

In this work a girl gazes dreamily – or thoughtfully – into space, as in many of Berthe's pictures. Her environment is an interesting mix: abstract areas of brushwork and colour punctuated by an elegant table supporting a still-life study.

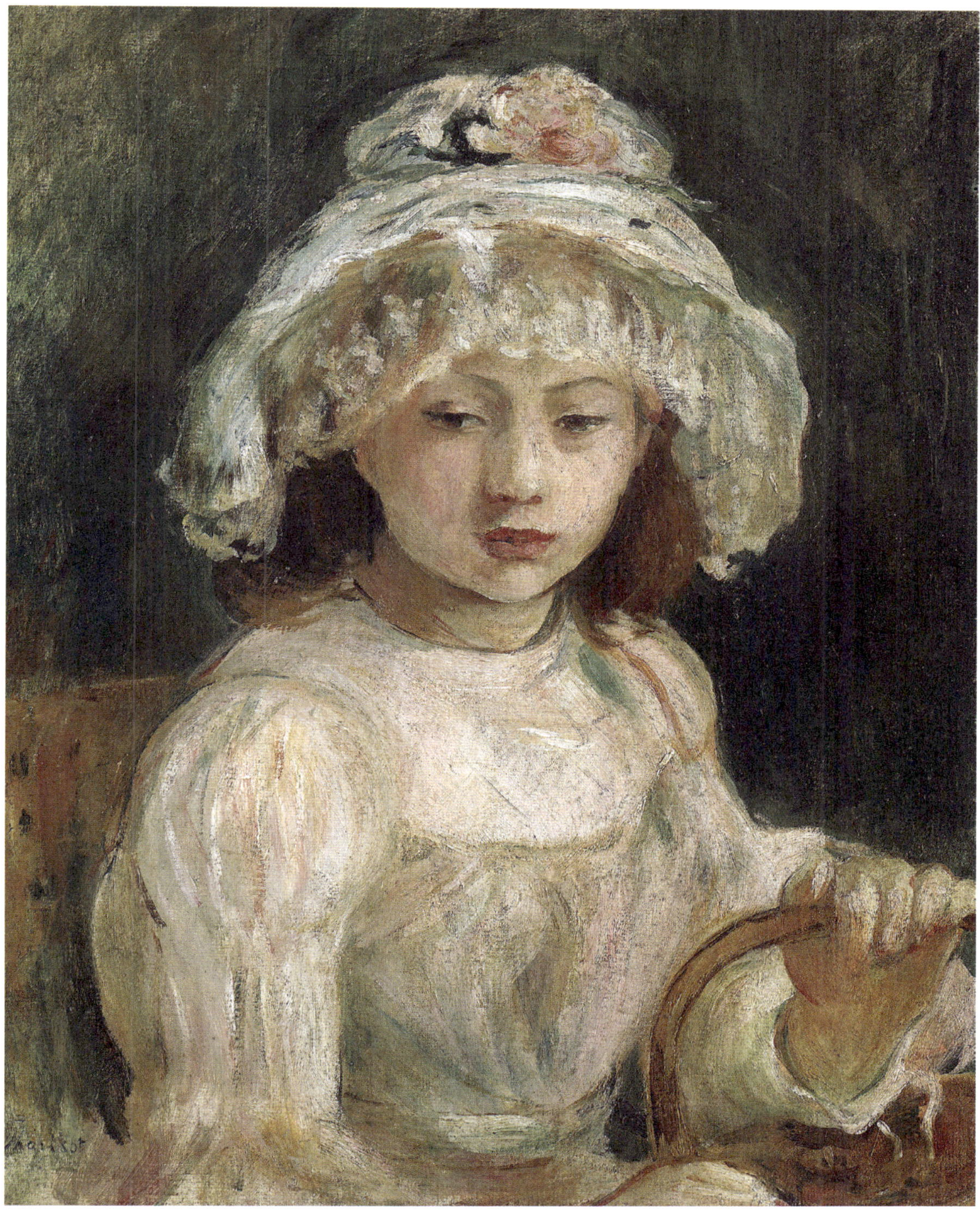

Young Girl with Hat, 1892
Oil on canvas, 56 × 47 cm (22 × 18½ in)
• The Art Institute of Chicago

The pretty pose with basket and hat suggests traditional portraiture. However, the Baroque contrasts of light and shade add a drama perhaps underlined by the girl's expression – does it hint at melancholy?

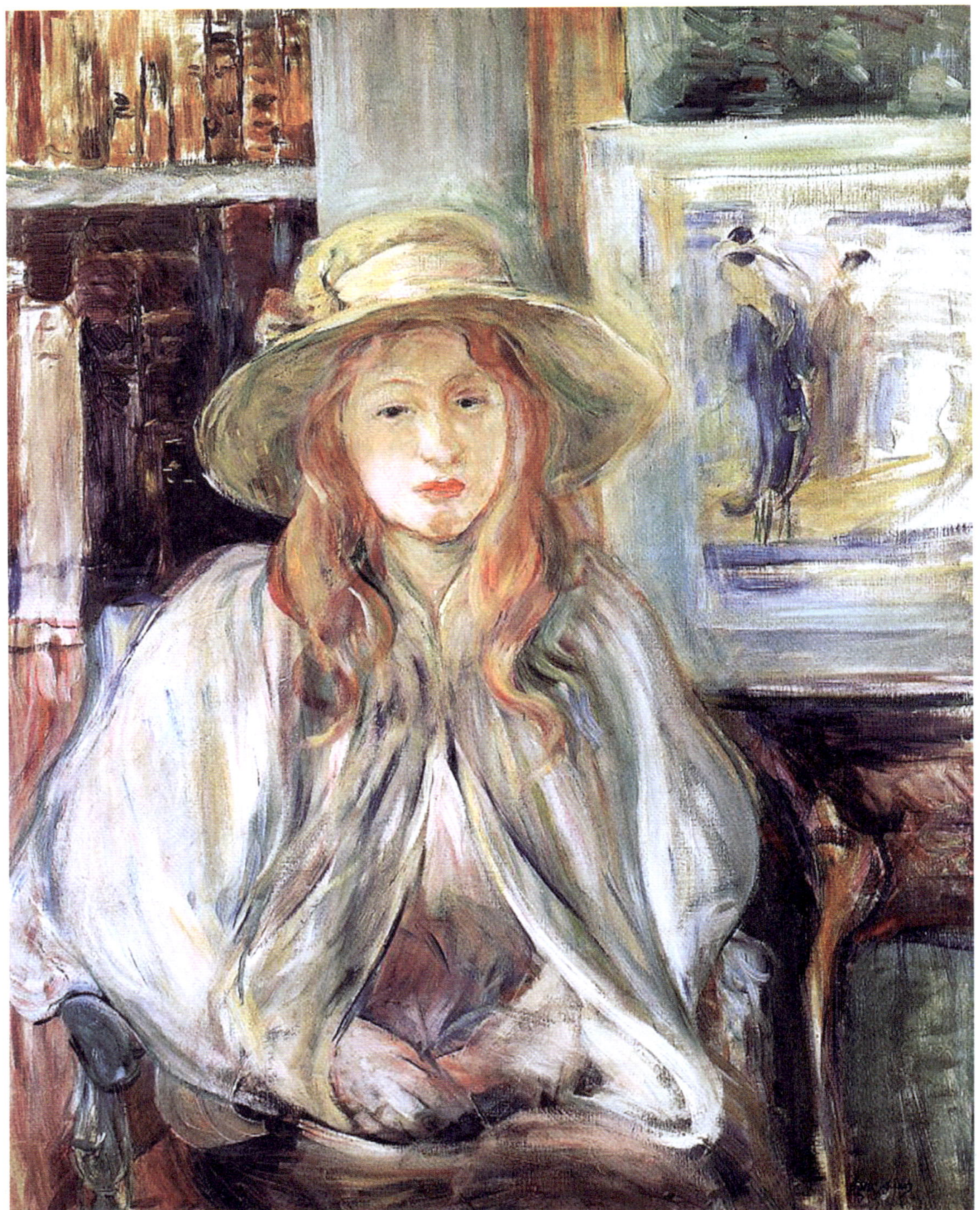

Julie Manet with a Straw Hat, 1892
Oil on canvas, dimensions unknown • Private Collection

This work is not simply a portrait but a study in shape, form and composition. Here the flowing lines of Julie's clothes and hair contrast effectively with the squared-up objects in the room around her.

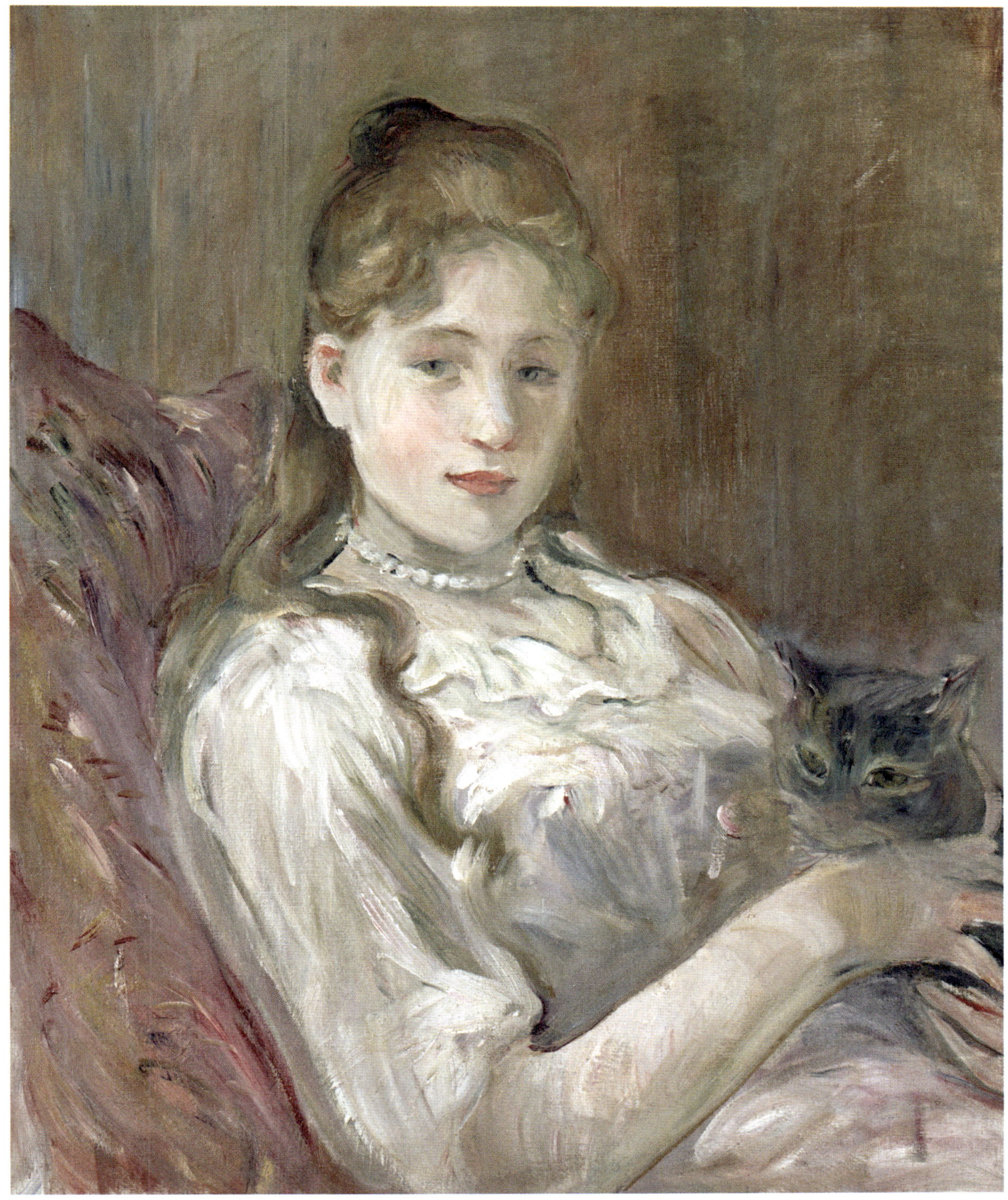

Young Girl with Cat, 1892
Oil on canvas, 55 x 46 cm (21⅔ x 18 in) • Private Collection

Berthe's fluid painting style here matches the relaxed feel of this portrait of professional artists' model Jeanne Fourmanoir. The smiling, some have said sexualized, girl reclines languidly as she holds and strokes her cat.

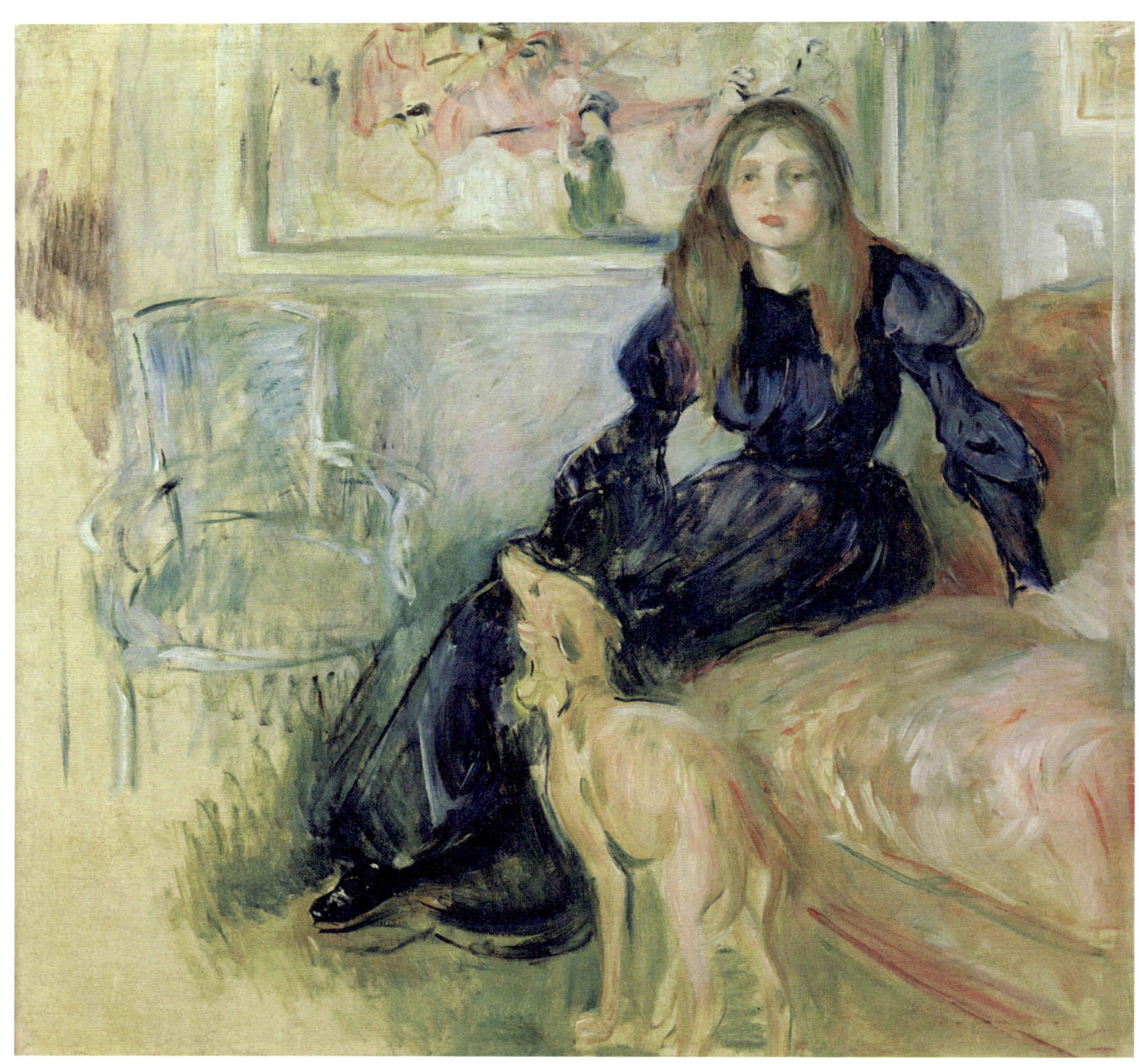

Julie Manet and Her Greyhound Laërte, 1893
Oil on canvas, 73 x 80 cm (28¾ x 31½ in)
• Musée Marmottan Monet, Paris

After Eugène's death in 1892, Berthe and Julie left Rue de Villejust for a small apartment on Rue Weber. Julie, still dressed in mourning, posed for this in the apartment's salon, elegantly furnished and with Japanese prints on the walls.

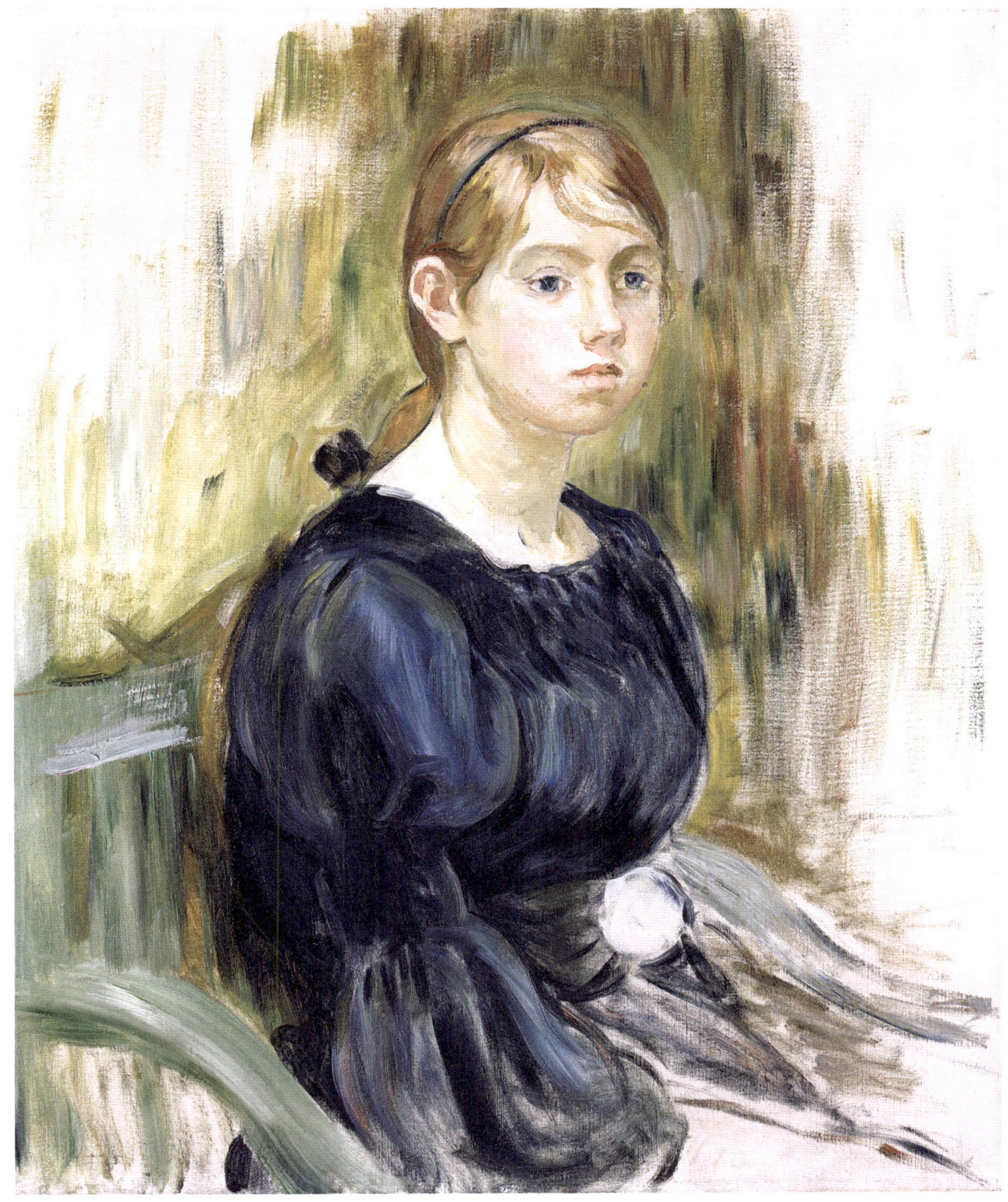

Jeannie Gobillard, 1895
Oil on canvas, 65.5 x 54.5 cm (25¾ x 21½ in) • Private Collection

Berthe often left images unfinished in the outer areas. Here she has focused on the skin tones and reddish hair of her niece, which form a bold contrast with the deep, strong colour and shine of her silk dress.

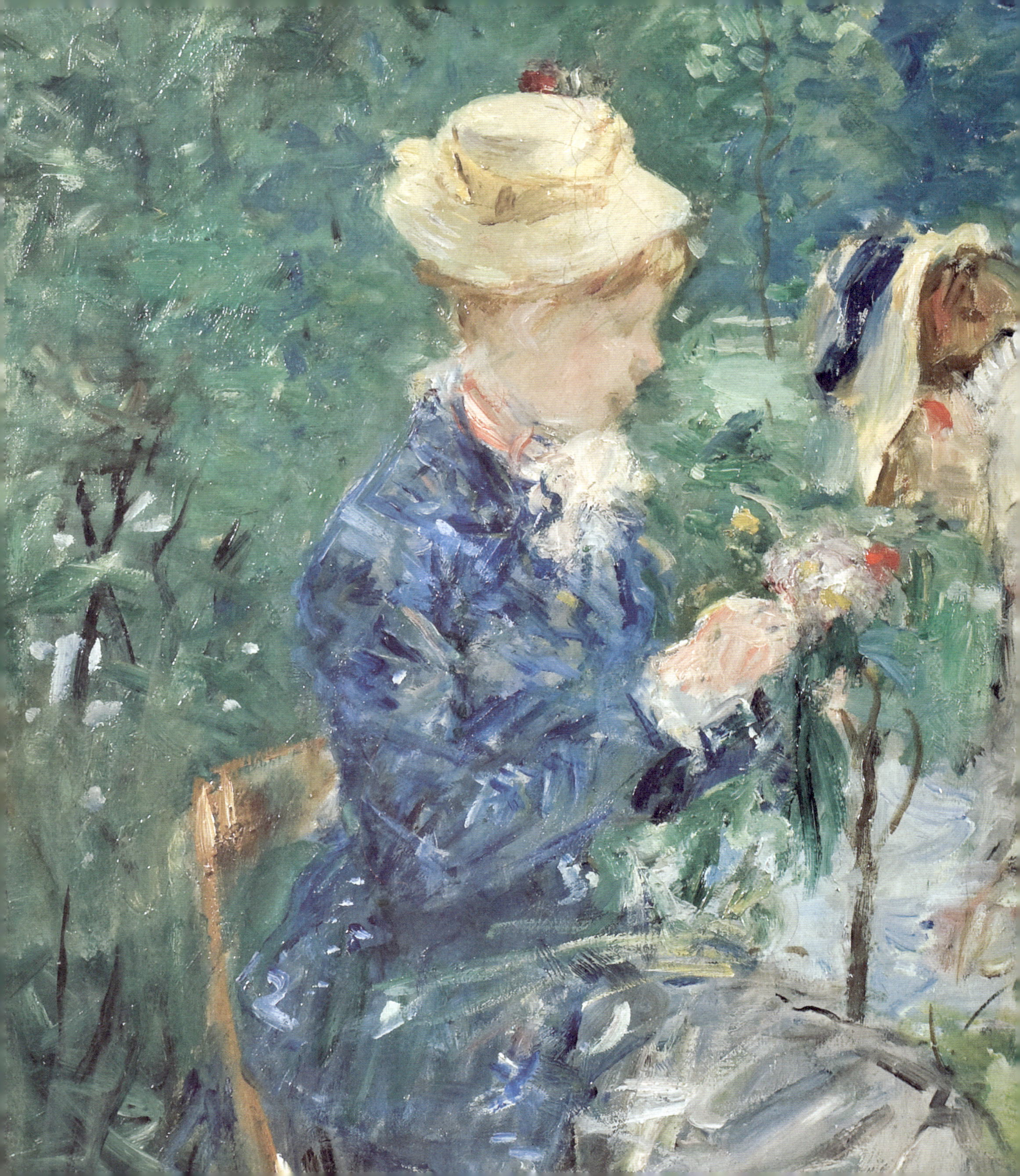

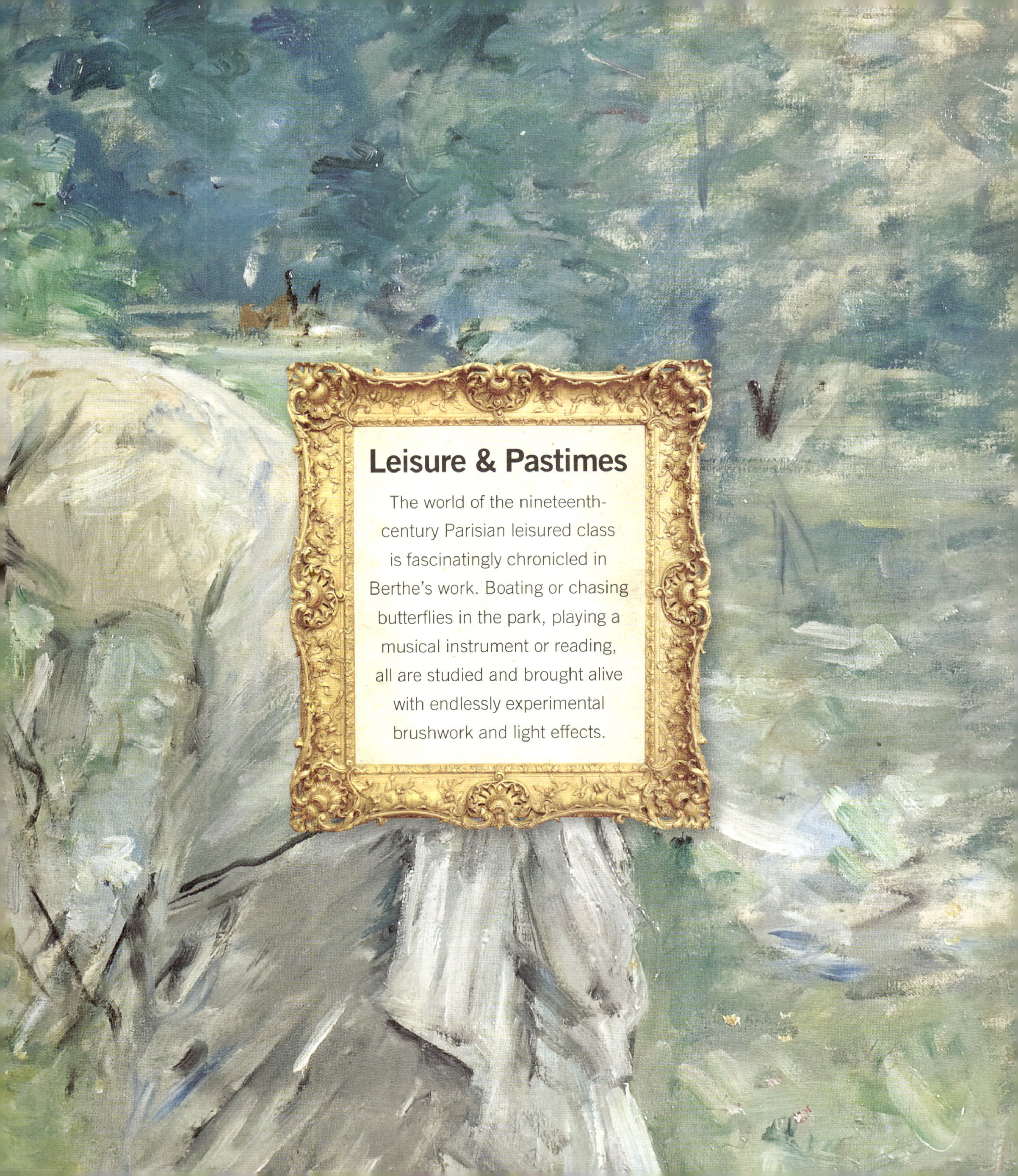

Leisure & Pastimes

The world of the nineteenth-
century Parisian leisured class
is fascinatingly chronicled in
Berthe's work. Boating or chasing
butterflies in the park, playing a
musical instrument or reading,
all are studied and brought alive
with endlessly experimental
brushwork and light effects.

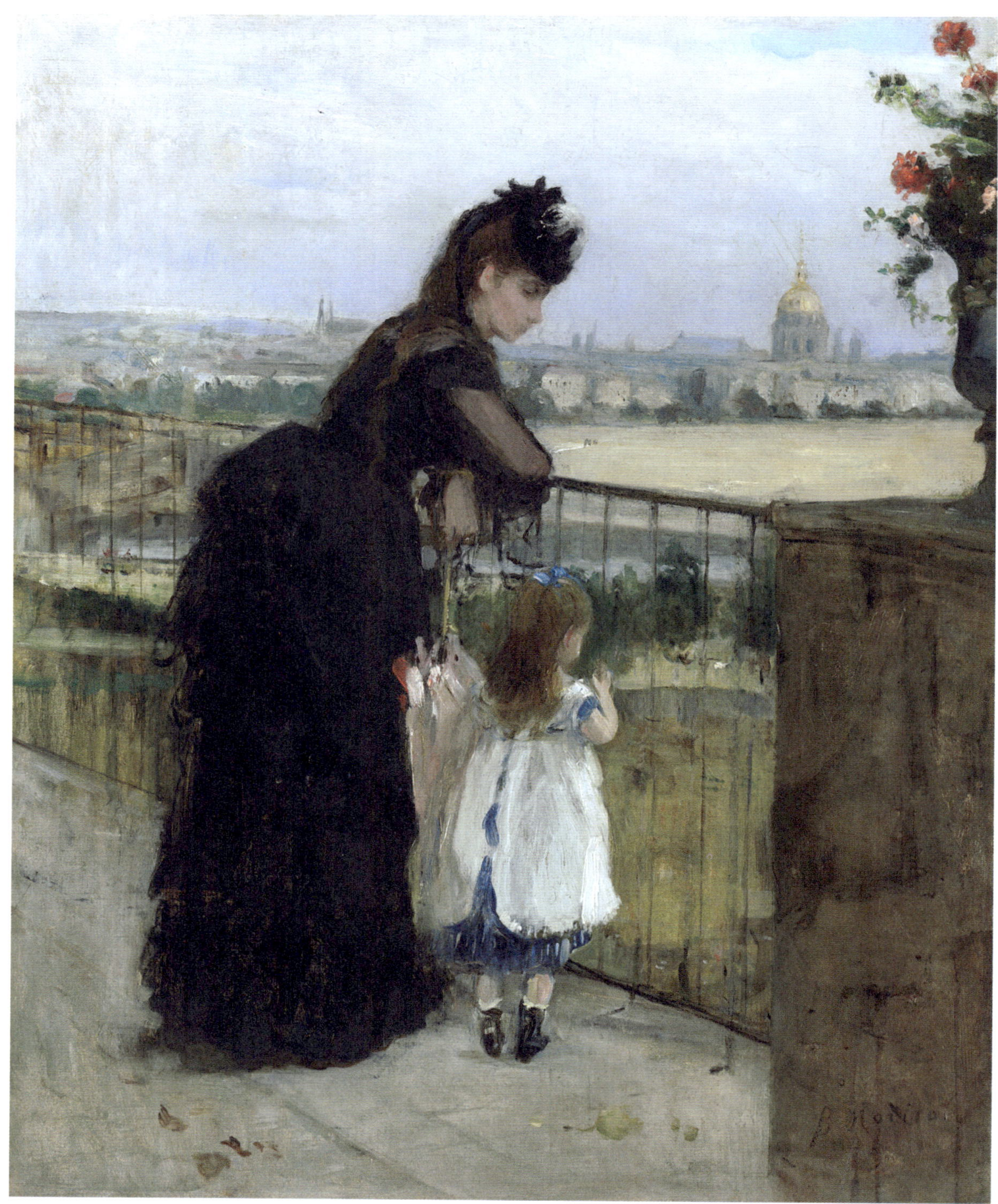

Woman and Child on a Balcony, 1872
Oil on canvas, 60 x 50 cm (23⅔ x 19¾ in) • Artizon Museum, Tokyo

A fairly early work, but one of Berthe's best known, this assured, Manet-esque picture is an informal evocation of stylish Parisian life. The little girl is Berthe's niece, Paule Gobillard.

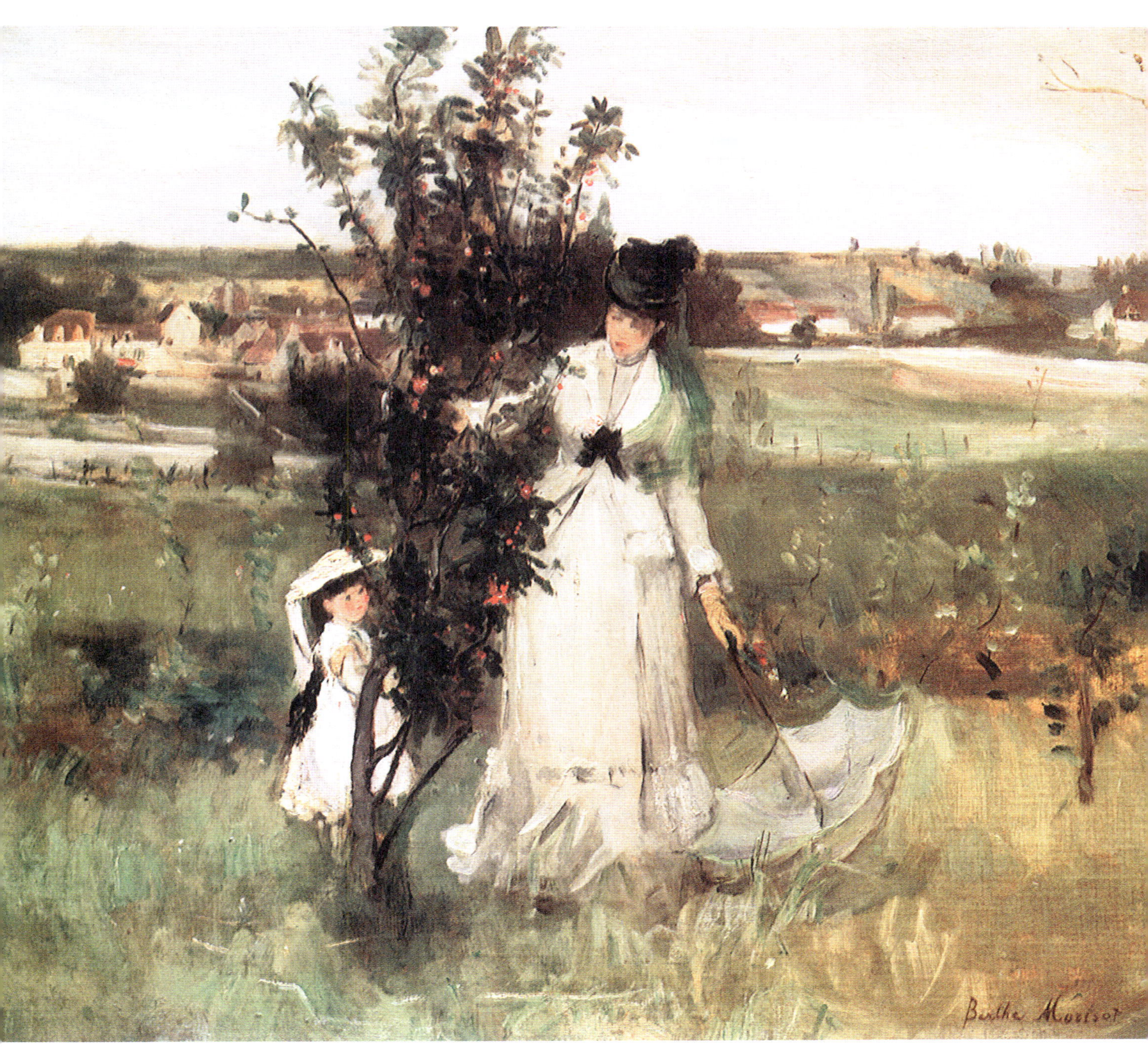

Hide and Seek, 1873
Oil on canvas, 45 x 55 cm (17¹¹⁄₁₆ x 21⅝ in) • Private Collection

Using sister Edma to model the woman, Berthe's playful picture shows her ability to paint a scene where figures and landscape seem mysteriously intertwined by palette and light effects. This would be even more pronounced in later works.

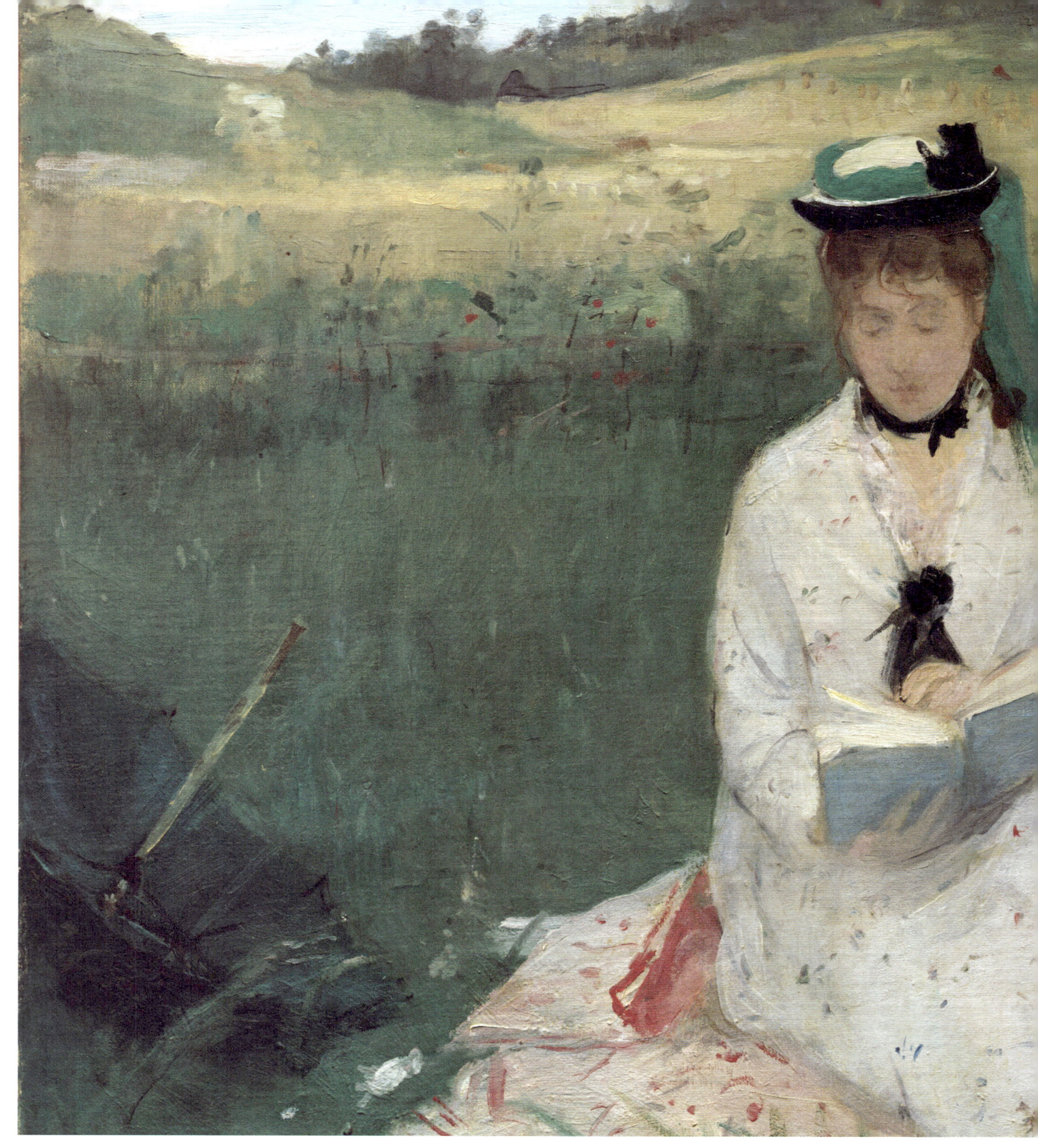

Reading, 1873
Oil on fabric, 46 x 71.8 cm (18 x 28¼ in)
• The Cleveland Museum of Art, Ohio

Painted with rapid strokes, this picture of Edma explores Berthe's interest in showing figures outdoors. The wonderfully lit pale dress is filled with subtle touches of many hues, displaying the very Impressionist concern with nature, light and colour.

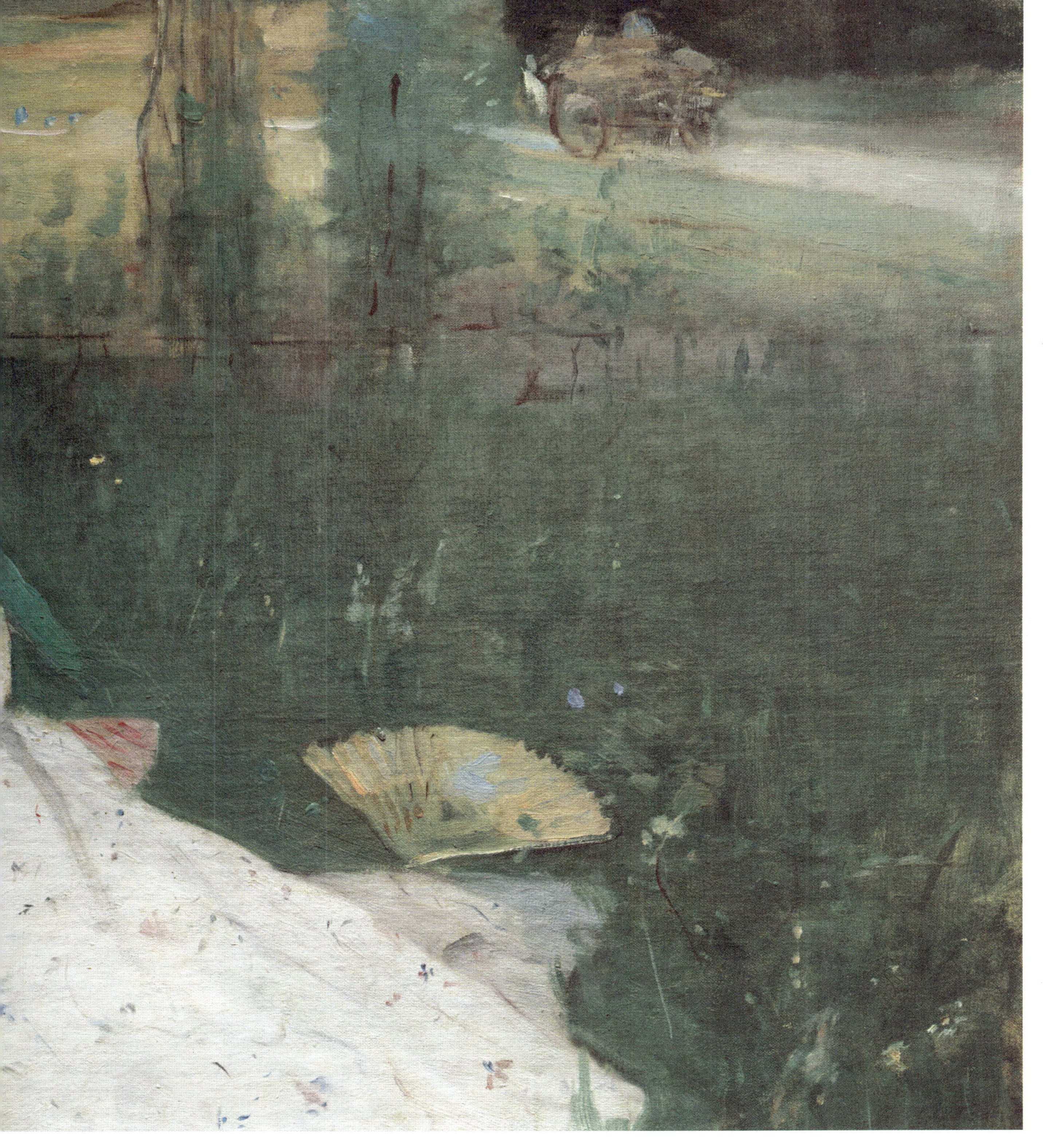

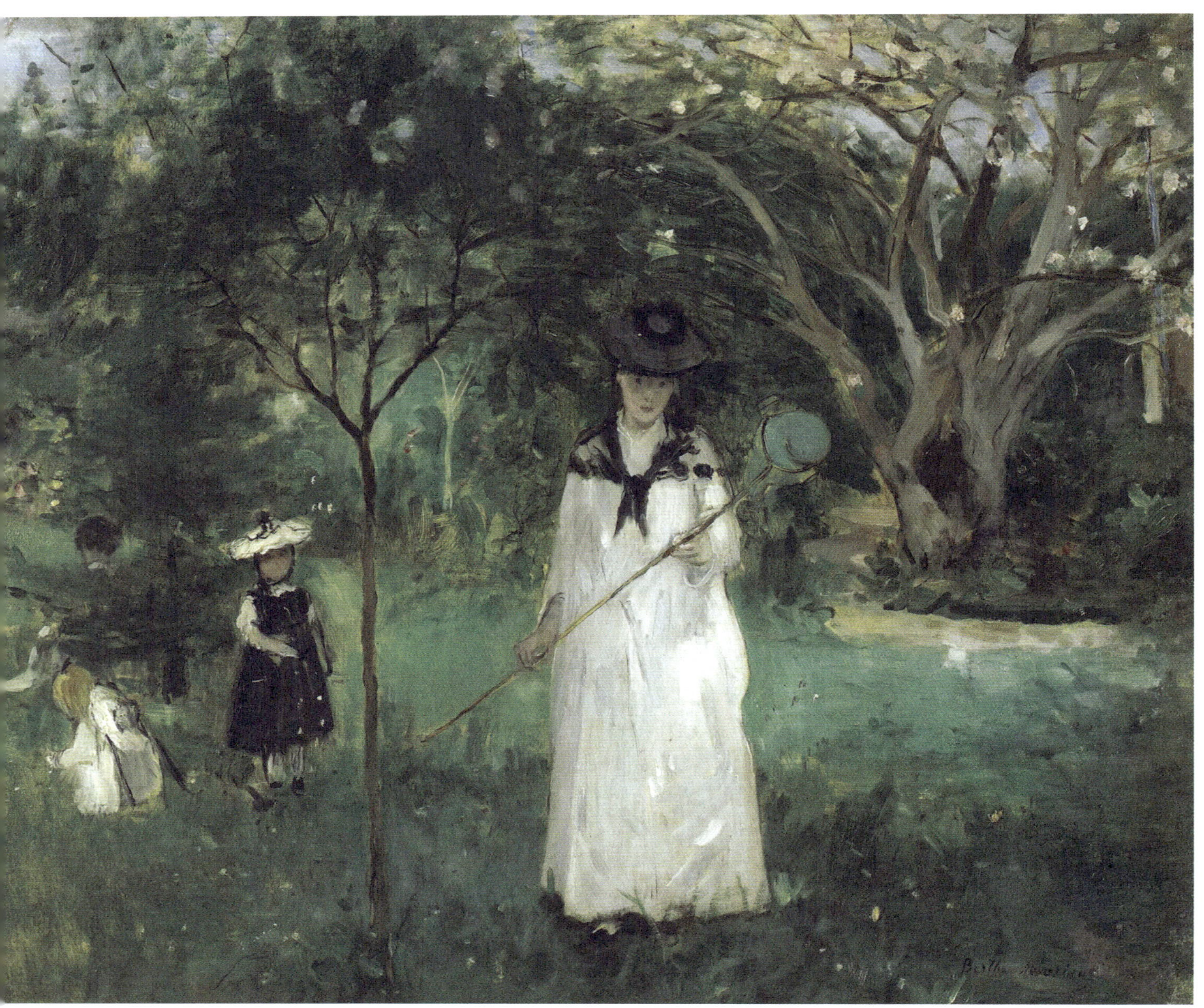

The Butterfly Hunt, 1874   This casual snapshot of family fun was modelled by Edma and her two daughters, Jeanne and Blanche.
Oil on canvas, 46 x 56 cm (18 x 22 in) • Musée d'Orsay, Paris   Facial features are left absent or undefined while the limited palette creates a natural harmony.

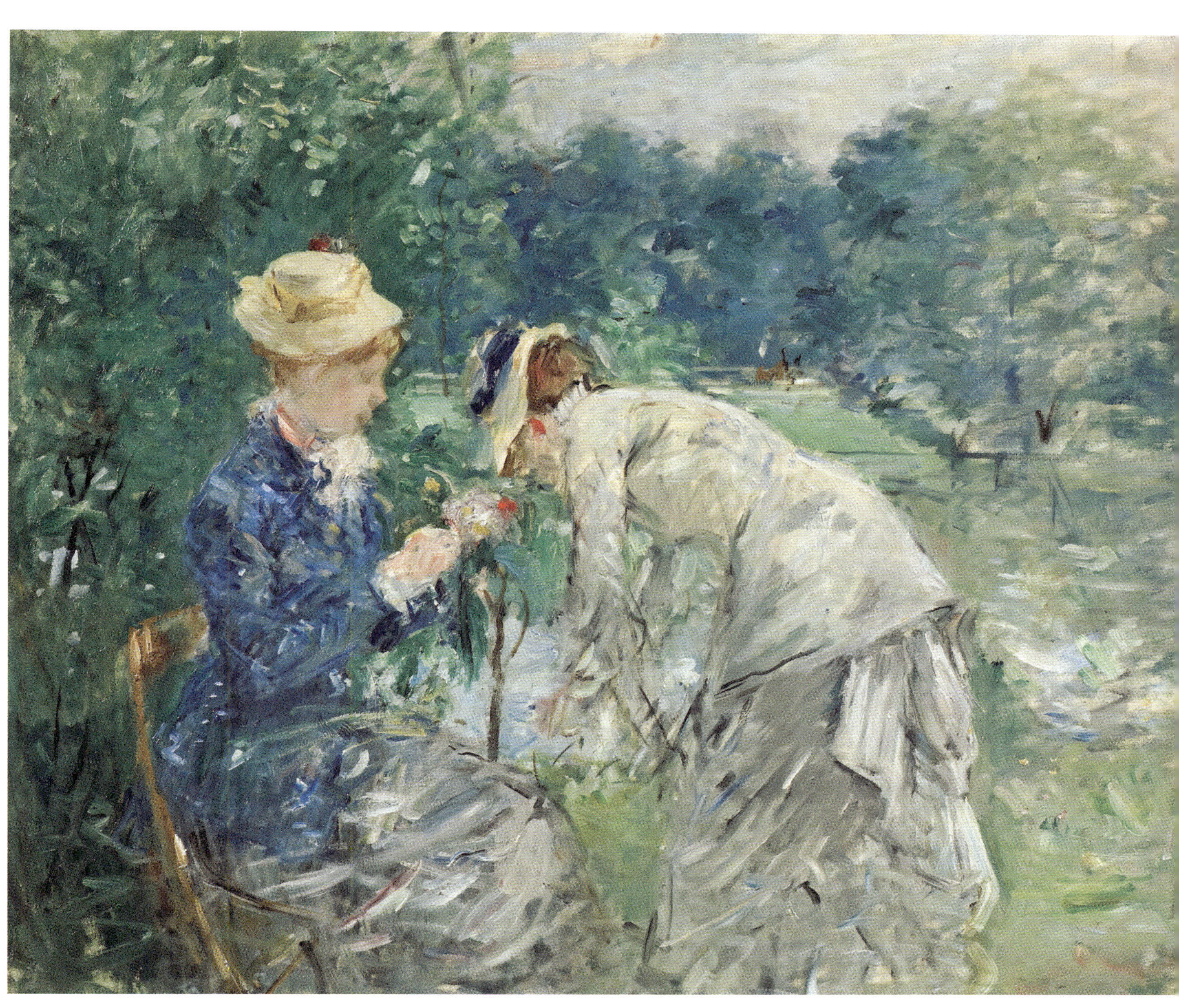

In the Bois de Boulogne, *c.* 1875–79
Oil on canvas, 61 x 73.5 cm (24 x 29 in)
• Nationalmuseum, Stockholm

Here bold strokes and dancing light effects make a direct sensory connection with the outdoors.
The setting is the Bois de Boulogne, in western Paris. It was hugely popular with middle-class
Parisians and Berthe, who lived nearby, often painted there.

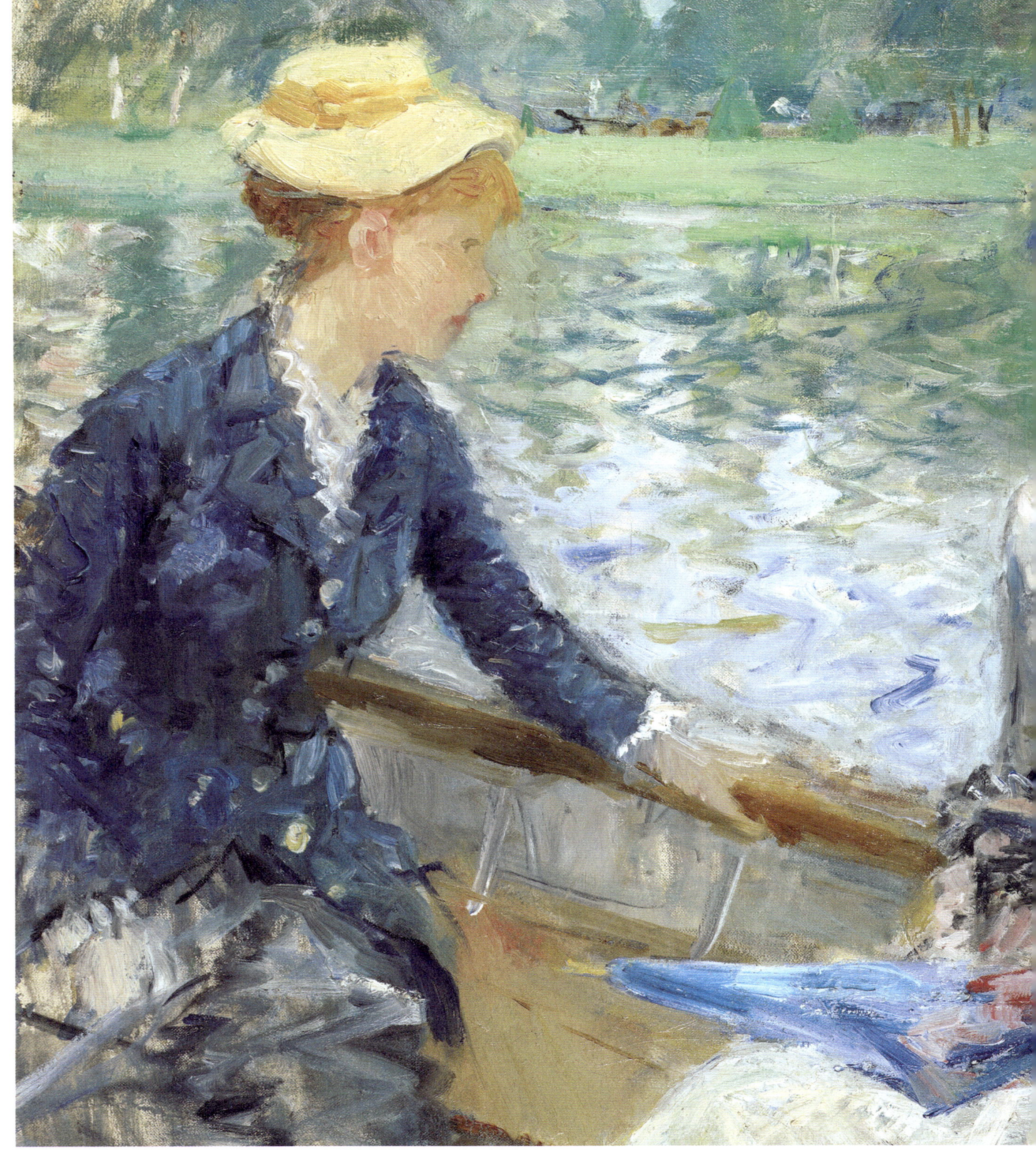

Summer's Day, *c.* **1879**
Oil on canvas, 45.7 x 75.2 cm (18 x 29⅔ in) • National Gallery, London

In another picture painted in the Bois de Boulogne, Berthe uses energy-filled zig-zagging strokes in varying hues to capture the dazzle of light on water. The two women shown may be professional models.

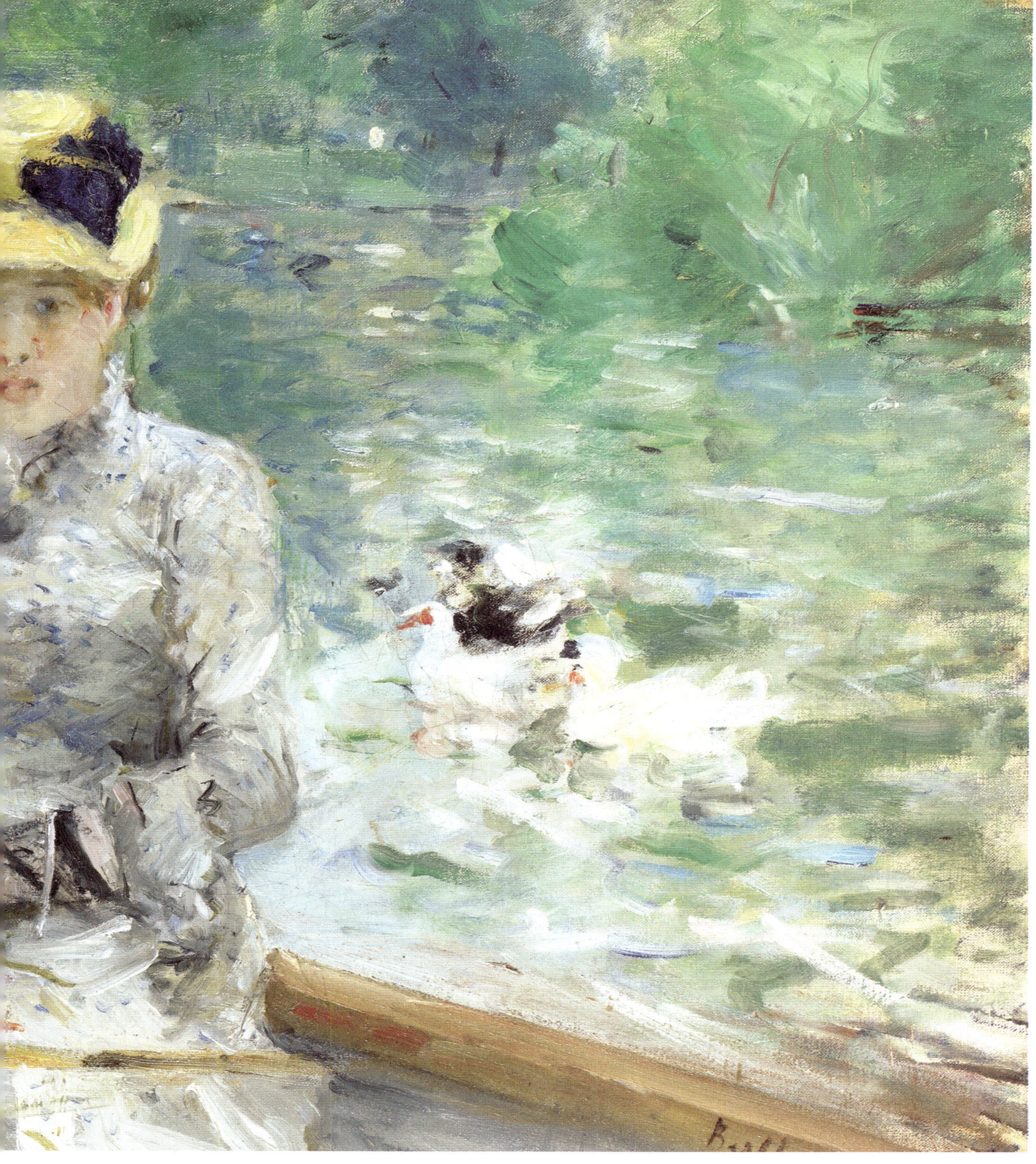

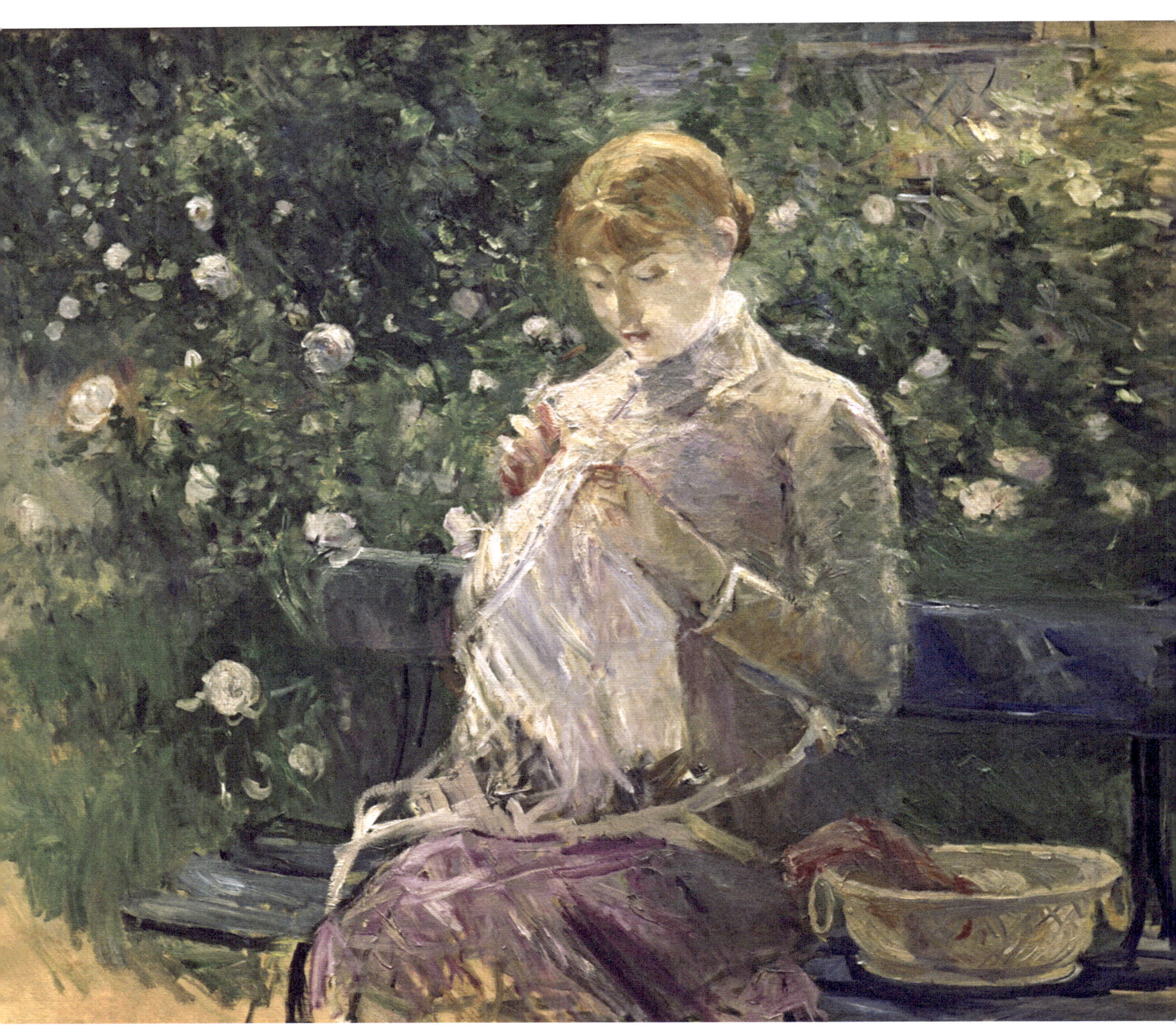

Pasie Sewing in the Garden at Bougival, 1881
Oil on canvas, 81 x 100 cm (32 x 39⅓ in)
• Musée des Beaux-Arts, Pau

Berthe's maid Pasie might be doing a household chore, but it seems to be providing her with an enjoyable and relaxed occupation. The picture pulsates with bright sunlight that cascades across this scene of the much-loved garden at Bougival.

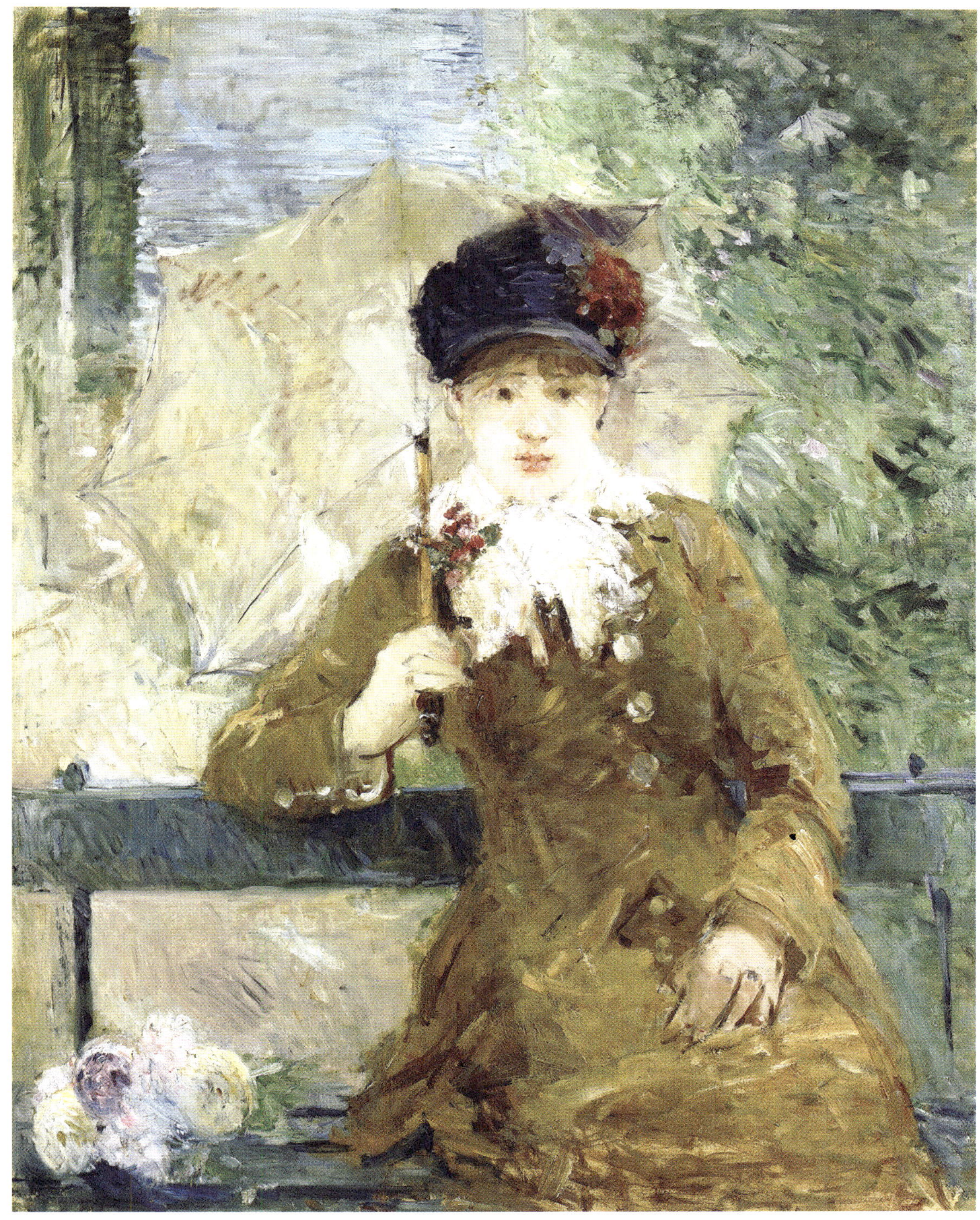

Woman with an Umbrella, 1881
Oil on canvas, 92 x 72.5 cm (36¼ x 28½ in) • Private Collection

Typically, there is little attempt at any detailed portrayal of the background greenery. However, light clearly picks out recognizable details on the model's dress – the buttons and cuffs – even though the strokes are very loose and rapid.

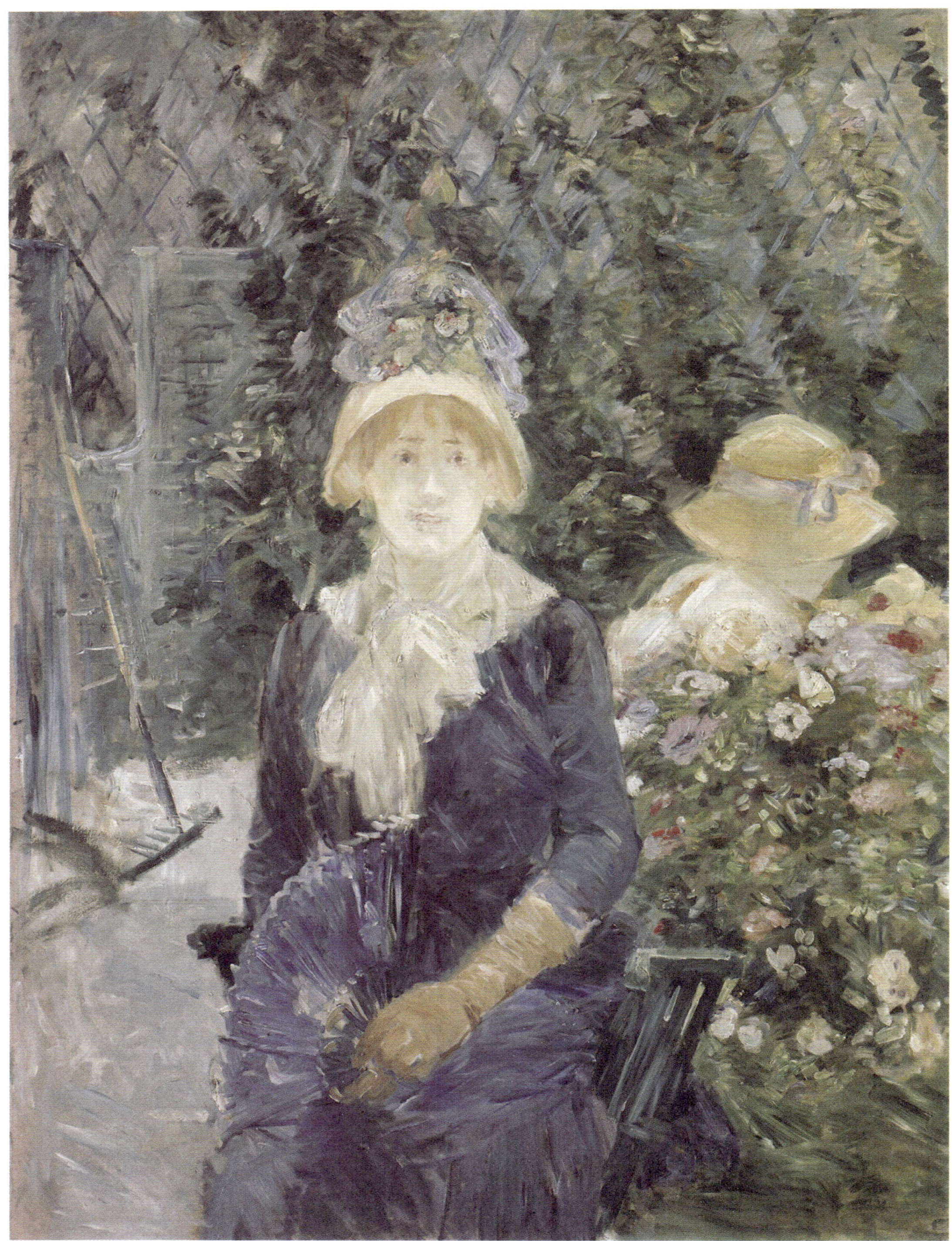

Woman in a Garden, 1882–83
Oil on canvas, 123 × 94 cm (48½ × 37 in)
• The Art Institute of Chicago, Illinois

Bright light blazes from this summery image, bleaching out the woman's face. Berthe's use of scumbling (applying different opaque hues partially over each other so that underlayers show through) is clearly seen here – much used by Degas too.

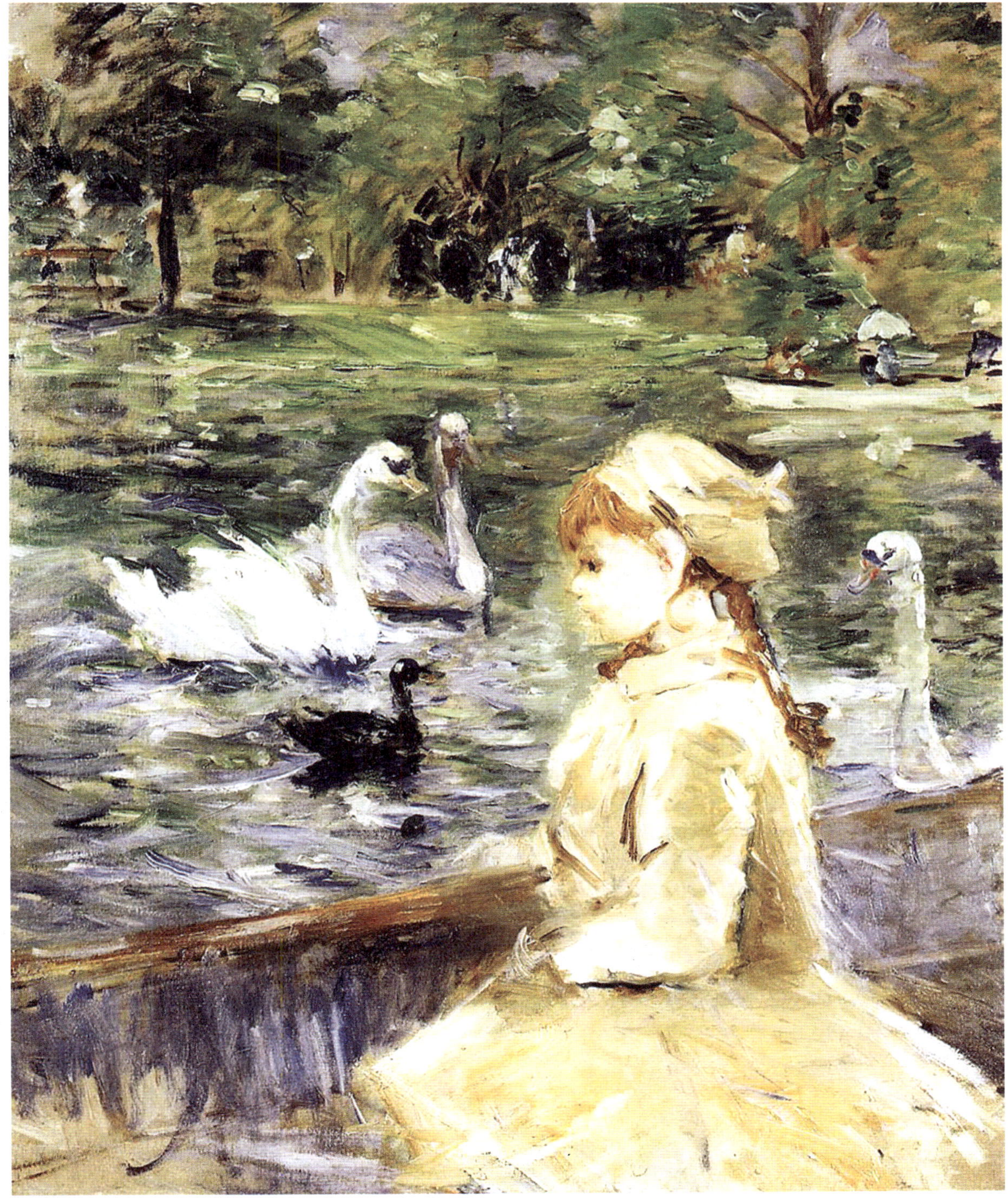

On the Lake, 1884
Oil on canvas, 65 x 54 cm (25⅔ x 21¼ in) • Private Collection

Boating on lakes in parks and gardens such as the Bois de Boulogne was extremely popular with the leisured classes. The way that Berthe's young model is dressed makes it clear that she is from a well-to-do background.

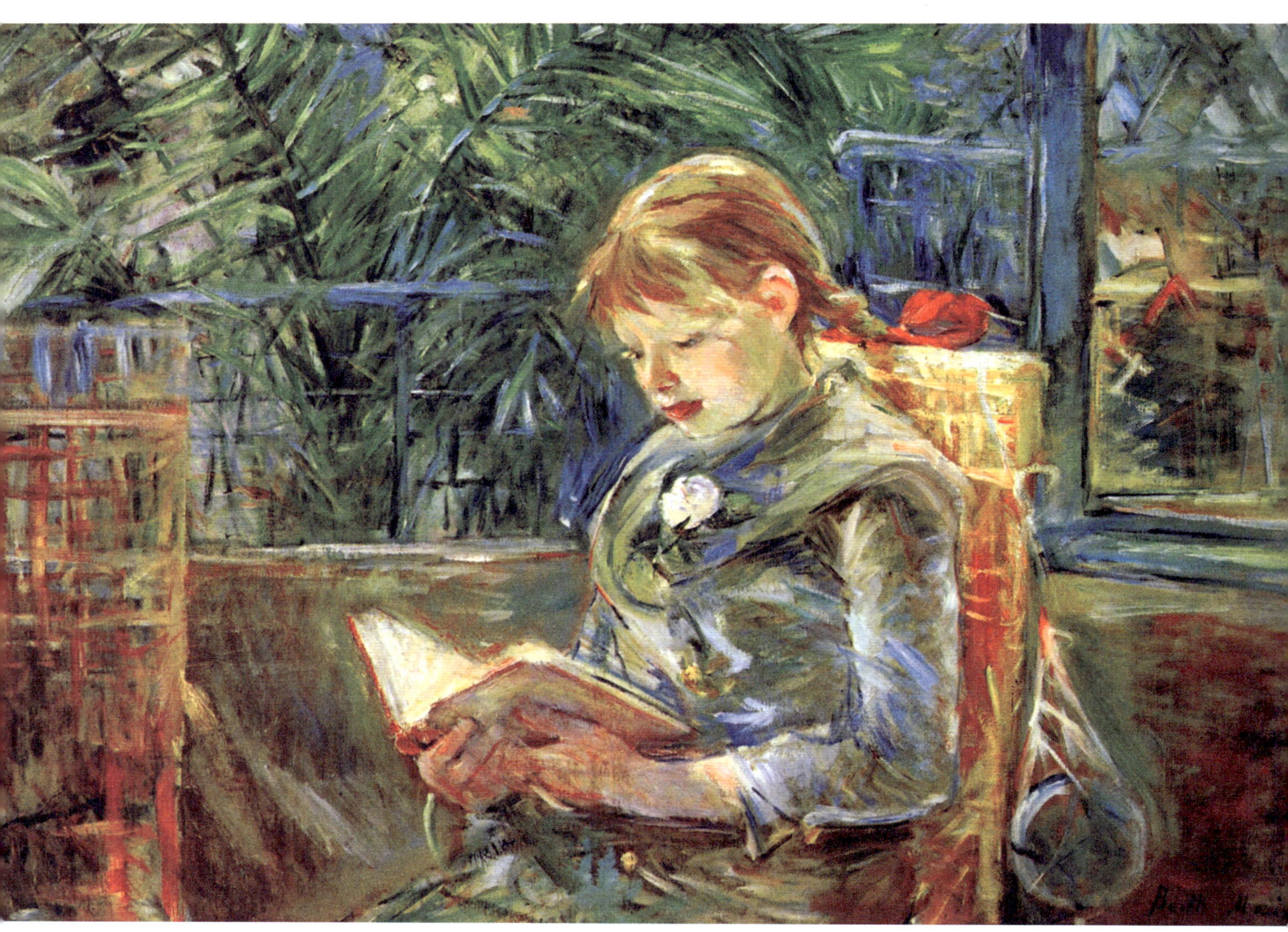

Reading, 1888
Oil on canvas, 74.3 x 92.7 cm (29¼ x 36½ in)
• Museum of Fine Arts, St Petersburg, Florida

A lovely blue-green palette and luminous lighting – both no doubt indebted to Corot – are wedded here to very modern thick and energetic strokes. The picture, whose sitter was called Jeanne Bonnet, shows what an instinctive colourist Berthe was.

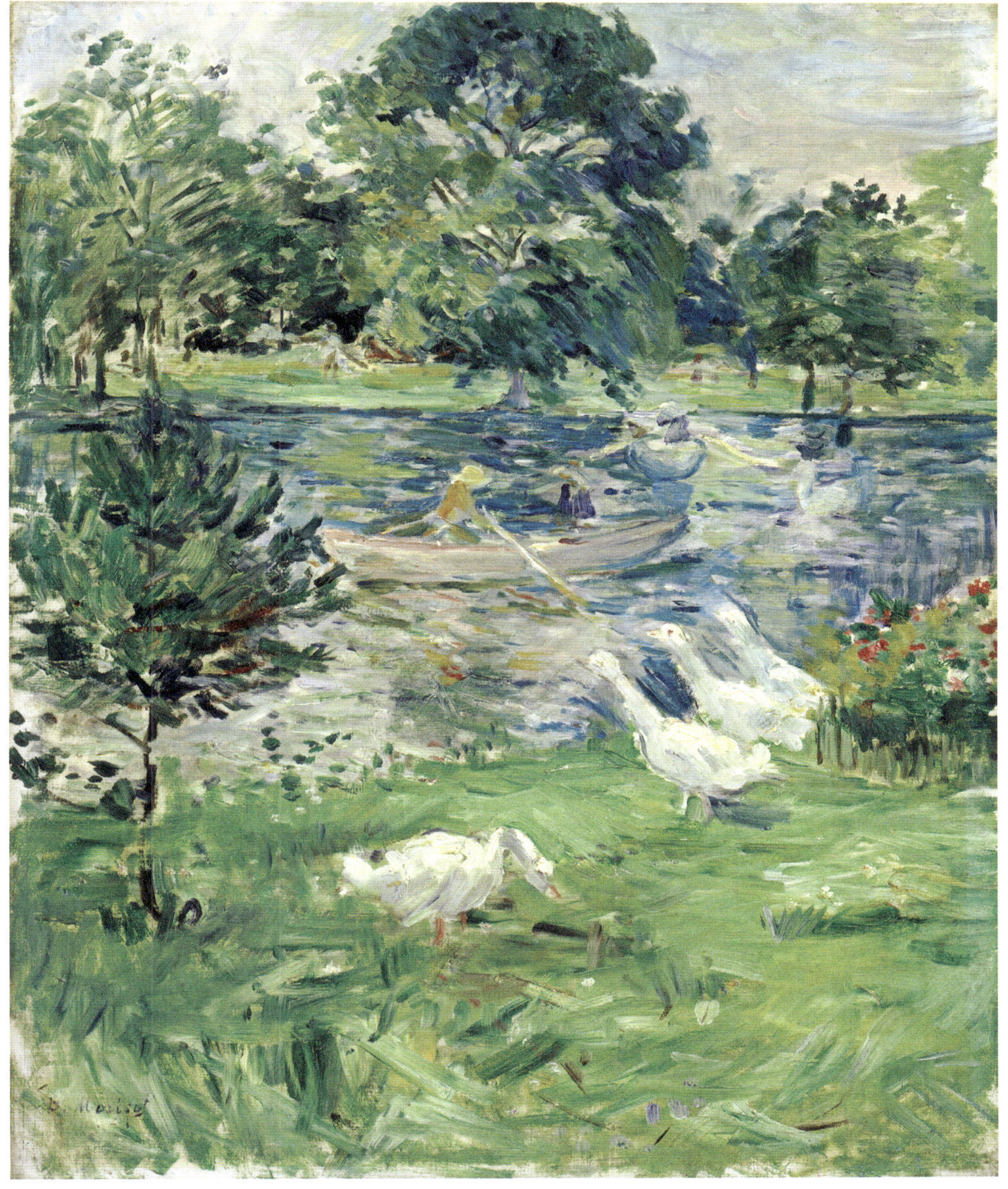

Girl in a Boat with Geese, _c._ 1889
Oil on canvas, 65.4 x 54.6 cm (25¾ x 21½ in)
• National Gallery of Art, Washington DC

Here another parkland boating scene generates a complex interweaving of blues and greens, uniting water, vegetation and sky into a kind of mirage. Deft loose strokes have caught the geese perfectly, from their sunlit backs to their shadowy undersides.

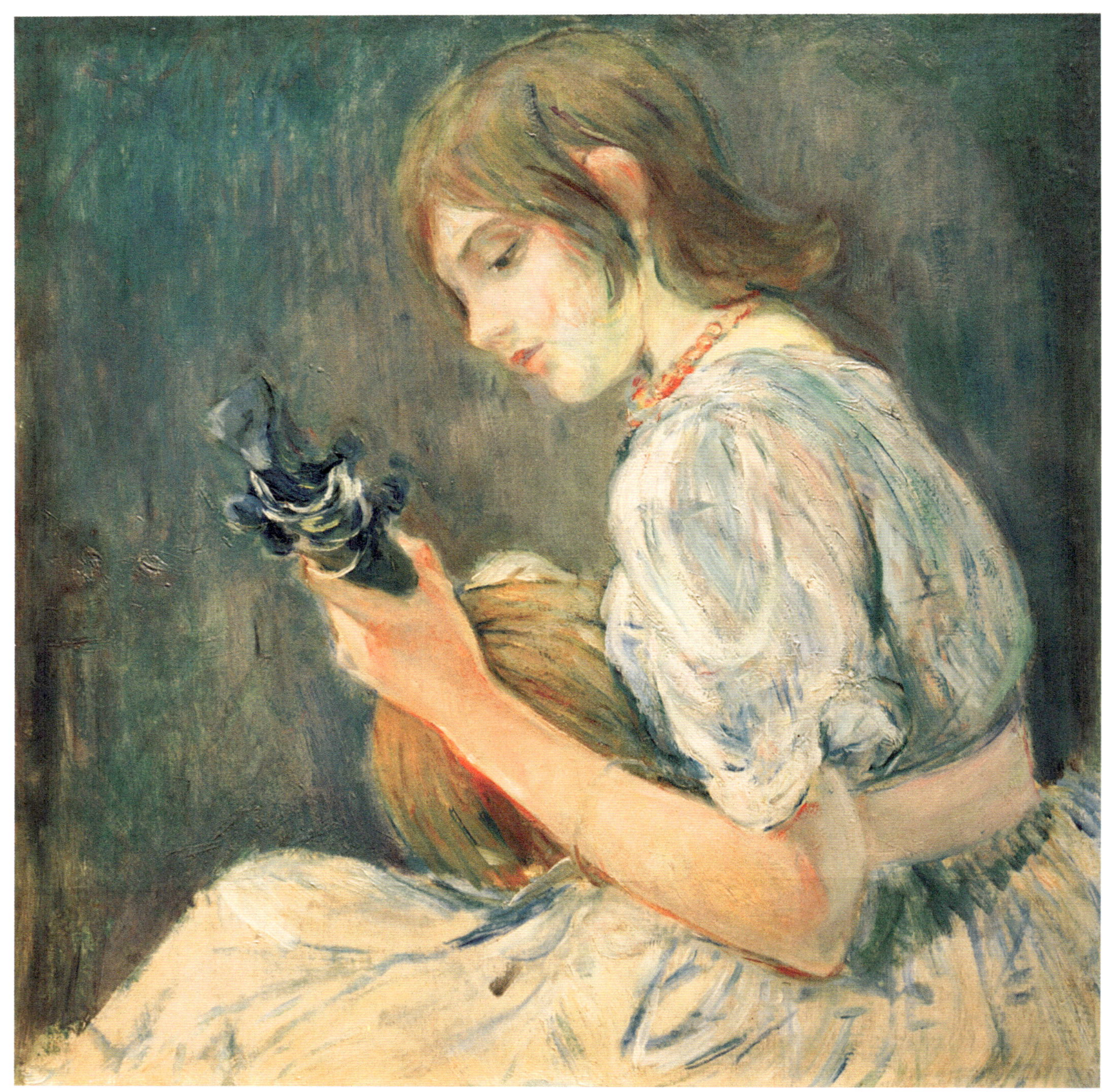

The Mandolin, 1889
Oil on canvas, 55 × 57 cm (21⅔ x 22½ in) • Private Collection

Playing musical instruments was considered a genteel accomplishment for middle-class girls. In images such as this, Berthe invests the activity with a casual yet sincere realism.

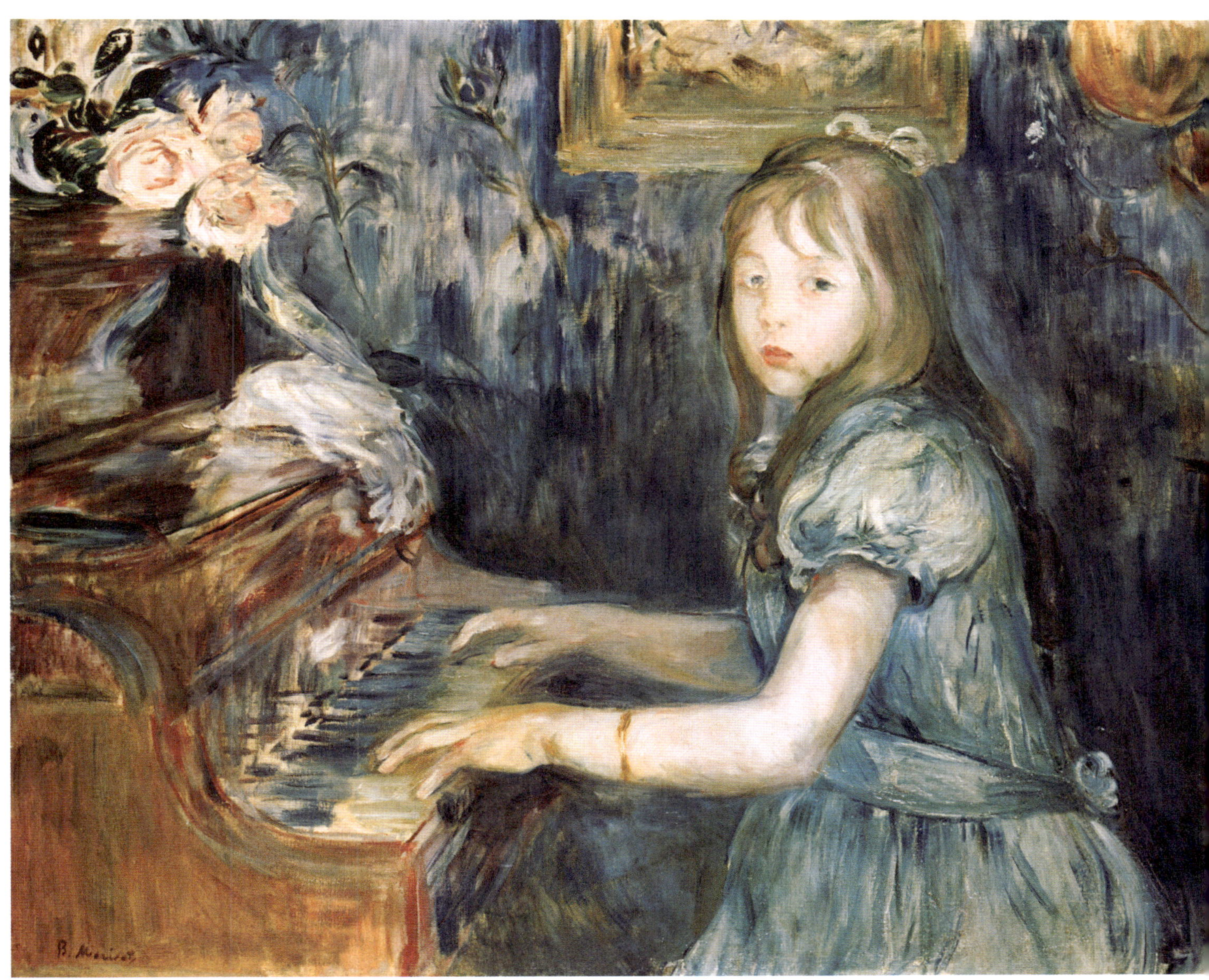

Lucie Léon at the Piano, 1892
Oil on canvas, 65 x 80 cm (25⅔ x 31½ in) • Private Collection

According to Julie Manet, Lucie was a reluctant sitter who would rather have been playing croquet.
Just a few years after this was painted, she was a prize-winning professional concert pianist – unusual
for women at this time.

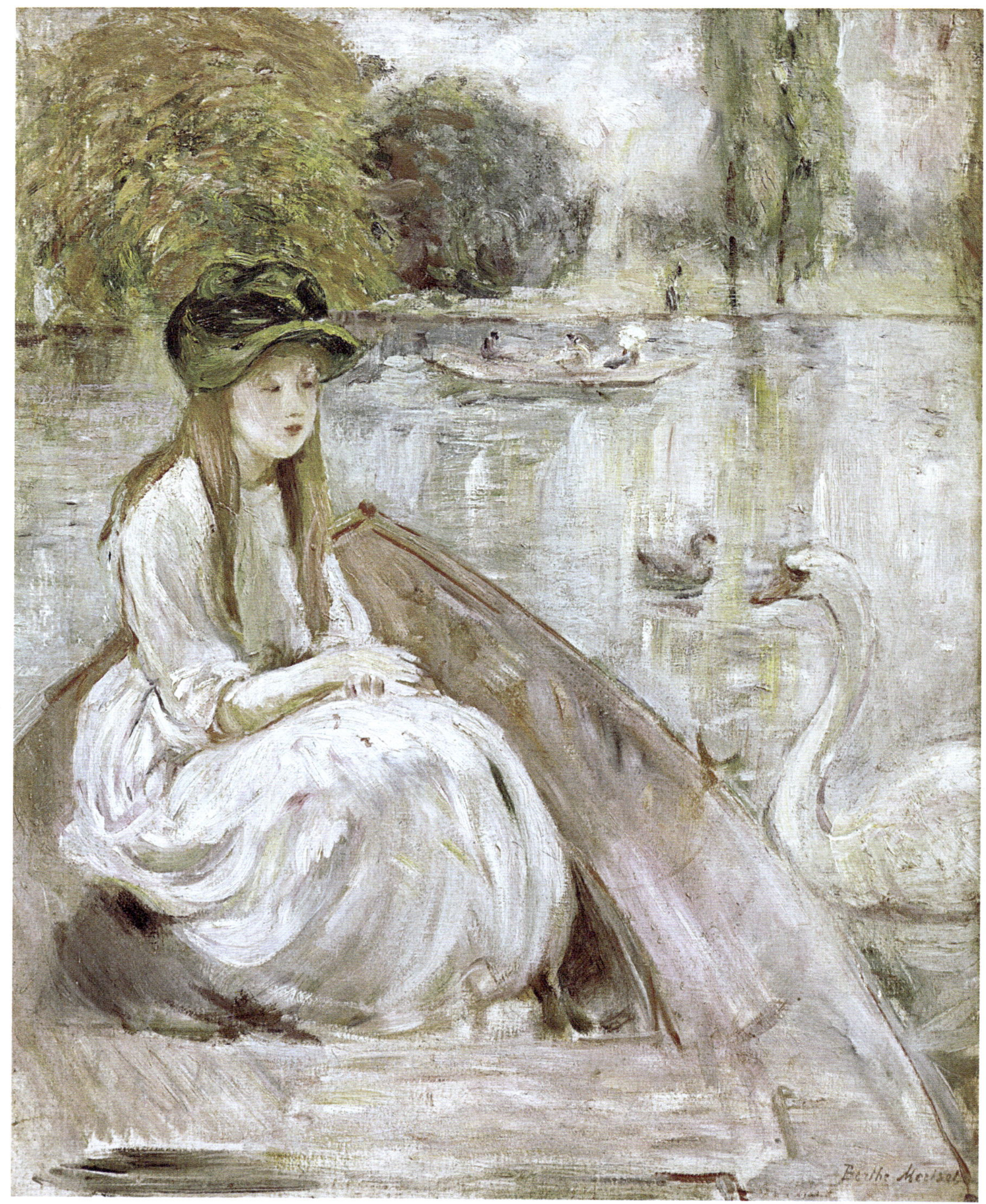

Jeanne Fourmanoir On the Lake, 1892
Oil on canvas, dimensions unknown
• Collezione Baron de Chollet, Fribourg

Jeanne Fourmanoir, also painted by Renoir, was a professional artists' model who was used for various figures by Berthe and was one of her favourite models. This image's delicate colouring recalls the artist's work in watercolour.

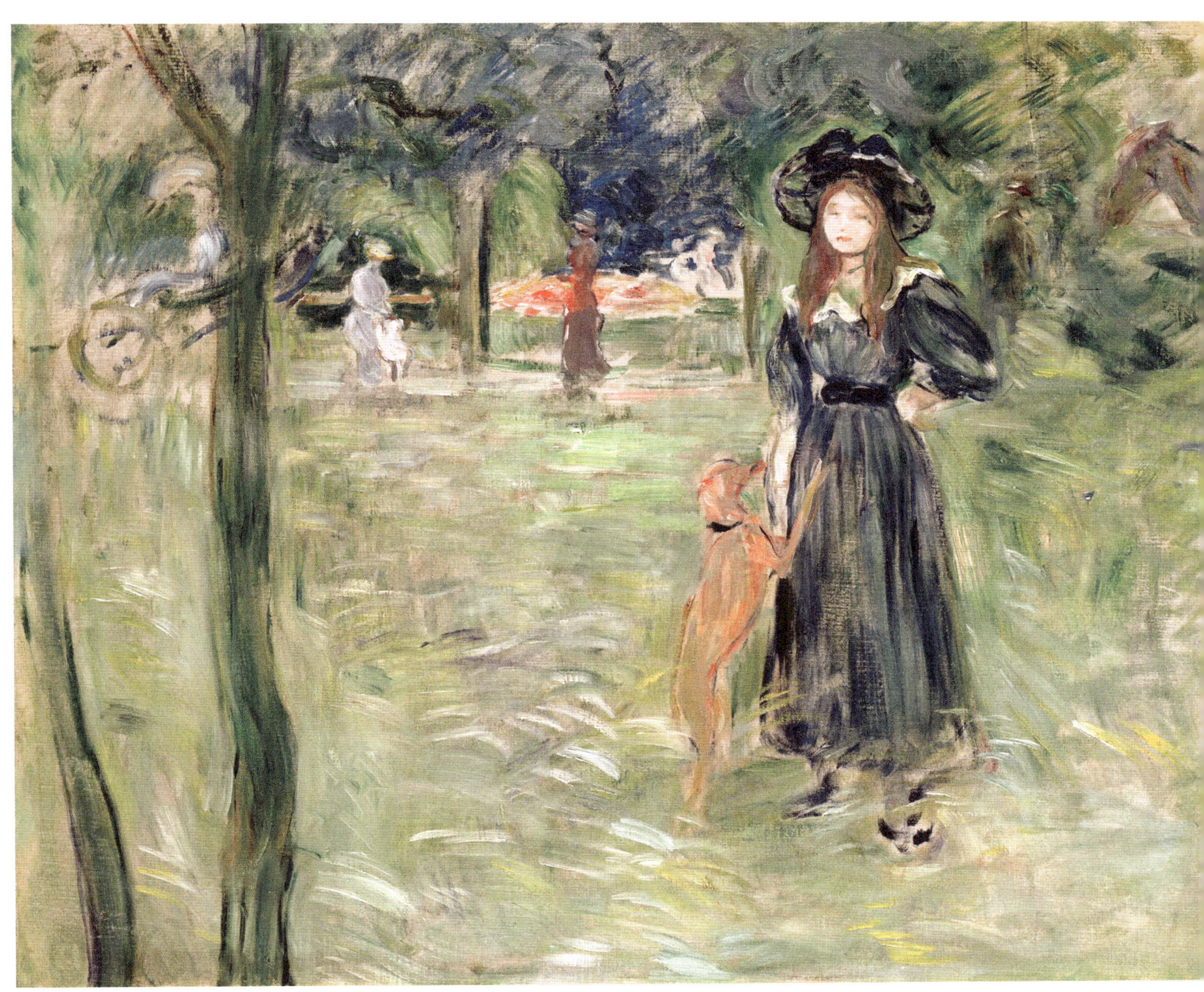

Bois de Boulogne, 1893
Oil on canvas, 50 x 61 cm (19⅔ x 24in)
• Musée Marmottan Monet, Paris

In this late portrayal of Julie and pet greyhound Laërte – a gift to her in 1893 from poet Stéphane Mallarmé – the loose, expressive brushwork and spatial uncertainty give the feel of an emotional work by Edvard Munch.

Indexes

Index of Works

Page numbers in *italics* indicate illustration captions.

General Index

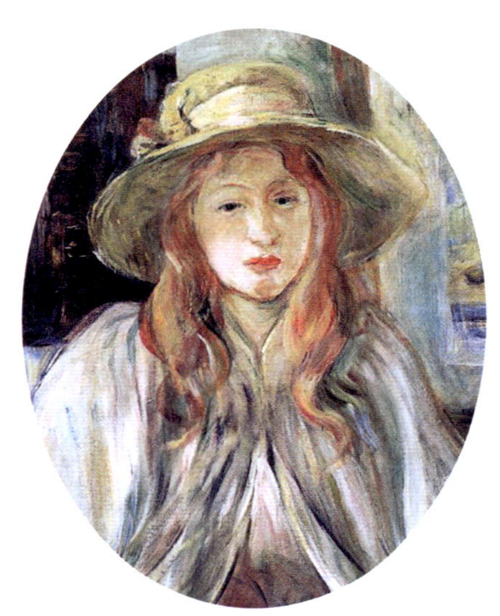

Masterpieces of Art
FLAME TREE PUBLISHING
A new series of carefully curated print and digital books covering the world's greatest art, artists and art movements.

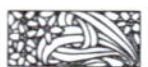

If you enjoyed this book please sign up for updates, information and offers on further titles in this series at

blog.flametreepublishing.com/art-of-fine-gifts/